5 0665 01001322 4

D1802264

DATE DUE

12/20/03			

Demco No. 62-0549

METROPOLITAN COLLEGE
OF NEW YORK LIBRARY
75 Varick Street 12th Fl.
New York, NY 10013

CHRISTIANITY, ISLAM AND ORIENTALISM

M.Faruk Zein

CHRISTIANITY, ISLAM

AND ORIENTALISM

SAQI

British Library Cataloguing-in-Publication Data
A catalogue record for this book is available from the
British Library

ISBN 0 86356 964 1

© M. Faruk Zein, 2003
This edition first published 2003

The right of M. Faruk Zein to be identified as the author of this work has been asserted by him in accordance with the Copyright, Designs and Patents Act of 1988

Saqi Books
26 Westbourne Grove
London W2 5RH
www.saqibooks.com

Contents

Introduction	9
1. Freedom of Religion, Freedom of Thought and Wars in Islam	13
Freedom of Thought and Religious Freedom	13
Wars in Islam	23
Jihad	29
2. The Bible, the Qur'an, and Progression of Divine Revelation	31
Definitions	31
The Old Testament	31
The New Testament	34
From the Q Gospel to the Narrative Gospels	38
Evolution of the Gospels	39
Versions of the Christian Bible	41
Historical Development	42
Authors and Editors of the Christian Bible	44
The Twelve Disciples and Bible Authorship	45
The Qur'an and the Bible	48
Credibility of the Qur'an	49
The Qur'anic Challenge	51
'De-dogmatization' and Appeal to Reason	52
3. Christianity and Hellenistic Culture	55
The Christian Enigma	55
Mythical Jesus of the Kerygma	57
The 'Apostle' Paul	60
From Nazarenes to Christians	64
The Council of Nicaea	66
The Christian Paradox	67
The Islamic View	68
4. The Nazarenes and the Christians	73
Who Were the Nazarenes?	73

Contents

The Jerusalem Church	75
The Nazarene–Christian Dilemma	76
Paul and the Heavenly Jesus	78
Trying to Bridge the Gap	79
The Nazarene Legacy	81
The Nicene Creed	83
Unitarianism in the Modern Age	85
The Islamic Perspective and the Gospel of Jesus	87

5. Christianity or Paulinism? ... 93
   Cardinal Features ... 93
   The Saviour ... 94
   The Eucharist ... 98
   The End of History ... 103
   Pauline Social Values ... 105
   Islam's Appeal to the Intellect ... 106

6. Jesus, the Messiah ... 111
   The Titles of Jesus According to the Gospels ... 111
   Titles of the Historical Jesus ... 112
   Titles of the Mythical Jesus ... 119
   The Islamic View ... 125

7. The Son of Man: Who Was He? ... 127
   Definitions ... 127
   The Messiah is Not the Deliverer ... 129
   Jesus the Messiah and the Hellenistic Chrestos ... 130
   The Messiah, Elias, and the Prophet ... 130
   Jesus Denies Being the Deliverer ... 131
   Sit Down, O Men of Israel ... 132
   The Coming of the Kingdom ... 133
   The Son of Man ... 137
   The 'Son of Man' Foretold by Jesus: the Islamic Perspective ... 140

8. The Crucifixion? ... 145
   The Evidence ... 145
   Passion Narratives ... 147
   Eyewitnesses ... 149
   Roman Justice ... 150
   A King's Triumphant Entry ... 151
   Contrast with Paul's Trial ... 153
   Three Women at the Sepulchre ... 155
   Jesus Reappears with the Disciples ... 157

Contents

Other Appearances	158
Jesus's Lifetime	159
The Islamic Viewpoint	160

9. The Book of Revelation, US Orientalism and Christian
   Fundamentalism — 165
   - Orientalism — 165
   - Revelation — 167
   - Emperor Nero — 170
   - Christian Persecutions — 171
   - John the Seer and his Revelation — 174
   - The Rapture — 175
   - The Middle Eastern Legacy of John the Seer — 176
   - John's Legacy on Palestine — 177
   - John's Legacy on Iraq, the Former Babylon — 181

10. The Protestant Reformation and Christian Fundamentalism — 185
    - Christian Fundamentalism — 185
    - The Catholic Viewpoint — 188
    - The Providential Plan According to Western Fundamentalism — 189
    - Pushing Forward the Providential Plan — 191
    - Awaiting the Messiah — 194
    - The International Christian Embassy — 196
    - The Islamic Perspective — 197
    - Islam and the Reforms of Luther — 198
    - Fundamentalism — 201

Appendix: Palestine and Jerusalem, Chronology of Conflict — 203
Select Bibliography — 207
Index — 210

Introduction

'And do not argue with the followers of earlier revelation otherwise than in a most kindly manner.' (Qur'an 29: 46)

The academic quest to disentangle the historical Jesus the Messiah, from Jesus Christ of the Church, started in the Western Hemisphere some two hundred years ago. Among famous pioneers on this quest was Thomas Jefferson (1743–1826), third President of the USA who endeavoured to produce a Bible purged of the notions of the mythical Christ, and retaining only those teachings and notions pertaining to the Jesus of history (Mack 1995 p. 2; Sanders 1993 p. 6). Over a time-span of some two centuries, and with many ups and downs, this quest gathered considerable momentum in the last three decades of the twentieth century (Parrinder 1992 p. 95). The result was the production of a considerable amount of new scholarly valuable material proving the existence of a vast gap between the mythical Christ of Pauline Christianity, and the historical Jesus of Nazareth (Funk 1993 pp. 2ff.). But in the words of one prominent Western academic: 'The ultra-orthodox Christians – Catholic or Protestant – are so anxious to preserve their religious faith intact, that they do not dare confront the conclusions of the last two hundred years of New Testament scholarship' (Wilson, A.N. 1992 p. xv).

In the words of the Qur'an: 'Those who are bent on denying the truth are enshrouding their hearts in order to hide from the truth of this divine writ' (Qur'an 11: 5), i.e. they allow their hearts and minds to remain wrapped up in prejudice, making it impervious to spiritual perception (Asad 1984, p. 311).

In the following chapters, the writer looks at the results of modern biblical criticism through Islam's perspective. The author also advances the view that Islam, while denying the mythical Christ of Pauline persuasion, had been more than twelve centuries ahead of biblical scholars in proclaiming the truth about the historical Jesus. Not only did the Qur'an preach the truth about the historical Jesus the Messiah, but it also did justice to, and made sense of, his historical prophetic mission on earth, something that the Pauline Church had mostly chosen to ignore.

Introduction

Fourteen centuries ago, the Qur'an highlighted the fact that the Nazarenes, the Nasa'ra, not the Christians, were the true followers of Jesus, a fact only recently raised and acknowledged by modern biblical scholarship. Since the first quarter of the seventh century, Islam has made a clear distinction between Jesus's historical title as the true Messiah, and Paul's notion of the mythical Greek title 'Chrestos' – in English, Christ – that Paul innovated as typical of mystical Graeco-Roman deities. In short, Islam drew a clear line between the prophetic mission of Jesus the Messiah on one hand, and Christianity as a religion that Paul inadvertently innovated reducing Jesus to a mere icon of his faith. Islam also made a clear distinction between the Nazarenes as the true followers of Jesus, and the Christians as followers of the Pauline faith.

The writer contends that modern biblical scholarly research, most valuable as it is, lacks a global outlook in that it does not include the Qur'an and the Muslim perspective within its quest for the truth on Jesus's mission. In matters of theology, 'objective' knowledge alone is not sufficient to arrive at the 'truth', unless it is supported by divine guidance. Man's arrogant conviction that one is self-sufficient and therefore above the need for divine guidance may partially, and understandably, have stemmed from disenchantment with the Church creed and Church practice over 2,000 years of its history. The reaction of intellectuals to the Church, taken to an extreme, has for some included a rejection in the belief of God and the Ultimate Judgement. Whereas 'None but those who are bent on denying the truth would call God's messages in question. But let it not deceive thee that they seem to do as they please on earth' (Qur'an 40: 4).

For two reasons, the Qur'an stands to address the predicament resulting from the Pauline faith. First, it is the last and final divine writ in the chain of divine revelations to mankind. Second, and contrasted with the Jewish and Christian Bibles, it is the only extant divine revelation remaining intact to this day in its original pristine form. In the author's view, the Qur'an's approach, appealing as it does to the human intellect and reason, is superior to the arbitrary attempt to invent a new Christianity or 're-shape' it, as proposed by some (see, for example, Spong 1998 p. 185).

While some biblical scholars may be sceptical about addressing the Islamic viewpoint on the historical Jesus, the Church establishment on the other hand, refuses to accept both the Islamic perspective and the findings of biblical scholarship. The net result to this attitude can only be what we see today of the rapid decline in religious belief in the West, especially among intellectuals who would only accept a religion based on reason, not on mythology.

The writer further contends that the remarkable agreement arising from Qur'anic revelation and many modern biblical findings can serve as a useful platform for further understanding, cooperation, and fruitful dialogue between

Introduction

Christians and Muslims. To this end, curious parallels between the Nazarene beliefs and the Qur'anic revelation are pointed out.

In the above context, the author looks at and interprets recent biblical findings through the perspective of Islam. To this end he briefly covers the origin of the Bible and the rise of Christianity, as related, or unrelated, to the historical prophetic mission of Jesus the Messiah. He describes the gradual triumph of Hellenistic Christianity over the early Jerusalem movement of the Nazarenes, the companions and disciples of Jesus and their followers. This triumph, which culminated officially at the Council of Nicaea in the year 325 CE, was reversed three centuries later with the advent of Islam, which redressed the injustice done to Jesus's prophetic mission in the same part of the world where he once preached his message. Christian Pauline dogma and Nazarene beliefs are both contrasted to the Islamic perspectives on every occasion.

The last two chapters address fundamentalist Christians' beliefs, in the Western Hemisphere in general and the USA in particular, which are believed to be a major driving force behind American policy towards Palestine and the Middle East.

The author felt it crucial to start this book with a first chapter that demonstrates a very important Islamic doctrine, repeated many times and in different forms in the Qur'an. Namely, that disagreements in matter of religion should be accepted as facts of life that people must accommodate and tolerate without necessarily becoming enemies.

M.Faruk Zein
October 2001

ONE

Freedom of Religion, Freedom of Thought and Wars in Islam

Because of this, then, summon – all mankind – and pursue the right course, as thou have been bidden – by God – and do not follow their likes and dislikes, but say: 'I believe in whatever revelation God has bestowed from on high; and I am bidden to bring about equity in your mutual views. God is our Sustainer as well as your Sustainer. To us shall be accounted our deeds, and to you your deeds. Let there be no contention between us and you; God will bring us all together; for with Him is all journey's end.' (Qur'an 42: 15)

Freedom of Thought and Religious Freedom

Not all God's apostles sent to various peoples and nations over the history of mankind are known to us. Certainly, they are not limited, neither to those mentioned in the Qur'an, nor to those mentioned in earlier extant revelations. The Qur'an states:

> And as We inspired apostles, whom We have mentioned to thee – in this divine writ – as well as other apostles whom We have not mentioned to thee, and as God spoke His word unto Moses. All these apostles – We have sent – as heralds of glad tidings and as warners, so that mankind, having had their apostles, might have no excuse before God (Qur'an 4: 164–65).

> And We sent forth Our apostles, one after another: – and – every time an apostle comes to his community, he is given the lie, and so We caused them to follow one another – into oblivion – and let them become – mere – tales: and so, away with the folk who would not believe (Qur'an 23: 44).

> By God – O Prophet – even before thy time have We sent apostles unto – various – communities, but – those who were bent on denying the truth have always refused to listen to Our messages because – Satan has made all

their deeds seem alluring to them, and he is as close to them today – as he was to the sinners of yore –, hence grievous suffering awaits them (Qur'an 16: 63).

Indeed in their stories – the prophets – there is a lesson for those endowed with insight. – As for this revelation – it could not possibly be a discourse invented – by man: nay indeed, it is – a divine writ – confirming the truth of whatever there still remains – of earlier revelations –, clearly spelling out everything and offering guidance and grace unto people who believe (Qur'an 12: 111).

The Qur'an presents itself as the last and final divine message in a long series of divine messages revealed to humankind: 'Have they, then, never tried to understand this discourse – the Qur'an? Or has there – now – come to them something that never came to their forefathers of old? Or is it, perchance, that they have not recognized their Apostle, and so they disavow him?' (Qur'an 23: 68–69). The implication is that it is impossible to disavow the Prophet – their Apostle – if one understands the Qur'an.

According to the Qur'an, an apostle's mission is no more than to deliver clearly the message entrusted to him. He is not to coerce people to believe against their will, nor is he to call them to account, nor punish them for failure to believe. Calling to account and punishment is up to God alone. People are to be left to their free will and free choice (Ali 1992 p. 1642). The Prophet is thus addressed:

Exhort them, thy task is only to exhort. Thou are not to compel them – to believe . . . Unto Us will be their return, and it is for Us to call them to account. (Qur'an 88: 21–22, 25–26)

Thy duty – O Prophet – is no more than to deliver the message; and it is for Us to call them to account. (Qur'an 13: 40)

Pay heed unto God, and pay heed unto the Apostle, and be ever on your guard – against evil – and if you turn away, then know that Our Apostle's only duty is a clear delivery of the message – entrusted to him. (Qur'an 5: 92)

No more is the Apostle bound to do than deliver the message – entrusted to him –, and God knows all that you do openly, and all that you would conceal. (Qur'an 5: 99)

But if they turn away – from thee O Prophet know that – We have not sent thee to be their keeper, thou are not bound to do more than deliver the message – entrusted to thee. (Qur'an 42: 48)

In consequence, Muslim jurists have concluded a negation of priesthood authority well known in other religions whereby religious leaders assume the prerogative of calling people to account for their beliefs. If the Prophet himself did not have such prerogative, how much less in authority are others of whatever status who endeavour to enforce their own beliefs, pretending that they have a monopoly on the 'truth'.

The Qur'an addresses the Prophet: 'And yet thy people have given the lie – to this divine writ – although it is the truth, say – then – "I am not responsible for your conduct. Every tiding – from God – has a term set for its fulfilment, and in time you will come to know – the truth"' (Qur'an 6: 66–67)

On turning away from such who indulge in blasphemous talk on the divine message, the Qur'an states: 'Now, whenever thou meet such as indulge in – blasphemous – talk about Our messages, turn away from them until they begin to talk of other things; and if Satan should ever cause thee to forget – thyself –, remain not, after recollection, in the company of such evil-doing folk' (Qur'an 6: 68). As they are held accountable to God only, the discourse continues: 'It is not for the righteous to call them to account in any way, but – their duty – is to remind them that they may become conscious of God' (Qur'an 6: 69).

The Qur'an further describes the believers as shying away from frivolous talk: 'And whenever they – the believers – hear frivolous talk – from the unbelievers – they turn away from it and say "Unto us shall be accounted our deeds, and unto you your deed. Peace be unto you, we do not seek such as are ignorant – of the meaning of right and wrong"' (Qur'an 28: 55).

Personal responsibility for one's beliefs and one's actions is emphasized: 'Obey God, and obey the Apostle, but if you turn away, he is only responsible for the duty placed on him, and you for that placed on you; if you obey him, you will be on the right path; the Apostle is not bound to do more than clearly deliver the message – entrusted to him' (Qur'an 24: 54).

The Prophet, much less anyone else, is not a keeper for mankind: 'Whoever pays heed unto the Apostle pays heed unto God thereby, and as for those who turn away, We have not sent thee – O Prophet – to be their keeper' (Qur'an 4: 80).

As for those who insist on denying the truth, the Qur'an states: 'And if they give thee the lie – O Prophet – even so, before thy time have – other – apostles been given the lie when they came with all evidence of the truth, and with books of divine wisdom, and with light-giving revelation' (Qur'an 3: 184).

It is only God – not the Prophet – who guides whom He wills. 'It is not for thee – O prophet – to make people follow the right path, since it is God – alone – who guides whom He wills' (Qur'an 2: 272).

For those who do not believe, no further step is required after delivering the message to them: 'But if they turn away – from thee, O Prophet, remember that – thy duty is a clear delivery of the message – entrusted to thee. They – who turn away from it – are fully aware of God's blessing, but none the less they refuse to acknowledge it, since most of them are bent on denying the truth' (Qur'an 16: 82–83).

And: 'Let, then, the deniers of the truth have their will, let them have their will for a little while' (Qur'an 86: 17), i.e. give them respite until they realize the truth, or until the day of judgement. In short, wait with gentle patience for His decision (Ali 1992 p. 1631).

To those who reject faith: 'Say: "O you who deny the truth! I do not worship that which you worship. And neither do you worship that which I worship. And I will not worship that which you have – ever – worshipped. And neither will you – ever – worship that which I worship. Unto you, your moral law, and unto me, mine"' (Qur'an 109: 1–6). Thus, no other course of action is required in case others are unwilling to abandon their disbelief. Any notion of coercion or persecution on account of one's faith or one's belief is excluded outright. While the *surah* (verse) stipulates a tolerant attitude, it simultaneously negates any possibility of compromise on faith (Ali 1992 p. 1707).

And: 'It may be that those who are bent on denying the truth, would like to become Muslims' (Qur'an 15: 2), i.e. had it not been for dogma, familial or social constraints, and worldly interests. In such case, the Qur'an advises on the course of action: 'Leave them alone; let them eat and enjoy themselves the while the hope – of vain delights – beguile them; for in time they will come to know – the truth' (Qur'an 15: 3).

The Prophet, and by implication any Muslim, is not to indulge in futile arguments on the message.

> Thus – O Prophet – if they argue with thee, say, 'I have surrendered my whole being unto God, and so have all who follow me', and ask those who have been vouchsafed revelation aforetime, as well all unlettered people 'have you too surrendered yourselves unto Him?' And if they surrender themselves unto Him, they are on the right path; but if they turn away – behold, thy duty is no more than to deliver the message, for God sees all that is in – the hearts of – His creatures. (Qur'an 3: 20)

And there are among them such as will in time come to believe in this – divine writ – just as there are among them such as will never believe in it, and Thy Lord is fully aware as to who are the spreaders of corruption. And – so, O Prophet – if they give you the lie, say: 'To me – shall be accounted – my actions, and to you your actions; you are not accountable for what I do, and I am not accountable for what you do'. (Qur'an 10: 40–41)

After such emphasis on individual freedom of choice, the manner through which the message is to be delivered unto mankind is spelled out in detail: 'Call – mankind – unto thy Lord's path following wisdom and goodly exhortation, and argue with them in the most kindly manner; for behold, thy Lord knows best as to who strays away from his path and He knows best who are the right guided' (Qur'an 16: 125). The emphasis is on kindness and tact, and hence on the use of reason alone in all religious discussions with adherents of other creeds. 'And do not argue with followers of earlier revelation otherwise than in the most kindly manner' (Qur'an 29: 46), 'unless it be such of them as are bent on evildoing' i.e. in such cases all disputes should be a priori avoided (Asad 1984 p. 613), 'and say, "we believe in that which has been bestowed from on high upon us, as well as that which has been bestowed upon you, for our God and your God is one and the same, and it is unto Him that we all surrender ourselves"' (Qur'an 29: 46).

On the substance of argument and what to do if the other party turns away:

Say 'O followers of earlier revelation! Come unto that tenet – divine manifesto – which we and you hold in common: that we shall worship none but God, and that we shall not ascribe divinity to aught beside Him, and that we shall not take human beings for our lords beside God." And if they turn away, then say, 'Bear witness that it is we who have surrendered ourselves unto Him'. (Qur'an 3: 64)

Tact and courtesy are emphasized. No more than a reminder is necessary: 'Remind, then, – others of the truth – if it would seem to be of use – to the other party' (Qur'an 87: 9).

The message of the Qur'an is described as a reminder: 'Nay, Verily, this – Qur'an – is but a reminder. And so, whoever is willing may remember Him' (Qur'an 80: 11). It is a reminder inasmuch it is meant to bring to light the instinctive realization, in man, of God's existence.

Noah is quoted by the Qur'an saying to his people,

Said – Noah – 'O my people! What do you think? If – it be true that – I am taking my stand on a clear evidence from my Lord, who has vouchsafed unto me grace from Himself, – a revelation – to which you have remained blind, – if this be true – can we force it on you even though it be hateful to you?' (Qur'an 11: 28)

Noah's stand is another reference to a cardinal Qur'anic principle that 'there shall be no coercion in matters of faith' (Qur'an 2: 256), and that a prophet's task is no more than to clearly deliver the message entrusted to him.

Similarly, Abraham declared to his people: 'And if you give me the lie – well, other communities have given the lie – to other prophets – before your time, but no more is an apostle bound to do than clearly deliver the message – entrusted to him –' (Qur'an 29: 18). In the same manner, Jesus addresses God:

> Nothing did I tell – my people – beyond what Thou – God – bid me to say, 'worship God, my Lord and your Lord', and I bore witness to what they did as long as I dwelt among their midst, but when Thou has caused me to die, Thou alone has been their keeper. For Thou are witness unto everything. (Qur'an 5: 117)

The following verse encapsulates the Qur'anic principle of freedom of religious belief: 'There shall be no coercion in matters of faith. Distinct has now become the right way, from – the way – of error. Hence, he who rejects the powers of evil and believes in God has indeed taken hold of a support most unfailing, which shall never give way, for God is all-hearing, all-knowing' (Qur'an 2: 256). Right and wrong having become distinct, faith can not be based on coercion, but on personal freedom and free choice.

More clearly: 'And say: "The truth has now come from your Sustainer, let, then, him who wills, believe in it, and let him who wills, reject it"' (Qur'an 18: 29).

Had it been the will of God that all mankind follow one belief, He could have made them so:

> And had thy Lord so willed, He could surely have made all mankind one single community, but – He willed it otherwise, and so – they continue to hold divergent views, – all of them – save those upon whom thy Lord has bestowed His Grace. And to this end has He created them – all – [i.e. to grant them free will and hence, divergence] ... But – as for those who refuse to avail themselves of divine guidance – that word of thy Lord shall be fulfilled, Most certainly will I fill hell with invisible beings as well as with humans, all together. (Qur'an 11: 118–19)

That is, the suffering of those who are bent on denying the truth will be a natural consequence of their choice and their deliberate failure to accept it.

Here again, the Qur'an emphasizes that continuing differences in people's views and ideas are not accidental but are a God-willed element of human existence. Had God willed that all human beings be of one persuasion, all intellectual progress would have been ruled out. People would be devoid of that relative free will that enables man to choose between right and wrong, and endows man's life with a moral meaning and a unique spiritual potential (Asad 1984 p. 335).

Such is one aspect of honour and dignity that God bestowed on mankind: 'Indeed, we have conferred dignity on human beings, and borne them over land and sea, and provided for them sustenance out of the good things of life, and favoured them far above most of Our creation' (Qur'an 17: 70).

Otherwise, all people could have been made believers in one single faith in one single community: 'And had thy Lord so willed, all those who live on earth would surely have attained to faith, all of them, do you then think that thou should compel people to believe' (Qur'an 10: 99). Thus the Qur'an stresses repeatedly the fact that 'had He willed, He would have guided you all aright' (Qur'an 6: 149), the obvious implication being that He has willed it otherwise, namely that He has endowed man with reason and freedom of choice between right and wrong, thus raising him to the status of a moral being as distinct from animals which can only follow their instincts.

On the other hand:

> Those who are bent on ascribing divinity to aught beside God will say, 'had God so willed, we would not have ascribed divinity to aught but Him, nor would our forefathers – have done so; and neither would we have declared as forbidden anything – that He had allowed'. Even so did those who lived before them gave the lie to the truth, until they came to taste Our judgement. (Qur'an 6: 148)

The reference is to the fact that God endowed man with the ability, and hence dignity, to choose between right and wrong. In this manner the Qur'an categorically rejects the doctrine of predestination in the commonly accepted sense of the word: 'Say, "have you any – certain – knowledge – about predestination – which you could proffer to us? You follow but – other people's – conjecture and you yourselves do nothing but guess". Say, "know – then, that the final evidence – of all truth – rests with God alone; and had He so willed, He would have guided you all aright"' (Qur'an 6: 148–49)

One of God's attributes is being Omniscient: His advance knowledge encompasses not only past and present but also the future, but this does not negate the free choice that man is endowed with. Morality and moral responsibility presupposes man's free will which in turn does not contradict

God's omniscience. And 'Had We so willed, We could have sent down unto them a message from the heavens, so that their necks would – be forced – to bow down before it in humility' (Qur'an 26: 4). In that case every individual without exception would forcibly believe, but this would negate man's moral choice in freedom, and would consequently deprive man's faith of all its moral significance (Asad 1984 pp. 197–98, 560).

In the same spirit, 'Had God so willed, He would indeed have gathered them all unto – His – guidance. Do not therefore allow thyself to be amongst those who are swayed by ignorance – of God's ways in creation –' (Qur'an 6: 35). God could have created mankind in the likeness of obedient angels, with no choice capability. But instead they are left to their own choice: 'Only those who listen – with an open mind – can respond to the call. As for the dead – those who are incapable of independent thinking – God will raise them from the dead – in the hereafter –, whereupon unto Him they shall return' (Qur'an 6: 36); and only then they will be able to understand.

God provides guidance and does not leave people unaware of the right choice: 'O Humankind, there has now come unto you an admonition from your Lord, and a cure for all – the ill – that may be in your hearts, and guidance and grace unto all who believe' (Qur'an 10: 57). The message of the Qur'an is described as a mere admonition, not compulsory. However it is a cure against doubt, uncertainty, misgivings and apprehension. In consequence, it provides guidance and bestows grace on those who choose to believe.

Consequently, it is not the Prophet's task – much less anyone else's – to ensure the choice outcome of other individuals: 'Say "O mankind, the truth from your Lord has now come unto you. Whoever therefore chooses to follow the right path, follows it to his own good, and whoever chooses to go astray, goes astray to his own detriment, and I am not set over you to ensure your choice"' (Qur'an 10: 108).

The Qur'an further addresses the Prophet: 'Yet if God so willed, they would not have ascribed divinity to aught beside Him': God could have obliged them to follow the right path between right and wrong. 'Hence We have not made thee their keeper', i.e to look after their affairs and ensure their correct belief. 'And neither are thou responsible for their conduct' (Qur'an 6: 107). It is up to God alone to call them to account.

Despite the Prophet's best effort and goodwill, most people will remain sceptical and unaware of many signs:

> Yet, most people will have no faith, however ardently thou may desire it. Although thou do not ask of them any reward, for it is but God's reminder unto all mankind. But then, how many a sign is there in the heavens and on earth, which they pass by – without appreciating its significance –, and to

which they turn their backs. And most of them do not even believe in God without ascribing divine powers to other beings besides Him. (Qur'an 12: 103–106)

And while the sceptics have closed their minds to the power of the Qur'an, the believers are most anxious of their coming to reason, although such matter rests wholly with God:

Yet even if – they should listen to – a divine discourse by which mountains could be moved, or the earth cleft asunder, or the dead made to speak – they who are bent on denying the truth would still refuse to believe in it –, nay, but God alone has the power to decide what shall be. Have, then, they who have attained to faith not yet reconciled themselves to the fact that, had God so willed, He would indeed have guided all mankind aright? (Qur'an 13: 31)

Again the reference is to the prerogative of man's free choice as a moral creature. But those who are bent on denying the truth will not believe even if the dead are raised and made to speak to them about the hereafter (see also Luke 16: 31).

Describing an adamant attitude: 'Yet even had We opened to them a gateway to heaven and they were to continue ascending therein; They would surely have said, "It is only that our eyes are spellbound! Nay we have been bewitched"' (Qur'an 15: 14–15).

But the universe and heavens were not created in vain, and as the reality becomes evident, in the hereafter, to those who did not take heed, their end will be a natural consequence to their free choice and deeds. As for this world, one is admonished to accommodate unbelievers through forbearance, making due allowance for their ignorance, arrogance, intransigence, and, perhaps, their feeling of self-sufficiency: 'And – remember – We have not created the heavens and the earth and all that is between them without – an inner – truth; but, behold, the Hour – when this will become clear to all – is yet to come indeed. Hence forgive – men's failings – with fair forbearance. Verily thy Lord is all-knowing Creator of all things' (Qur'an 15: 85–86).

Having delivered the message, leaving alone those who insist on turning their back to it is emphasized: 'Hence, proclaim openly all that thou has been bidden – to say –, and leave alone all those who ascribe divinity to aught beside God. Verily, We shall suffice thee against all who – now – deride – this message –' (Qur'an 15: 94–95).

Urging forbearance towards others is specifically detailed in the following verse: 'Accept what is easily forthcoming – from man's nature –, and enjoin the doing of what is right; and leave alone all those who choose to remain ignorant' (Qur'an 7: 199). The injunction is to leave alone those who wilfully insist on remaining deaf to moral truths, but not those who are simply unaware of them.

In short, a believer is responsible for himself: 'O you who have attained to faith! It is – but – for your own selves that you are responsible; those who go astray can do you no harm if you are on the right path. Unto God you must all return; and then He will make you – truly – understand all that you were doing in – life –' (Qur'an 5: 105). A believer, having fulfilled his duty of reminding others, will not be held responsible for their disbelief.

On the same theme: 'As for him who believes himself to be self-sufficient. To him did thou – O Prophet – give your whole attention. Although thou are not accountable for his failure to attain to purity' (Qur'an 80: 5–7). The address to the Prophet is by implication applicable to all believers.

Explicitly forbidding man to punish other people who deny the truth, the Qur'an addresses the believers: 'Leave Me alone – to deal – with him whom I have created alone' (Qur'an 74: 11), thus reserving punishment of unbelievers exclusively to God. Also: 'Hence, leave Me alone with such as give the lie to this Message. We shall bring them low, step by step, without their perceiving how it has come about' (Qur'an 68: 44), i.e. God alone has the right to decide whether or how to chastise them.

'And have patience with what they say, and leave them with noble dignity. And leave Me alone – to deal – with those who give the lie to the truth, those who enjoy the blessing of life – without any thought of God –; and bear thou with them for a little while' (Qur'an 73: 10–11), i.e. leave them to the day of Judgement. In this regard it is stated further: 'Your Sustainer is fully aware of what you are – and what you deserve –, if He so wills, He will bestow His grace upon you; and if He so wills, He will chastise you; hence, We have not sent thee – unto men, O Prophet – with the power to determine their fate' (Qur'an 17: 54).

As for what still remains of previous revelations to Prophets of past:

And unto thee – O Prophet – We have vouchsafed this divine writ, setting forth the truth, confirming whatever truth there still remains of earlier revelations and determining what is true therein. Judge, then, between the followers of earlier revelation in accordance with what God has bestowed from on high, and do not follow their errant views forsaking the truth that has come unto thee. For every one of you We appointed a – different – law and way of life. And if God had so willed, He could surely have made you all one single community, but – He willed it otherwise – in order to test you by means of what He has vouchsafed unto you. Vie, then, with one another in doing good works. Unto God you all must return, and then He will make you truly understand all that on which you were wont to differ. (Qur'an 5: 48)

Richness in thought and diversity, rather than uniformity, is shown to be intentional in the divine scheme. The search for uniformity envisaged by some mentalities entails 'heresy' by necessity. Whereas, vying between ethnic and religious communities should be in good deeds only, not in enmity or mutual hostility. Complete uniformity is never envisaged by the Qur'an. Ultimately everyone will return to God whereby he or she will know the truth behind his or her belief and ideological conflicts. The test of human beings is their willingness to surrender themselves to the will of God, and obey Him in accordance with the sequence of divine messages, so that they can grow socially, intellectually, and spiritually in accordance with God's will for the creation (Asad 1984 p. 153).

This is spelled out with more detail in the following verse: 'Verily, those who have attained to faith – in this divine writ – as well as those who follow the Jewish faith, and the Nazarenes, and the Sabians, all who believe in God and the Last Day and do righteous deeds, shall have their reward with their Sustainer; and no fear shall they have, and neither shall they grieve' (Qur'an 2: 62). Thus, salvation is conditional on: belief in God, belief in the Day of Judgement, and righteous deeds in this life. This thesis categorically rejects the Jewish and Christians claims that salvation is due to them alone. The Jewish claim to exclusive salvation by virtue of their descent from Abraham is specifically rejected.

As to the judgement between various religious groups: 'Verily, as for those who have attained to faith – in this divine writ – and those who follow the Jewish faith, and the Sabians, and the Nazarenes, and the Magians, and those who are bent on ascribing divinity to aught but God; verily, God will decide between them on Resurrection Day' (Qur'an 22: 17). The 'Sabians' referred to in the above two verses are the followers of John the Baptist (Eisenman 1997 pp. 326, 331; Schonfield 1993 p. 131; Dawud 1990 p. 143; Knight and Lomas 1998 p. 141).

Wars in Islam

In contrast to the Qur'anic quotations stated above, some may be inclined to invoke such Qur'anic verses urging believers to fight polytheists. For example: 'And so when the sacred months are over, slay the Pagans wherever you may come upon them, and take them captive, and besiege them, and lie in wait for them at every conceivable place. Yet if they repent, and take to prayer, and practice regular charity, then let them go their way. For God is Oft-Forgiving, Most Merciful' (Qur'an 9: 5). 'And fight the Pagans all together, as they fight you – O believers – all together, and know that God is with those who are conscious of Him' (Qur'an 9: 36).

The above verses taken out of context, are labelled by some as 'the sword verses'. Some like to claim that they abrogated many verses pertaining to forgiveness, peaceful co-existence, freedom of religion, and leaving polytheists and the ignorant alone; whereas in fact, they abrogated nothing. That this ruling is applicable solely to the pagans of Arabia is clear from the context. To this one can add that the theory of abrogation is dubious and almost most certainly invalid. A saying attributed to the Prophet is:

> I am empowered to fight people until they accept the tenet that, 'God is The Only Deity, and Muhammad is His messenger', and until they establish prayer, and practise regular charity. Only then, their persons and properties are safe as far as I am concerned, and, then, it is for God alone to take them to account – for their inner motives.

Clearly, the Prophet was referring solely to the people of Arabia. Qur'an 9: 1–28 strongly support this argument. The intention that only the population in Arabia should be Muslim in totality is very clear. Those residing in Arabia while rejecting Islam were at liberty to leave. This point is substantiated by another saying of the Prophet that: 'Arabia shall not accommodate two religions simultaneously'. It was not conceivable that those ascribing divinity to aught but God should reside in Arabia and practice polytheism. In contrast, Qur'an 5: 29–34 clearly define the policy of Islam towards people outside of Arabia.

People outside of Arabia are not meant by Qur'an 9: 1–28 and 9: 36. Rather, it is the more general doctrine that applies to them: 'There shall be no coercion in matters of faith; distinct has now become the right way from – the way – of error' (Qur'an 2: 256). There are many verses that guarantee religious freedom, forbid aggression, advocate peace over war (e.g. Qur'an 2: 190–93; 4: 91; 8: 61; 60: 8–9). There are many other verses that establish Islam on a footing of reason, scientific clues, and intellect, while rejecting coercion, dogma, and tradition. Such policy was indeed implemented by Muslims during their first conquests whence they left local populations outside of Arabia to their original faith. The subsequent conversion to Islam on the part of non-Muslims was a slow and gradual process following personal free choice, conviction, and satisfaction. In many countries the locals adhered to their religion for hundreds of years whereby Muslims remained in the minority, as for example in Spain (Lang

p. 185). This was one reason why Muslim conquests spread within 90 years from China in the east to Spain and France in the west. Local inhabitants welcomed Muslims as liberators from religious persecution, something they endured under their previous masters. As such, Islamic conquests were predicated by the necessity to guarantee 'human rights' as expressed in today's terminology.

The Qur'an order to fight 'people of earlier scriptures', e.g. Jews and Christians (9: 29–34), should be read in the context of the overall Qur'anic Law that fighting should be conducted only in defence, and for the sole purpose of preventing religious persecution, coercion, and ethnic cleansing. The Qur'an clearly states the objective of war: 'And fight against them until there is no more oppression and all worship is devoted to God alone', i.e. until man is free to worship God, 'But if they desist', i.e from repression and persecution, 'behold, God sees all that they do.' (Qur'an 8: 39), i.e. He knows all their motives, and He alone will call them to account.

The Qur'an injunction to Muslims to incline to peace – having prepared for war – is stated as follows: 'But if they incline to peace, incline thou to it as well, and place thy trust in God' (Qur'an 8: 61). And: 'As for such – of the unbelievers – as do not fight against you – on account of your faith –, and neither drive you out of your homeland, God does not forbid you to show them kindness and to behave towards them with full equity, for verily, God loves those who act equitably' (Qur'an 60: 8).

'And never let your hatred of people, who would bar you from the Inviolable House of Worship, lead you into the sin of aggression; but rather cooperate in furthering virtue and God-consciousness, and do not cooperate in furthering evil and enmity, and remain conscious of God, for God is strict in retribution' (Qur'an 5: 2). This injunction, of general timeless import, refers to anybody who might endeavour to bar believers from the exercise of their religious duties – symbolized by the Inviolable House of Worship – and thus try to lead them away from their faith. The injunction states that another party's error does not justify aggression.

In short, wars that are waged for purposes of coercion, aggression, material gains, or for vengeance and 'religious' grudge (crusades), or to usurp the material wealth of other nations (imperialist wars), all such wars are forbidden in Islam. The following verse makes this point very clear: 'And be not like those who went forth from their homeland – setting forth for war – full of self conceit and a desire to be seen and praised by men; trying to turn others away from the path of God; the while God encompassed all their doings' (Qur'an 8: 47).

War is made lawful only when the objective is to defend the oppressed and maintain justice. Wars designed for aggression are utterly forbidden: 'And fight in God's cause against those who wage war against you, but do not commit aggression, for verily God does not love aggressors' (Qur'an 2: 190). The purpose of lawful war is explicitly stated: 'Hence, fight against them until there is no more oppression and all worship is devoted to God alone, but if they desist, then all hostility shall cease, save against those who – wilfully – do wrong' (Qur'an 2: 193), i.e. until God alone can be worshipped without fear of persecution, and none is compelled to bow down in awe before another human being (Asad 1992 pp. 41, 244).

> Hence, make ready against them whatever force and war mounts you are able to muster, so that you might deter thereby the enemies of God, who are your enemies as well, and others beside them of whom you may be unaware – but – of whom God is aware; and whatever you may expend in God's cause shall be repaid to you in full, and you shall not be wronged. (Qur'an 8: 60)

This verse constitutes an injunction to be prepared for opposing aggression and oppression. For it is immediately followed by: 'But if they incline to peace, incline thou to it as well, and place thy trust in God' (Qur'an 8: 61). In compliance with this injunction, Muslims always made peace treaties with the most generous of terms even when they had the upper hand.

Although the enemy may be offering peace with a view to deceiving the Muslims, the peace offer must nevertheless be accepted: 'And should they seek but to deceive thee – by their peace offer – behold, God is enough for thee' (Qur'an 8: 62). In other words, in such a case, judgement should be based on outward evidence alone. Mere suspicion cannot be an excuse for rejecting an offer of peace, notwithstanding the offer might be made in bad faith. Because in the end 'such evil scheming will engulf none but its authors' (Qur'an 35: 43).

In compliance with the above, all the Prophet's encounters with his enemies were conducted in self-defence. True, he did, in many cases, take the initiative but only to abort an aggressive enemy plan. His Tabuk expedition (October 630 CE) is one very clear example. Byzantium became wary of the rise of Islam and the prospect of unifying all of Arabia under one leadership, and therefore prepared to invade the Hijaz – western Arabia – where Islam was budding. The Prophet on his part was not in the habit of passively waiting for events to happen to Muslims. He therefore took the initiative by mobilizing some thirty thousand men whom he led north to Tabuk, only to find that the Byzantine Emperor Heraclius had withdrawn having received news of the Prophet's advance. The Prophet on his part deemed it sufficient to make peace treaties with the Arab tribes in the region and remained with them for twenty days before returning to Madinah. The Tabuk expedition was in perfect compliance with the Qur'anic injunction:

Permission – to fight – is given to those against whom war is being wrongfully waged, and verily, God has indeed the power to succour them. Those who have been driven from their homelands against all right for no other reason than their saying, 'Our Sustainer is God'. For if God had not enabled people to defend themselves against one another, monasteries and churches and synagogues and mosques in – all of – which God's name is abundantly extolled, would surely have been destroyed. God will most certainly succour him who succours His cause, for verily God is most powerful, almighty. (Qur'an 22: 39)

The permission to fight is clearly made conditional on responding to aggression.

The following verse specifies which deniers of the truth are to be fought: 'O you who have attained to faith, fight against those deniers of the truth who are near you, and let them find firmness in you, and know that God is with those who are conscious of Him' (Qur'an 9: 123). Deniers of the truth 'who are near' refer to those who lived in Arabia at the prophet's time, because Arabia's population was destined to be totally Muslim as already explained. Outside of Arabia the reference is to those who come from afar, approaching Muslim countries with the intent of aggression.

The Prophet's injunction to his lieutenant Mua'z Ben Jabal, whom he sent to the Yemen, is noteworthy:

You will find there some people of previous scriptures [e.g. Jews or Christians]. Invite them to profess that 'God is the only Deity, and that Muhammad is His messenger'. If they go along, tell them that God has ordained on them five prayers every day and night. If they go along tell them that God has ordained that charity be taken from their rich to be given to their poor. If they go along, beware of giving the best of their possessions to the poor – as charity –. And beware of the supplication of him who has been wronged. For there is no barrier between God, and a wronged person's supplication.

One cannot fail to notice the repetition of the Prophet's phrase: 'If they go along' three times, emphasizing their freedom of choice. Finally, he warned Mua'z against any wrong-doing to them, for fear that a wronged man's supplication has direct access to God.

In another instance, the Prophet sent a letter to Heraclius, the Byzantine Emperor, inviting him to accept Islam stating: 'Surrender – to God – and you will achieve peace, otherwise you will bear a share of the sin of persecuting the Arians.' It is both interesting and important that the Prophet's letter did not threaten war if the Emperor failed to accept Islam; only that the Emperor would share in the sin of Arian persecutions that apparently persisted to Heraclius' time! Thus, he emphasized again the defensive nature of war in Islam, and that Heraclius, having been reminded, was accountable to God alone.

Similarly, wars fought by the Prophet's successors were defensive in that the political environment of their day was summarized in a situation of 'conquer or be conquered' (Lang 1997 p. 133). Byzantium and Persia were locked in costly military conflict over Iraq, Syria, and Egypt long before the rise of Islam, but when a new power rose in Arabia both Byzantium and Persia had their misgivings about it. Heraclius mobilized his forces to attack the Hijaz – western Arabia – while Persia prepared to take the Gulf area – eastern Arabia. Omar, the second successor to the Prophet was reported to have said: 'I only wish that there could be a barrier of fire between us and them [the Persians], so that they do not reach us, and we do not reach them.' As for the disputed Islamic jurisprudence on the so-called 'abode of peace' and 'abode of war' among Muslim Jurists, it merely reflected the status quo of their time, and did not reflect a conceptualization of how things should ideally and perpetually be (Lang 1997 p. 134).

Some may like to refer to the tribute – *jizya* – levied on non-Muslims, by the Muslim state of the time, as a sign of imposed capitulation. Nothing could be further from the truth. The tribute was simply a means of equating non-Muslims to Muslims in the duty of defending the country. Since the state was based on religion and ideology, it was not conceivable that a non-Muslim could join a Muslim army in defence of the country. In return for exemption from military service the *jizya* was levied on every able bodied non-Muslim male. Women were exempted, as were children not of military age, the old, the sick, the handicapped, and the clergy. In return for the *jizya*, every non-Muslim became a *zummi*, meaning someone entitled to the protection of the Islamic State. In any case, the amount of *jizya* was much less than the *zakat*, the purifying alms paid to the state by Muslims.

One Qur'an exegete, a famous jurist Al-Razi, wrote in his exegesis of verse 9: 30: 'God has accepted *jizya* from Jews and Christians because they have, on the face of it, attached themselves to Moses and Jesus. And so in due regard and respect for these two great prophets and their Holy Scriptures, God ruled that *jizya* is to be accepted from them.'

Jihad

It is nowadays common in the media to use the phrase *jihad* rather inaccurately (Hoffman 1993 pp. 161–66) and in a fashion that has no support in the Qur'an nor in the Traditions of the Prophet. For example, the media translates *jihad* to mean what they term 'holy war' although in Islam there is no such thing as holy war, or unholy war, nor holy *jihad*! There is simply *jihad* to repel aggression. The term 'holy war' is indeed a Christian term first advanced by Pope Urban II who in 1095 summoned the Christians of Europe to carry the cross and their swords to recover Jerusalem from the hands of the 'infidels' – Muslims. Thus, the First Crusade was to become the first 'holy war'.

In Islam the etymology of *jihad* derives from the verb 'to strive' or 'exert effort'. Thus to perform *jihad* means simply to strive and exert effort, and this exertion of effort is applicable in every facet of life, for example in learning and research, not merely in fighting aggression.

Quotations from the Qur'an help to illustrate the point: 'But as for those who strive in Our cause, We shall most certainly guide them onto paths that lead unto Us; for, behold, God is indeed with those who do good' (Qur'an 29: 69). The point made is that those who strive to research for definitive knowledge, e.g. free from dogma, and strive against evil will be led to a cognizance of God. The plurality in 'paths' indicates that there are many, rather than a unique path. Also: 'Hence, whoever strives – in God's cause – does so for his own good, for, verily, God does not stand in need of anything in all the worlds' (Qur'an 29: 6).

And 'Hence, do not defer to – the likes and dislikes of – those who deny the truth, but rather strive against them by means of this – divine writ – with utmost striving' (Qur'an 25: 52). Striving by means of the Qur'an means intellectually to understand its meanings and follow its directions in argument with others while setting the best of practical examples as elucidated in the following:

> O you who have attained to faith! Bow down and prostrate yourselves, and worship your Sustainer, and do good, so that you might attain to a happy state. And strive hard in God's cause with all the striving that is due to Him. It is He who has elected you – to carry His message –, and has laid no hardship on you in – anything that pertains to – religion. (Qur'an 22: 77–78)

The way to deal with both the deniers of the truth and the hypocrites is spelled out as follows: 'O Prophet, Strive hard against the deniers of the truth and the hypocrites, and be adamant with them; and – if they do not repent –

their goal shall be hell – and how vile a journey's end' (Qur'an 9: 73). Being adamant with both parties precludes accepting ideological compromise. The verse deals with both deniers of the truth and the hypocrites. Striving – *jihad* – in this particular case precludes fighting, because Islam considers an outward profession of faith to be sufficient even though it may be made in bad faith as in the case of the hypocrites. The verse therefore requires that *jihad* should be pursued through intellectual discussions and reasoning.

The Qur'an clearly forbids fighting anyone who has not had the opportunity to receive the message, or having received it, did not accept it: 'And if anyone of those who ascribe divinity to aught beside God seeks thy protection, grant him protection', meaning it is unlawful to fight or kill him, 'so that he might – be able to – hear the word of God – from thee –, and thereupon – if he fails to accept Islam – convey him to a place where he can feel secure' even though he is a non-believer. 'This – order to grant them protection – because such people do not know – or appreciate the truth' (Qur'an 9: 6). Al-Razi wrote:

> This verse is clear proof that, as far as Islam is concerned, dogma is insufficient and that intellectual clues, reason, and intellectual effort are mandatory. If dogma were sufficient, respite could not have been allowed to a non-believer. A non-believer would then have been addressed: 'either you believe as we do, or we will kill you'. But the Qur'an forbids this course of action, making it clear that dogma is insufficient for matters of belief, and that it is mandatory to provide convincing argument and valid reason, and, in addition, to provide respite for the other party to contemplate and think.

There is little doubt that early Muslims fully understood this point with the result that Islam spread as easily as it did in their time.

TWO

The Bible, the Qur'an, and Progression of Divine Revelation

> Behold, from on high have We bestowed upon thee this divine writ, setting forth the truth for – the benefit – of mankind. And whoever chooses to be guided – thereby – does so for his own good, and whoever chooses to go astray, goes but astray to his own hurt; and thou are not set over them to dispose their affairs. (Qur'an 39: 41)

Definitions

The fundamental beliefs of Christianity are maintained in two collections of books, together called the Holy Bible, or simply the Bible. The first of these two collections comprises the Jewish scriptures, referred to collectively, as the Old Testament (OT), or the Jewish Bible. The second is called the New Testament (NT), sometimes referred to alone as the Christian Bible. It includes fourteen epistles of Paul, four narrative gospels about the life of Jesus written under the influence of Pauline theology, the Acts of the Apostles whose hero is Paul, and eight other treatises.

The Old Testament

The 'Old Testament' is a Christian term used in contradistinction to the 'New Testament'. It is a collection of Jewish 'Holy Scriptures' (thirty-nine books) referred to collectively as the Jewish Bible. Christians accept it as an important part of their Bible preserving the message of Jewry, on condition that it is interpreted in accordance with Christian theology. Prior to the fixing of the NT in 325 CE, Christians made special use of the OT as their principal sacred book (Dawes 1999 p. 91; Freke and Gandy 1999 p. 222). This was both important and necessary because the advent and the events of Jesus's life were presented as a fulfilment of the 'prophecies' of the OT. Pauline Christianity was keen to preserve continuity with the old tradition to give weight to its own theology. If it rejected Judaism and the OT outright it would lose 'proof' of Jesus as Christ, and lose proof that the events of Jesus's life occurred 'in accordance with the scriptures'. On this point the Qur'an states: 'Who has bestowed from on high the divine writ which Moses brought unto men as a light and a guidance, and which you treat as mere leaves of paper making a show of them the while you conceal so much' (Qur'an 6: 91).

The first five books of the Old Testament are collectively called the 'Pentateuch' meaning the five books of Moses. They are also metaphorically labelled as the 'Torah' meaning the Law of Moses. This 'Torah' does not necessarily correspond to the 'Taurah' divinely inspired to Moses as referred to in the Qur'an (Ali 1992 p. 288; Spong 1992 p. 41), except perhaps for a few scattered subjects and clauses of the text that may have survived from the original. The Torah contains a 'historical' and legendary narrative of the history of the world from the Creation to the time of arrival of the Jews in the Promised Land. It contains some beautiful idylls but also stories of incest, cruelty, and treachery, not always disapproved of. A great part of the Mosaic Law is embodied in the narrative. The Pentateuch was authored during and after the period of Babylonian Exile (586–539 BCE) when the Jews were deported to Babylon under the Babylonian king Nebuchadnezzar (Rhymer 1996 p. 62).

It is noteworthy that in Luke 24: 44 Jesus refers to the Law of Moses, the Prophets and the Psalms. In Matthew 7: 12 Jesus refers to the Law and the Prophets as summing up the whole scripture. It is also noteworthy that II Chronicles 34: 30 refers to the 'Book of the Covenant' as the original Law: the Covenant of God. This is interesting as the Qur'an also refers to the Covenant with the Jews. Indeed the modern Christian terms of 'Old Testament' and 'New Testament' are substitutes for 'Old Covenant' and 'New Covenant'. Muslims believe in the mission of Moses as a Prophet to the Children of Israel and that Moses was inspired with the Taurah which was afterwards distorted or mostly lost. The Jewish religious establishment, at various stages of history, attempted to reconstruct the Taurah, but to no avail.

The prevailing present opinion of Biblical scholars is that Jewish Scriptures were edited and rewritten from four sources labelled by the scholars as Y-E-D-P meaning YHWH – Elohim – Deuteronomy – Prophets (Spong 1992 pp. 40–57; Friedman 1987).

The earliest source which is called Yahwist – from Yahweh, i.e. God – is supposed to have been written during the reign of King Solomon in Jerusalem (960–920 BCE), some three hundred years after the death of Moses. The second source labelled Elohist – from Elohim, also meaning God – was written in

Samaria around the year 850 BCE, after the split of Israel into two kingdoms north and south. The third source labelled Deuteronomist – from Deuteronomy, meaning the second Law – was supposed to be a discovery in Jerusalem of a scroll of Law in 621 BCE, purported to have been written by Moses himself. The fourth part of Old Testament books is labelled P, for Prophets-Psalms-Proverbs, all of which were written between the sixth century BCE and the birth of Jesus. Their authors are not necessarily the prophets to whom the books are ascribed; one reason for calling them apocrypha. Ascribing names of prophets to such books, although quite common, was mostly guesswork or pious wishful thinking. Indeed it was a merit of Islam to have rejected the validity of the 'Old Testament' in its present form.

In summary, books of the Old Testament were written during a period extending several hundred years after the death of Moses, and much of the OT constitutes a description of the national history of the Jewish people – mostly biased. This explains late Jewish concepts about God being a tribal deity embodying the prejudices of the Jewish people. It is significant that the oldest extant parts of the Hebrew Bible were found among the Qumran documents – discovered near the Dead Sea in 1947, now dated to the second century BCE (Livingstone 2000 p. 160; Funk 1996 pp. 25, 70).

The Old Testament was translated into the Greek language in Alexandria, presumably for the sake of the Jewish community in Egypt when Greek was the lingua franca of the Hellenistic world. This Greek translation, labelled Septuagint (from the Latin septuaginta, meaning seventy), abbreviated LXX, is the earliest extant Greek translation of the Old Testament of the original Hebrew. The name was derived from the legend that there were 72 translators, six from each of the twelve tribes of Israel. The story is that the translators were sent to Alexandria by Eleazar, the high priest at Jerusalem, at the request of the Ptolemaic king of Egypt, Ptolemy II Philadelphus (285–246 BCE). In fact the translators were Hellenized Jews who took the opportunity to create and insert similarities and synthesis between Jewish and pagan mythology. The Septuagint, at later times, greatly influenced the authorship of the New Testament.

The Jewish religious establishment continued writing 'Holy Scriptures' after the advent of Christianity, thus producing the Talmud, the code of Jewish law, between the second and fourth centuries CE (Vermes 1998 p. 43; Freke and Gandy 1999 p. 196). But Christians do not acknowledge Jewish scriptures produced later than the birth of Jesus, thus placing the Talmud on the same level as pagan mythology (Le Glay 1997 p. 524).

The New Testament

The New Testament, comprising 27 books, is accepted by the Christians as their own 'Holy Scriptures', and together with the Old Testament constitutes the Christian Holy Bible.

The first four books of the New Testament, attributed to Matthew, Mark, Luke and John, are called gospels. Gospels are narratives, supposed to cover the life of Jesus, though unevenly. These four gospels were amongst tens of other gospels circulating in early Christianity. In 325 CE, the consul of Nicaea, convened under the auspices of the then heathen, Byzantine emperor Constantine, 'canonized' these four gospels, and abrogated and ordered the destruction of all others.

None of the material of the New Testament was written during Jesus's lifetime. Moreover, the arrangement of material in the New Testament does not reflect their chronological order of writing. The first of the NT material to have been written, were the epistles (letters) of Paul about 50–60 CE, followed by the Gospel According to Mark written about 70–80 CE, then the Gospel According to Matthew and the Gospel According to Luke in the mid-eighties (Funk 1993 pp. 18, 128). Last to have been written was the Gospel According to John, about 110–30 CE. Other letters and materials of the New Testament were written as late as 140–50 CE (Mack 1995 p. 5). Some authors contend that the book of Acts, plus Luke's gospel, was written in the early second century, some 75 years after Jesus's death (Mack 1995 pp. 45, 228). At the time of production of the New Testament material expectations were high among Pauline Christians that Jesus was about to return to earth as a powerful king to fulfil militarily what they considered he did not accomplish in his first coming. Paul had predicted that Jesus would return to earth during Paul's own lifetime and the lifetime of his own contemporaries.

At the time of its writing, the New Testament material was considered neither sacred, nor 'Holy Scripture' (Spong 1992 pp. 80–81, 89; Funk 1996 p. 111). It is even doubtful whether the Christians of that time would have been willing to subscribe to later developed church creeds such as the Nicene Creed of 325 CE. Only towards the beginning of the third century, did Christians begin to think of such treatises as holy. The four gospels of the New Testament were not the only gospels or scriptures circulating during the first four centuries. Many other gospels had been written exceeding twenty in number and perhaps much more (Funk 1993 p. 29; Funk 1996 p. 57; Parrinder 1992 p. 82). In addition, there must have been hundreds of epistles in circulation containing exposition of doctrine interpreted differently by different groups and churches. It was a wild body of unharmonized unmethodical literature, casual in nature. Choosing which of the many scriptures to be included in the Christian 'Holy Bible' had to wait until the fourth century. The choice was made subsequent to the council of Nicaea in 325CE in favour of the four canonical gospels plus twenty-three other treatises. Indeed, the New Testament turned out to be a very small collection of texts from a large body of literature produced by various religious groups. Still, this accredited book, oddly misnamed the 'Word of God', gave the church its credentials for its subsequent role, not only in Constantine's empire, but also for future generations (Mack 1995 pp. 6, 15). It is remarkable that most of the texts of the Christian Bible now unquestioned by today's Christian institutions were, during the first four centuries, considered to be either forged or heretical (Freke and Gandy 1999 p. 224).

Considering that Jesus is reckoned to have died in the year 30 CE at the earliest, or in the year 37 CE at the latest (Sanders 1993 p. 286), and his birth having been between 4 and 7 BCE (Sanders 1993 pp. 11, 282), it follows that Paul wrote his epistles some 20–30 years after the death of Jesus, and that the four gospels were written some 40–100 years after his death. Obviously, their authors had to write depending on memory recollections and meagre sources many decades after the events took place. None of the authors was eyewitness to first-hand knowledge, or to events when it took place. This is one reason why the gospels, on many issues, are widely divergent, contradictory, and impossible to harmonize or reconcile. These include important issues, not the least of which are the stories of Jesus's nativity, the annunciation to Mary, the virgin birth, and the 'genealogies' of Jesus.

Ironically, Paul's letters, the first to have been written, included very little information about Jesus's life or message. This is explained by the fact that Paul himself was neither a disciple of Jesus nor an eyewitness to his life, not to mention Paul's indifference to Jesus's earthly message (Funk 1993 p. 7; Mack 1995 p. 75). For information about the life of Jesus, many more decades had to elapse after Paul's death for contradictory narrative abridged gospels to emerge. The synoptic gospels, for example, place most of Jesus's mission in Galilee and give the impression that it lasted no more than one year, a rather conspicuous detail. On the other hand, the fourth gospel places a good part of Jesus's mission in Judaea and gives the impression that it lasted more than two years (Sanders 1993 pp. 66–67). This is an added reason why the gospels cannot be viewed as objective realistic history (Funk 1993 p. 11).

The four gospels of Matthew, Mark, Luke, and John are narratives purporting to document the life of Jesus. Unfortunately this documentation, several decades after the events took place, was based on hearsay. Indeed the information documented may have passed through many anonymous parties before coming to the notice of the author, himself anonymous (Funk 1993 p. 16).

It is therefore difficult to consider the gospels as biographies of Jesus. Not all stages of his lifetime are described, and wherever they are, the attention given to each stage is not balanced. The central theme of the gospels seems to be that of Jesus's future 'passion' with most of the emphasis placed on his last week in Jerusalem. The preceding stages of his life are portrayed as mere preludes to this final week. Jesus himself is mostly portrayed as a passive recipient of events, rarely if ever as taking the initiative. Very little attention is devoted to his prophetic message or Messianic mission on earth. The impression is given that his death was more important than his life and his message on earth.

Another difficulty with the material of the New Testament is its origin in the Greek language at its inception. This is to be contrasted with the fact that Jesus spoke Aramaic (Vermes 1998 p. 53; Vermes 2000 p. 2; Eisenman 1997), the language of Palestine at the time. The net result of initial Greek authorship was that all Christian tradition had to undergo translation from oral Aramaic into written Greek. What was lost, changed, and modified in the process of translation will never be known (Funk 1993 p. 27; Spong 1992 p. 79). But what we do know is how much mutilation the message of Jesus has undergone, with the obvious result that the odd naming of the Christian Bible as the 'Word of God', is merely a fantasy, or pious wishful thinking dictated by religious compulsion (Spong 1992 pp. 77, 79; Spong 1996 p. 6; Funk 1996 pp. 100, 111). The actual 'Word of God' divinely inspired to Jesus had been mostly lost forever.

With the exception of the epistles of Paul, authors of other parts of the New Testament are anonymous, and are most probably not associated with the apostles or evangelists bearing their names. It was quite common at the time to write material and attribute it to names other than the real author. Such practice was not considered dishonest (Funk 1993 p. 22; Sanders 1993 pp. 63–66; Mack 1995 pp. 7–8). This explains why each gospel bears the heading: 'Gospel According to', due to the uncertainty of its author. It is only out of convenience that one states 'the gospel of Mark' or 'the gospel of John' etc. Mark, Matthew, Luke, and John are mere titles employed only to distinguish which gospel one is talking about, without actually subscribing to the authorship of one or the other. This fact should be kept in mind whenever reference is made to any of the gospels. In summary, virtually nothing is known about the gospel authors whom, for convenience only, we call Matthew, Mark, Luke and John (Funk 1993 pp. 8, 20; Mack 1995 p. 153; Pagels 1989 p. 17).

Yet, the four gospels are termed 'canonical', because they were sanctioned by the Council of Nicaea, from amongst many others in circulation (Funk 1993 p. 29; Allegro 1992 p. xxv; Pagels 1989 p. xxiii). Subsequent to the Council of Nicaea, Emperor Constantine ordered the destruction of all gospels besides the four canonized. 'By the end of the fourth century it was all over. Books had been banned and burned, temples destroyed, and martyrs killed' (Mack 1995 p. 277).

The first three of the canonical gospels are labelled 'synoptic' because of their similarity and the common ground that they cover, although their extent is different. Mark, the most compact, starts with story of the public ministry of John the Baptist and the baptism of Jesus by the former. It concludes with Jesus's resurrection and the three women fleeing from an empty tomb. Matthew starts with the so-called genealogy of Jesus, his nativity and childhood, his baptism by John, and ends with the appearance of the resurrected Jesus to his disciples. Luke extends his account further in both directions starting with the angel's prophecy on the birth of John the Baptist, passing through Jesus's genealogy, which is substantially different from that presented by Matthew, and ending with a detailed account of apparitions of a resurrected Jesus.

The fourth canonical gospel – according to John – is distinct from the first three in matters of theology (Funk 1993 p. 3). It has a higher degree of 'Christology', a belief that Jesus was a pre-existent Logos, the eternal Word of God, or an incarnation of God who had taken flesh and roamed among humans while concealing his 'true' nature. It is almost certain that this was the last of the canonical gospels to have been written, perhaps as late as 130 CE, representing advanced and late theological developments (Wilson, A.N. 1992 p. 48; Spong 1996 p. 13).

The fifth book included in the Christian Bible is called 'Acts of the Apostles' and attributed to Luke. The title gives the impression that the book is about the twelve Apostles of Jesus. But the title is misleading because Acts is dominated mainly by the story of Paul, who was not even an apostle. With the exception of Peter, almost nothing is mentioned in Acts about other disciples of Jesus. Even Peter is introduced in the narrative with the sole intention of providing alleged continuity and unity between the message of Jesus and the new Pauline theology. In the words of one Bible authority (Eisenman 1997 p. 95), 'Acts is not history. It is not even particularly good narrative, romance, or fiction.' This point becomes clearer when one learns that Luke himself, not a disciple of Jesus, was one of Paul's converts. Small wonder that Luke depicts Paul as the hero of Acts.

To recap, the Christian Bible, or any of the four gospels, is *not* the Evangel four times mentioned in the Qur'an. Rather, the Qur'an refers to the original divine revelation bestowed upon Jesus and known to his contemporaries, the Nazarenes, under its Greek name 'Evangelion' (Good Tidings), from which the Arabic term '*enjil*' is derived. Islam maintains that the Gospel *of* Jesus, is not the same as the gospels *about* Jesus. This does not preclude that the Christian Bible in its present form may have derived some of its material from the Gospel of Jesus, reflecting his true message.

The Gospel of Jesus, the '*enjil*', is explicitly referred to in the Qur'an as follows:

> And We caused Jesus, the son of Mary, to follow in the footsteps of those – earlier prophets – confirming the truth of whatever still remained of the Torah; and We vouchsafed unto him the Gospel – the *enjil* –, wherein there was guidance and light, confirming the truth of whatever still remained of the Torah, and a guidance and admonition unto the God – conscious. (Qur'an 5: 46)

From the Q Gospel to the Narrative Gospels

From studying the four canonical gospels, scholars have noticed that both Matthew and Luke have included in their gospels substantial parts from Mark. Matthew reproduced about 90 per cent of Mark's material in his gospel. Luke used about half of Mark's material (Funk 1993 p. 10). All gospels agree that Mark was not a disciple of Jesus, but he was the first amongst the four evangelists to have written a narrative, in about 70 CE, after the destruction of Jerusalem.

In addition, scholars have noticed that a substantial part of the non-Markan material in both Matthew and Luke has striking similarity, and that these common parts involve the teachings of Jesus. Since it is believed that Matthew and Luke wrote independently and did not know one another, it was therefore postulated that there must have been a separate non-narrative written source on which both Matthew and Luke relied. On the other hand, there are areas of disagreement between the gospels of Matthew and Luke, which may point to Jesus's own distinctive views on which Matthew and Luke superimposed his own Christology (Funk 1993 p. 17).

The non-Markan common source of Matthew and Luke, was postulated by the scholars to have been a Sayings gospel, labelled 'Q' (from German Quelle, meaning source) which comprises the sayings of Jesus. The 'Q' label was chosen because most of the pioneer literature on the subject was German. Scholars have subsequently reconstructed Q from Matthew and Luke. There are no extant copies of the original Q gospel. However, the discovery at Nag Hammadi in Egypt, in 1945, of the Coptic gospel of Thomas has reinforced the 'Q' hypothesis as will be discussed (Funk 1993 p. 15; Funk 1996 pp. 61, 124). Coptic Thomas's gospel was a real manuscript with a composition similar to

Q, proving that Jesus's followers, the Nazarenes, had preserved in writing a gospel comprising only the teachings of Jesus (Funk 1993 p. 13ff.)

Since the Q source that scholars have postulated contains a compendium of Jesus's sayings only, and if this Q theory is correct, then the Q gospel may be comparable, in principle, though not in detail, to the 'Enjil' mentioned in the Qur'an. Alternatively, it may be more like the category of 'Hadith', that is, the authentic sayings of the Prophet. The Q gospel may also be viewed as the Gospel *of* Jesus contrasted with the four narratives, which are gospels *about* Jesus. There are several reconstructed editions of the Q gospel now available for general use. This is not saying that a reconstructed Q gospel contains 100 per cent authentic sayings of Jesus, but only that scholars have selected and compiled in Q what they deemed the most probable authentic sayings of Jesus.

The Q gospel must have been in circulation at an early date, perhaps about 50 CE (Funk 1996 p. 135; Pagels 1989 p. xvii), before the eruption of Paul's activity on the scene. If Q' had originally been compiled by the Nazarenes of Jerusalem, then it must by necesity be much closer to the message of Jesus, having escaped the theological innovations of Paul. For example, Q does not accord Jesus any divinity, only that Jesus was a Prophet sent by God to preach repentance before the final judgement. Jesus in Q does not die on a cross as first claimed by Mark forty years after Jesus's death (Funk 1996 p. 238). In this respect, it is worth noting that the Nazarenes had their own gospel in Hebrew called the 'gospel of the Nazarenes' (Eisenman 1997 p. 249; Freke and Gandy 1999 p. 172).

The discovery at Nag Hammadi of the so-called Nag Hammadi Library was one of the most important discoveries in modern times. It included a complete text of a new gospel in Coptic, the gospel of Thomas, which proved to be of extraordinary importance. The Coptic gospel of Thomas is a fourth-century manuscript based on original Greek fragments dating back to the last quarter of the first century (Mack 1995 p. 60). Coptic Thomas is a collection of 114 sayings of Jesus. It contains minimal dialogue and virtually no narrative. Remarkably, Thomas lacks any reference to the passion story. It looks very much like the Sayings gospel Q, and there is about 40 per cent overlap between the sayings in both gospels (Funk 1996 pp. 71, 134ff.). Coptic Thomas and its Greek fragments had obviously escaped burning by the Pauline Church during the persecutions after the Council of Nicaea.

Evolution of the Gospels

Hellenistic Christianity dominated the process of gospel composition. In the Gospel According to John, Jesus the Prophet was replaced by the myth of

Chrestos – Christ – the Divine. He was made to be co-eternal with the 'Father'. In addition, this fourth gospel included the myths of a conflict between Light and Darkness, and the identification of Jesus with the Eternal Logos, both clearly Hellenistic, and having their origin in the Mithraic cult (Larson 1977 pp. 186, 188; Wilson, A.N. 1997 p. 32).

As for Mark, all gospels are in agreement that he was not one of Jesus's disciples; yet Mark, a representative of Hellenistic Christianity, was the first to produce a written narrative gospel some forty years after Jesus death. In his presentation, Mark dissipated the message of Jesus within the Hellenistic kerygma. The kerygmatic Jesus represents the Hellenistic myth of a dying/rising god of some Hellenistic mystery cults. Mark was not, of course, the pioneer of the Hellenistic Chrestos myth. He had followed in the footsteps of Paul, and it was natural for him to document the myth being himself an exponent of Hellenistic Christianity. At a later stage both Matthew and Luke, in producing their own gospels, relied heavily on Mark as we have already seen (Kelber 1997 p. 5; Dawes 1999 pp. 94, 115–16, 129).

Gospel authors typically attributed to Jesus ideas and sayings of their own belief, with the intention of circulating what they deemed as the proper thing to have been said by Jesus, while actually reflecting their own beliefs for propaganda or doctrinal purposes (Funk 1996 p. 241ff.; Kelber 1997 p. 4ff.). The intent was to write gospels reflecting the authors' own beliefs to the extent of providing a radical alternative to the original faith of Jesus. Thus, in Hellenistic Christianity, the only thing remaining from Jesus's prophetic mission was his name. Jesus was maintained as a mere icon of the new faith.

To summarize, the chronology in which the 'Christian Scriptures' had evolved was in the following order: first, the Q gospel emanating from the historical Jesus the Prophet; second, Paul's letters replacing the historical Jesus with a mythical Chrestos in the context of a pagan Hellenistic milieu; and third, the narrative gospels, which merged the historical figure of Jesus the Prophet, with a mythical Chrestos of Pauline invention. All authors of the canonical gospels were exponents of Pauline theology.

In addition, excerpts from the Greek Jewish Bible, the Septuagint, were frequently extracted, modified, and inserted in the gospels to prove particular views. Scriptures were altered to ensure its fulfilment. It seems to have been accepted practice to rewrite texts from the Jewish Bible, insert them in the gospels, and re-interpret them in new ways according to new situations having nothing to do with their original context. In this manner, the New Testament could be tailored to fulfil Old Testament prophecies (Funk 1993 p. 23; Funk 1996 p. 231ff.; Dawes 1999 p. 77)

The controversy in the first centuries as to what material should be considered 'orthodox' led to schismatic movements within Pauline

Christianity. For example Marcion (d. 160) taught that the Jewish Bible should be abandoned. He theorized that the God of the Jewish Bible is different from the God of the gospels. Marcion's canon included only Luke's gospel and the epistles of Paul. Obviously this was not acceptable to the Orthodox Church, which needed the Jewish Bible as 'proof' of Jesus's Messiahship. It was this continuity that was required to give weight to Pauline Christianity. Eventually the Orthodox Church concluded that it must decide which of the many circulating scriptures of the time should be considered legitimate. This was not an easy task and the decision had to wait first until the Council of Nicaea in 325 CE and then until 387 CE after the 'Ecumenical' Council of Constantinople (Wilson, B. 1999 p. 36).

The Christian theologian-philosopher of the third century, Origen, acknowledged that scriptures were subjected to editing, deletions and additions, so as to suit the theological climate of those who set themselves up as 'correctors' (Freke and Gandy 1999 p. 145).

For all these reasons the gospels can neither be considered history nor 'Word of God'. Christian dogma did not emanate from the historical Jesus but quite the contrary. Scripture were based from the start on Pauline theology and history was either adapted or fabricated accordingly. Canonical gospels are mere narratives evolving from late religious groups who adopted Pauline beliefs about Jesus, including: that he died on the cross; that he instituted the Eucharist; that he was the saviour and redeemer of humanity from eternal sin; that he founded a 'Christian Church' with priestly hierarchy; and that, according to the fourth gospel, he was some deity incarnate.

It is of the utmost irony that the Christian Church was bent on making Paul's writings and doctrines a basis for a new religion that it attributed not to Paul, but to Jesus.

Versions of the Christian Bible

Versions of the Bible are not necessarily identical, as they change from time to time, and from one Christian denomination to another. For example the Roman Catholic Version, RCV for short, includes seven additional books which Protestants do not acknowledge and deem as apocrypha. Responding to the Protestants, these books are called 'deutero-canonical' by the Roman Catholics and the Orthodox churches, meaning they are a second canonical corpus (Mack 1995 p. 4). Thus the RCV includes 73 books compared with 66 books in the Protestant Bible.

It is noteworthy that the printing press determines to a great extent which books should be included or excluded from the Bible, a practice that continues to this day. From the start it was common practice to exclude material not conforming to particular Church views (Funk 1996 p. 107).

Historical Development

The language that Jesus spoke was the language that was at his time common in Palestine: Aramaic. Hebrew was one offshoot-dialect of Aramaic. However, the Christian Bible, in its entirety, and from the very start, was composed in Greek. The oldest scriptures that we possess today are in Greek, not in Aramaic, the language spoken by Jesus. Scholars are therefore faced with a daunting situation: how Jesus sayings, spoken first in Aramaic, were, for the purpose of writing gospels, translated into Greek. Added to this difficulty is the fact that the oldest extant Greek scriptures of the New Testament are fragments dating later than 200 CE (Funk 1996 pp. 25, 107).

The Latin Bible version, which is called 'Vulgate' meaning popular, was translated from Greek by Jerome in 382 CE. The Latin Vulgate became the official Bible for the Latin Church (Funk 1996 pp. 78, 115; Mack 1995 p. 290).

The present day Aramaic version called 'Peshitta', meaning 'simple', written in the Syriac dialect (an offshoot of Aramaic), is not an original, but has been translated from the Greek during the period 411–433 CE. The translation was made in Edessa the Syriac capital south-east of Asia Minor. The Peshitta became the official version of the Orthodox Eastern Church which separated from the Church of Rome after the Council of Ephesus in 431 CE. The Peshitta comprises only twenty-two books compared with the twenty-seven books of the Latin Vulgate. Conspicuously, the book of Revelation is not included in the Peshitta.

As for Arabic versions, Father R.P. Chediac wrote that the first Arabic translation of the Christian Bible dates back to the year 1060 CE, a scripture present in St Petersburg library (Ben Nabi 1986 p. 247). Other sources state that the oldest Arabic fragments that survive of Arabic translations of the gospels date from the ninth century. In consequence, Christian teachings in Arabia before the ninth century CE were communicated either verbally, or from Syriac and Ethiopic texts (Parrinder 1979 pp. 146, 161).

The first English version of the Bible and the first to be printed, was that of William Tyndale in 1524. Tyndale, an instructor at the University of Cambridge, was first prevented by the Church in England from translating the Bible. He then went to Germany taking advantage of the Protestant Reformation, which was starting under Martin Luther. In Germany he completed the first English translation of the New Testament, which was published first in Cologne, copies of which started reaching England in 1526.

Tyndale moved away from the doctrine of justification by faith only towards double justification by faith and works. He met bitter opposition from the Church and was finally arrested before being able to complete the translation of the Old Testament. In October 1536, he was publicly executed by burning at the stake, with his translation of the NT suppressed. Yet, Tyndale's work became the basis for subsequent English versions.

Almost simultaneously in Germany, Martin Luther was at work translating the Bible into German. He completed the New Testament translation in 1522, and the Old Testament was then translated in 1534. This and other doctrinal differences with the Catholic Church led to Luther's excommunication by the Pope who considered Luther's work and ideas to be 'heretical'.

In spite of the Church's opposition several Protestant translations were subsequently produced and circulated. In response, and as an alternative to the Protestant translations, the Roman Catholic Church decided to issue its own 'authoritative' Roman Catholic English version of the Bible. Thus, a NT English translation based on the Latin Vulgate was published in 1582 at Rheims, France. Shortly afterwards, the OT was translated into English and published in 1609, at Douai, also in France. Thus, the Roman Catholic version was called the Rheims–Douai version. This Roman Catholic version contained many polemic notes against Protestant 'heresies'.

In turn, in 1611, the Church of England issued its own English version called the 'King James Version' (KJV), also called 'The Authorized Version' (AV). Thus in the sixteenth and seventeenth centuries, and for the first time in history, Christians were buying and reading Bibles on their own. King James Version was first issued including the seven deutero-canonical books but thereafter without them (Funk 1996 p. 116).

In 1881, the Church modified the Authorized Version and a Revised Version, RV, was issued. In 1952 it was revised again and the so-called 'Revised Standard Version', RSV, was issued. Revised again in 1971, the new version maintained the same label: RSV. The publishers (Collins) in their notes on the RSV had the following to state: 'This Bible, RSV, is the product of thirty-two scholars of the highest eminence, assisted by an advisory committee representing fifty co-operating denominations.' (Deedat 1994 p. 85)

The following was also stated in the RSV preface by way of comment on the Authorized Version: 'The King James Version has grave defects ... these defects are so many and so serious as to call for revision.' One important point to note is that this last RSV expunged from the Holy Bible the only reference to Trinity in the New Testament, (I John 5: 7). The other reference to the Trinitarian formula in Matthew 28: 19 can safely be discarded as belonging to a late stage of doctrinal evolution obviously having nothing to do with the Jesus of history (Vermes 1998 p. 200).

In 1993, the so-called 'Scholar's Version' of the New Testament was issued in the USA under the name 'The Five Gospels', comprising the four canonical gospels plus the recently discovered Sayings gospel of Thomas. More than two hundred theologians and Doctors of Divinity from different parts of the USA, calling themselves 'The Jesus Seminar', cooperated to produce 'The Five Gospels'. The Jesus Seminar decided that in excess of 82 per cent of the sayings attributed to Jesus in the four canonical gospels were put in his mouth, and were most likely untrue (Funk 1993 p. 5; Dawes 1999 p. 58).

In this regard, it is interesting that Muslim scholars thirteen centuries ago conducted a similar study on the traditions of the Prophet. They classified the sayings attributed to the Prophet into categories such as true, weak or dubious, and false, with many shades in between, including many sub-divisions. Obviously, there is no guarantee on the complete soundness of the results, only that the scholars, at that early time, endeavoured to sift objectively the true from the dubious. Their methodology included the study of the personality of narrators, their biography, and therefore the credibility of each narrator. The chain of transmission for each tradition was thus of utmost importance. Traditions with a single chain of transmission were considered weaker than those with more than one chain. But this was not their only criterion. They also checked the text of each tradition to ascertain whether or not it fit within the general context of the Prophet's message.

Authors and Editors of the Christian Bible

We have already seen that St Paul, the founder of present-day Christianity, was the author of substantial parts of the New Testament, namely the Pauline epistles. Paul was not an apostle although he claimed to be one. No one believes that Paul was a disciple of Jesus. As far as Paul was concerned, Jesus's mission did not represent any meaningful message for future humanity but was merely a symbol of mythical Hellenistic ideas. Obviously, Jesus was not the first Christian in the sense of present-day Christianity, nor was he a Christian at all for that matter. Yet Christians attribute to him sayings that make him a Christian according to Pauline beliefs, notwithstanding the immense gap between the teaching and message of Jesus, and the doctrines of Christianity. Little wonder that present-day Christianity is labelled 'Pauline Christianity'.

At the time of Paul's death not a single gospel had been written. Furthermore, when Paul died, none of his letters were regarded as 'Holy Scripture'. Gospels were written, many decades after Paul's death, under the influence of proliferating Pauline doctrines with the result that the Christian Bible is much more dominated by Paul's thought than is apparent on the surface. A reader of the New Testament first encounters the four gospels, which attempted to narrate Jesus's life. Next comes the story of Paul under the heading 'Acts of the Apostles', although very little is mentioned about the apostles aside from the self-appointed Paul. Then one reads Paul's letters. But as we have already noted, the arrangement of the Bible does not correspond to its chronological authorship. We already know that the earliest writings of the Christian Bible were Paul's letters. For this reason Paul's ideas, theories, and doctrines became the basis for future gospels. Gospel authors and editors were exponents of the Pauline belief, and it was natural that they reflected and expounded Paul's theology in their narratives about Jesus (Maccoby 1998 p. 4).

Although the writing of gospels started after the year 70 CE, the oldest scripture fragments that we possess today date to some 175 years after the death of Jesus. These scriptures are so different from one another that no two are alike. More than seventy thousand meaningful variants are estimated to exist in the manuscripts of the Greek New Testament (Funk 1996 p. 94). In addition, the Septuagint LXX, the Greek translation of the Old Testament, substantially influenced gospel authorship. For example, Mark, who was an exponent of Pauline Hellenistic persuasion, and had written the first of the canonical gospels from hearsay long after the events took place, had put into the mouth of Jesus his own 'Christian doctrines'. Examples are the prophesies attributed to Jesus about his 'future sufferings' (Mark 8: 31; 9: 31; 10: 33). All Bible authors typically attributed to Jesus ideas and concepts of their own persuasion (Kelber 1997 p. 5).

In short, the gospels grew out of a conflict between the mission of Jesus the Messiah and that of the self-appointed 'apostle' Paul, in which Paul's views emerged victorious. Following the triumph of the Pauline Church, Nazarene ideology and doctrines that originally had been the orthodox views, became 'heretical' because of their opposition to Pauline doctrines. Thereafter they were either not included in or expunged from the final versions of the Bible adopted by the Pauline Church.

The Twelve Disciples and Bible Authorship

According to the four canonical gospels, the twelve disciples of Jesus were: Simon, renamed Peter 'cephas', Peter's brother Andrew, who was, according to the fourth gospel, the first of Jesus's disciples, James and John, sons of the Galilean fisherman Zebedee, Philip, Bartholomew, Matthew, Thomas, James the son of Alphaeus, Thaddeus, Simon the Zealot and Judas Iscariot (Matthew 10: 2–4; Mark 3: 16–19; Luke 6: 14–16; John 6: 67–71; Acts 1: 13).

The Christian Church claims that authors of the gospels were eyewitnesses to events, and that they wrote from first-hand information. But even if one accepts the pretence that the gospels' authors were disciples of Jesus, it will be noticed from the outset, that Mark and Luke, two of the supposed authors of the gospels bearing their names, are not among the twelve. And in their respective gospels, Mark and Luke did not ever claim that they were among the disciples.

For his part, Mark, the first to have written a gospel, was a strong exponent of Pauline doctrines. As for Luke, he acknowledged at the start of his gospel that he was not eyewitness to the events he was recounting, 'Even as they delivered them unto us, which from the beginning were eyewitnesses and ministers of the word' (Luke 1: 2), thus ascribing eyewitnessing to others. This is an explicit acknowledgement by Luke that he was not a disciple of Jesus. On the contrary he was one of Paul's converts, referred to in Colossians 4: 14 as the 'beloved physician'. Ironically, Luke, who was addressing his treatise on the life of Jesus to an acquaintance, had no inkling that his treatise would be regarded as gospel, or Holy Scripture, by later generations, only that it seemed good to him to write to his 'most excellent Theophilus', presumably a Roman official (Wilson, A.N. 1997 p. 62). 'It seemed good to me also, having had perfect understanding of all things from the very first, to write unto thee in order, most excellent Theophilus' (Luke 1: 3). The same can be said about the book of Acts, also authored by Luke. It was addressed to his 'Dear Theophilus' as well (Acts 1: 1).

Furthermore, we notice that John, to whom is attributed the authorship of the fourth gospel, is most certainly not the disciple of Jesus (Spong 1992 p. 193). The fourth gospel was written in Greek at a very late date, about 110–30 CE, which makes it quite improbable that John the son of Zebedee had lived that long, or if in fact he had, that he should have waited 80 years after the death of Jesus to write his gospel. The author of the fourth gospel, whoever he was, seems to have been familiar with the doctrine of the Hellenistic Jewish philosopher Philo concerning the Logos (Word), and was a strong believer and advocate of the Logos doctrine. The fourth gospel is theologically the most developed of the New Testament writings, and is a mixture of Jewish and Hellenistic elements. It is therefore impossible to reconcile with the three synoptics.

Substantial interaction between the spiritual doctrines of the Jewish Bible and the materialism of pagan Greece had evolved following the conquests of Palestine and Egypt by Alexander the Great in the year 320 BCE. Greek art and philosophy began to be admired and studied by Jewish scholars both in Palestine and Egypt where there had been a prominent Jewish community. The

Jewish Bible was translated into the Greek 'Septuagint' version for the benefit of the Hellenistic Jews.

Jewish scriptures began to be read in Greek in the prayers and in the synagogues of Egypt and other countries. This was a radical impact of Greek culture onto Jewish religious thought. Jewish philosophers such as Philo had delighted themselves in finding points of comparison and agreement between the Jewish concept of God and the Greek ideas of the deity or the 'Good'. The theory of 'ideas' that originally sprang from the mind of Plato was adjusted to the Logos (word) invented by Philo. The 'Word of God' was transformed into 'God the Word'. This Hellenistic pagan influence is displayed at the opening of the fourth gospel which states: 'In the beginning was the Word, and the Word was God' (John 1: 1). It is impossible to believe that a Jewish disciple of Jesus could have written such blasphemy. The Divine Word means the Word of God, and *not* God the Word (Dawud 1990 pp. 152–53; Dawes 1999 p. 91).

Dwelling on John, it is also impossible that the Revelation of St John, the twenty-seventh book of the Christian Bible, could have been authored by the disciple John son of Zebedee. It must have been another John, not a disciple of Jesus, who authored Revelation. The disciples of Jesus were Hebrews who lived in Jerusalem forming after him the so-called 'Jerusalem Church', or the Nazarenes. By contrast John the author of Revelation was a Hellenistic Jew who lived in Rome during the reign of Emperor Nero, some thirty years after Jesus death. Moreover, a simple reading of Revelation makes it more than clear that a disciple of Jesus could not have written it.

By way of summary, the scholars participating in the Jesus Seminar had the following to say on the authorship of the four canonical gospels: 'All gospels were originally circulating without a known author until the first Church decided to assign an author to each one of them. In most cases the assignment was a result of guesswork or pious wishful thinking' (Funk 1993 p. 20). The gospels remained untitled until the second half of the second century, about the year 180 CE. At that time there were many gospels in circulation, not just four. According to the tradition of the time an anonymous book implicitly claimed sound knowledge and reliability. It would have impaired the value of the gospel of any one author had he written 'this is my version' instead of 'this is what Jesus said and did' (Sanders 1993 p. 66).

The only parts of the Christian Bible to which a known author can be attributed, with any degree of certainty, are the letters of the self-appointed apostle Paul. But Paul never planned to initiate a new religion for future generations. He had never imagined that his letters, written for transient needs, would become Holy Scripture in a future Holy Bible. Still less, he never imagined that there would be a Holy Christian Bible, consisting of four canonical gospels, followed by his story in Acts, followed by his own letters, other epistles, and one apocalypse! Paul's sole task had been to prepare the world for what he was convinced was the imminent end that was supposed to happen in his own days. Indeed, he would have been horrified to learn that the world would last at least two millennia after him!

The Qur'an and the Bible

The Qur'an, revealed to Muhammad during the period 610–32 CE, was more than twelve centuries ahead of Bible scholars in uncovering the fact that the Bible which we read today is not divinely inspired, but indeed authored by humans. The Qur'an was also far ahead of scholars in sifting the Bible, separating truth from falsehood. It is noteworthy, as we have seen, that at the time of Qur'anic revelation the only known versions of the Bible were the Syriac Peshitta, and the Latin Vulgate, neither of which were accessible to the Prophet, or, if indeed they were, they could not have been read or studied by him. The Prophet was illiterate even in his own native Arabic tongue.

One conspicuous verse of the Qur'an concisely and clearly summarizes the above discussion: 'Woe, then, unto those who write down, with their own hands, – something which they claim to be – divine writ, and then say, 'this is from God' in order to acquire a trifling gain thereby, woe unto them for what their hands have written, and woe unto them for all that they may have gained' (Qur'an 2: 79).

Another says: 'And, behold, there are indeed some among them who distort the Bible with their tongues, so as to make you think that – what they say – is from the Bible, the while it is not from the Bible; and who say, "This is from God", the while it is not from God; and thus do they tell a lie about God, being well aware – that it is a lie' (Qur'an 3: 78).

On this subject, Professor Funk, founder of the Jesus Seminar, wrote that 'the New Testament should be declared as a highly uneven and biased record of various early attempts to invent Christianity ... the question of what documents belong among the founding witnesses should be reopened' (Funk 1996 p. 314).

Another Qur'an verse alludes to the lost divine writ, and to the persistent claim of the Jews that they are 'God's chosen people', and their belief that His forgiveness and grace are assured to them irrespective:

> And they have been succeeded by – new – generations who, – in spite of – having inherited the divine writ, clutch but at the fleeting good of this lower world and say, 'we shall be forgiven', the while they are ready, if another fleeting good should come their way, to clutch at it – and sin again

– Have they not been solemnly pledged through the divine writ not to attribute unto God but what is true, but having studied the writ they simultaneously destroyed it. (Qur'an 7: 169)

Attributing to God what is not true is at the heart of the Bible problem. Polycarp (69–155 CE) Bishop of Smyrna, deplored men who 'pervert the sayings of the Lord to their own lusts' and he wanted to turn to 'the Word handed down to us from the beginning', thus referring to a book or tradition much earlier than the gospels (Ali 1992 p. 291).

Since the Bible is a mixture of human composition and remnants of divine revelation, the Qur'an set out to confirm whatever true revelation remains in the Bible: 'And unto thee – O Prophet – We have vouchsafed this divine writ, setting forth the truth, confirming the truth of whatever there still remains of earlier revelations and determining what is true therein' (Qur'an 5: 48).

In another verse: 'Step by step has He bestowed upon thee from on high this divine writ, setting forth the truth which confirms whatever there still remains of earlier – revelations –, for it is He who has bestowed from on high the Torah and the Gospel' (Qur'an 3: 3). In this manner, the Qur'an functions to sift human fabrication from divine revelation.

Still, those who are bent on denying the truth, will accept neither the Qur'an, nor whatever truth remains in earlier revelations. 'And – yet – those who are bent on denying the truth do say, "we shall never believe in this Qur'an, and neither in whatever there still remains of earlier revelations"' (Qur'an 34: 31).

Another feature of the Qur'an is its decision on religious disputes among peoples of earlier revelations: 'Behold, this Qur'an explains to the children of Israel most of that whereon they hold divergent views' (Qur'an 27: 76). The implication is where they differ from the truth made evident to them in their own scriptures. The term Children of Israel, in this instance, comprises Jews as well as Christians inasmuch as both follow the Old Testament, albeit in corrupted form. And it is because of this corruption that the Qur'an sets out to explain to both religious communities the truth behind their divergent views. The reference to 'most' and not all problems has to do with the fact that metaphysical questions will only become clear in the hereafter (Asad 1984 p. 586).

Credibility of the Qur'an

The Qur'an, inspired to the Prophet as the Standard to discern truth from falsehood in previous revelations, holds within itself the proof of its own credibility: 'Now this Qur'an could not have been possibly devised by anyone save God: nay indeed, it confirms the truth of whatever there still remains – of earlier revelations – and clearly spells out the revelation – which comes –, let there be no doubt about it, from the sustainer of all the worlds' (Qur'an 10: 37). Not only does the Qur'an confirm whatever truth remains in earlier revelations, but it also transcends it to spelling out clearly the new revelation.

By its own testimony, the Qur'an predicts the impossibility of its being penetrated by falsehood: 'No falsehood can ever attain to it openly, and neither in a stealthy manner. Bestowed from on high by One who is truly Wise, ever to be praised' (Qur'an 41: 42). This means it can not be openly changed by means of additions or omissions, and nor surreptitiously, by hostile or deliberate confusing interpretations.

The Qur'an, in stark contrast to the Bible, is the preserved last and final divine revelation, bestowed on the Last Prophet. It has been literally preserved, word for word. It had anticipated its own preservation from the time it was revealed: 'For it is We, without doubt, who have bestowed from on high, step by step, this Reminder – the Qur'an –, and We will assuredly guard it – from all corruption –' (Qur'an 15: 9). This Qur'anic prophecy has been strikingly confirmed by the fact that the text of the Qur'an remained free of any alteration, however trivial, ever since its revelation to the Prophet. There is no other instance of any old book, of whatever description, which has been similarly preserved for fourteen centuries. The early-noted variants in the reading of certain words of the Qur'an, occasionally referred to by the classical commentators, represent no more than differences in respect of the diacritical marks or of vocalization, and, as a rule, do not affect the meaning of the passage in question. 'Nay, but this – divine writ which they reject – is a discourse sublime, Upon an imperishable tablet preserved' (Qur'an 85: 21–22). The implied metaphorical allusion is to God's promise that the Qur'an will never be corrupted; a natural corollary of its being the final divine revelation to humankind (Asad 1984 p. 383).

Based on their own scriptures some of the recipients of earlier revelations will no doubt recognize the truth of the final revelation: 'Those who shall follow the – Last – Apostle, the unlettered Prophet whom they find described in the Torah – Taurah – that is with them, and later on in the Gospel – of Jesus – ... Believe, then, in God and His Apostle, the unlettered Prophet, who believes in God and His words, and follow him, so that you might find guidance' (Qur'an 7: 157–58). The emphasis on the Prophet having been unlettered, meaning unable to read and write Arabic, serves to bring out the fact that all his knowledge of earlier prophets was wholly due to divine inspiration, and not to supposed familiarity with the Bible, which at his time was, in any case, available only in two versions: the Syriac Peshitta, and the Latin Vulgate.

This historical piece of information is conspicuously confirmed in the Qur'an: 'For – O Muhammad – thou have never been able to recite any divine writ before This one, nor did thou ever transcribe one with your own hand, or else, they who try to disprove the truth – of This revelation – might indeed have had cause to doubt – it.' (Qur'an 29: 48)

The Qur'anic Challenge

One corollary of the perfect preservation of the Qur'an throughout the centuries, and in fact a testimony to its perfection, is its complete harmony and absolute conformity with scientific progress and scientific discoveries evolving with time. To this end the Qur'an repeatedly urges people to assess its content without prior preconception: 'Will they not, then, ponder over this Qur'an? or are there locks upon their hearts?' (Qur'an 47: 24). And: 'Will they not, then, try to understand this Qur'an? Had it issued from any but God, they would surely have found in it many an inner contradiction' (Qur'an 4: 82). Being devoid of any contradiction points to the impossibility of human authorship, a charge so common not only among the Prophet's contemporaries but also among non-believers of later times.

Inviting people of all times to objectively make use of their intellect to study and assess the message of the Qur'an on its own merit is an often recurrent theme of the Qur'an. This being the case, it is impossible that the unlettered Prophet could have produced the Qur'an. Indeed, all mankind plus all 'invisible beings' put together, could not have achieved such a task: 'If all mankind and all invisible beings should come together with a purpose to producing the like of this Qur'an, they could not produce its like, even if they were to exert all their effort in aiding one another' (Qur'an 17: 88). Implied in the challenge is an exhortation to mankind to make the Qur'an the subject of their intellectual inquiry, something unique among all religions.

'Will you not, then, use your reason?' (Qur'an 23: 80) is an often repeated Qur'anic exhortation. 'We have now bestowed upon you – O Men – from on high a divine writ containing all that you ought to bear in mind: will you not then use your reason?' (Qur'an 21: 10) alludes indirectly to the dignity and peace of mind to which man may attain by following the spiritual and social precepts laid down in the Qur'an (Asad 1984 p. 488).

'Or do they say that he – the Prophet – has fabricated this message? Nay, but they are not willing to believe. But then, – if they deem it the work of a mere mortal – let them produce another discourse like it, if what they say is true'

(Qur'an 52: 33–34), i.e. a consistent discourse devoid of contradictions with the passage of time. Implied again is the non-believers' denial, altogether, of the possibility of divine revelation or inspiration from God.

Not only are humans unable to produce a similar discourse, but they are unable to produce one chapter thereof: 'And yet – those who are bent on denying the truth – assert that Muhammad has invented – the Qur'an –. Say unto them, produce then, one chapter of similar merit – and to this end – call to your aid whomever you can, besides God, if what you say is true' (Qur'an 10: 38). The challenge implies that their hypothetical literary effort can never be equal to any part of the Qur'an. This challenge is repeated in different forms in two other verses: 2: 23 and 11: 13.

'De-dogmatization' and Appeal to Reason

Not only do they refrain from reason but those who deny the truth are also bent on blindly accepting the doctrines of their forebears and predecessors: 'And thus it is: whenever We sent, before thy time – O Prophet – a warner to any community, those of its people who had lost themselves entirely in the pursuit of pleasures would always say, "behold we found our forefathers agreed on what to believe, and verily it is but on their footsteps that we follow"' (Qur'an 43: 23).

Thus for most people the only justification for rejecting the truth is accepting inherited beliefs and dogmas at face value without recourse to one's own intellect, something which the Qur'an repeatedly condemns.

On this very point the founder of the Jesus Seminar Professor Robert Funk wrote,

> We can no longer rest our faith on the faith of Peter or the faith of Paul. I do not want my faith to be secondhand. I do not want to be misled by what Jesus's followers did. I am fundamentally dissatisfied with versions of the faith that trace their origins only so far as the first believers. True faith, fundamental faith, must be related in some way directly to Jesus of Nazareth.
>
> Jesus himself is not the proper object of faith. That would be the idolatry of the first believers. The proper object of faith inspired by Jesus is to trust what Jesus trusted. To call for faith in Jesus is to substitute the agent for the reality, the proclaimer for the proclaimed.
>
> Must the decisions of Constantine and the voting that took place at Nicaea and other councils be accepted as final? The creedal formulations of the second, third and fourth centuries should be de-dogmatized and Jesus

should be permitted to emerge in his own right. Jesus, rather than the Bible or the creeds, should become the norm by which other views and practices are to be measured. Jesus deeds should be the basis on which to formulate a new version of faith. Creedalism is a religion that supersedes Jesus, replaces him or perhaps displaces him, with a mythology that depends on nothing that Jesus said or did. Jesus has contributed little, if anything, to the religion that regards him as its founder. We have to start all over again with a clean theological slate. (Funk 1996 pp. 300–05)

Repeatedly the Qur'an appeals to the human intellect and reason, and stigmatizes those who don't believe as people of no intelligence, persons incapable of the intellectual effort needed to cast off dogma and routine thinking: 'When they are told, "Follow what God has bestowed from on high", some answer, "Nay, we shall follow – only – that which we found our forefathers believing in and doing." Why, even if their forefathers did not use their reason at all, and were devoid of all guidance?' (Qur'an 2: 170; Lang 1995 p. 23).

And: 'Verily, the vilest creatures in the sight of God are those who are bent on denying the truth and therefore do not believe' (Qur'an 8: 55). The reference is clearly to those who do not make proper use of their intellect. Their disbelief is a direct consequence of their denying the truth. And: 'Verily, the vilest of all creatures in the sight of God are those deaf, those dumb ones who do not use their reason' (Qur'an 8: 22).

In this respect they are like cattle: 'And so, the parable of those who are bent on denying the truth is that of the beast which hears the shepherd's cry, and hears in it nothing but calls and cries. Deaf are they, and dumb, and blind, for they do not use their reason' (Qur'an 2: 171). This means they are captive to their inherited thoughts and dogma, not prepared to assess the worth of what they are told. And so they are deaf to proper understanding, dumb to declare the truth, and blind to the signs.

They are also like inanimate statues: 'And there are among them those who listen – but can not hear –, can thou cause the deaf to hearken, even though they will not use their reason? And there are among them those who look – but cannot see –, can thou show the right way to the blind, even though they are unable to see – the truth?' (Qur'an 10: 42–43).

They are also incapable of pondering the awesome signs of the universe around them, and fail to benefit from lessons of history: 'Have they, then, never journeyed about the earth, letting their hearts gain wisdom, and causing their ears to hear? Yet verily, it is not their eyes that have become blind, but blind have become the hearts that are in their breasts' (Qur'an 22: 46).

For those of childish mentality who, rather than use their intellect, require supernatural miracles in order to believe, the Qur'an states: 'Why – is it not enough for them that We have bestowed this divine writ on thee from on high, to be conveyed to them? For verily, in it is manifested Our grace, and a reminder to people who will believe' (Qur'an 29: 51). Thus, the emphasis is on the contents of the Qur'an, which should be enough for those endowed with reason and intellect to make them grasp its intrinsic truth, without the help of external 'miraculous' proof of its divine origin (Asad 1984 p. 614).

Geoffrey Parrinder in his book *Jesus in the Qur'an* (1979 pp. 171, 173) concluded that

> Deep and significant implications of the Qur'an are unknown to the average Christian. Its prophetic witness to the unity of God, and in general to the humanity of Jesus and his mother, was a needful corrective which the church [badly needed but] largely ignored. Christian terms like Son of God, Trinity, and Salvation need to be re-shaped and given new point. Concepts of prophecy, inspiration and revelation must be re-examined in view of the undoubted revelation of God in Muhammad and in the Qur'an. The example of Islam towards other people of the book often puts us to shame.

Dogmatists and those who worship a multiplicity of gods will offer predestination as an excuse for their belief and conduct:

> Those who are bent on ascribing divinity to aught beside God will say, "Had God so willed, we would not have ascribed divinity to aught but Him, nor would our forefathers – have done so– and neither would we have declared as forbidden anything – that He has allowed –" Even so did those who lived before them give the lie to the truth until they came to taste Our punishment. Say: "Have you any – certain – knowledge which you could proffer to us? You follow but conjecture, and you yourselves do nothing but guess". (Qur'an 6: 148)

It is notable that the verse states their excuse in the future tense, expecting in advance their typical pretence of denying the role of human reason and intellect. It is also interesting that the verse constitutes a categorical rejection of the doctrine of predestination and rather emphasizes that man should go only by definitive knowledge, not by mere conjecture.

'For most of them follow nothing but conjecture: and behold, conjecture can never be a substitute for truth' (Qur'an 10: 36). For either they are dogmatists holding to inherited beliefs, or they are innovating theories without basis. In both cases the role of human reason and intellect is denied. 'Verily God has full knowledge of all that they do' (Qur'an 10: 36), meaning that belief should be coupled with deeds.

THREE

Christianity and Hellenistic Culture

Now as for those who take aught beside Him for their protectors – God watches over them, and thou are not responsible for their conduct. (Qur'an 42: 6)

The Christian Enigma

The question as to the origin of Christianity is taken for granted by the majority of people, Christians and non-Christians alike. But researchers and intellectuals have, for centuries, faced serious questions on this issue. The big question is whether Christianity originated with Jesus or with Paul, and who was the first Christian, Jesus or Paul? More clearly: was Jesus a Christian at all in the sense of today's Christianity. Was Jesus a 'Christ', in the Hellenistic sense understood by Paul and the Pauline Church? Or was he *the* awaited Messiah in the Jewish sense? Did Christianity begin during Jesus's lifetime, or during the lifetime of Paul? Or did it grow after Paul who, by necessity of his mission, was preaching the 'End of History'? How and why did the council of Nicaea elaborate the Christian Creed? And what, if any, is the relationship between Jesus and Christianity later formed in his name? What would he say about it and about the Nicene Creed? Why is Christianity attributed to Paul and not to Jesus? What was the driving force behind Paul's missionary efforts? And why did he choose to attribute his own theology to Jesus? Why did Paul transform Jesus *the* Messiah, into a Hellenistic 'Chrestos'?

Why is it that most people are in the dark about the Christian reality? Why is the church adamant, now as in the past, in claiming Paul as the sole interpreter of Jesus's mission (Funk 1993 p. 24)? Did the Nazarenes – the early followers and companions of Jesus – understand Jesus's message in the same sense that Paul imagined? It is now well known that late Pauline divinity concepts bestowed on Jesus were not known to the Nazarenes, the early Jesus's followers described in the book of Acts as the 'Jerusalem church'. How was it then possible that a strict monotheistic religion forbidding any compromise with pagan concepts such as multiplicity of gods should give birth to such concepts? Does it make sense that a monotheistic Jewish Prophet-Messiah could have entertained such beliefs? And if not, why is the Church unable or unwilling to disentangle Jesus's message from Paul's theology and from later ecumenical councils' formulations.

We have already noted that out of the twenty-seven books that comprise the New Testament, only four canonical gospels are about Jesus, and that these four gospels are no more than unbalanced narratives written under Pauline theological influence long after events took place. Their authors were not eyewitnesses to the events that they purport to describe. In fact the authors are anonymous and do not correspond to the persons to whom authorship is attributed (Funk 1993 p. 20). In addition, the essence of the narrative gospels is structured on Pauline theology, namely that Jesus was a saviour whose 'death on the cross' became a sacrifice for the 'sins of humanity'. As for the remaining New Testament materials they are mostly letters of Paul, which he wrote for transient needs while he was expecting the 'End of History' in his own days.

Why then does the Christian Church pretend that the Bible is the 'word of God'? 'And they say "This is from God", the while it is not from God: and thus do they tell a lie about God, being well aware – that it is a lie –' (Qur'an 3: 78). Why did Paul preach a Jesus of his own, one that was not recognized by Jesus's closest companions and disciples who knew Jesus better than anyone else? Why did Paul label Jesus's disciples in Jerusalem as 'false brethren'? Why did they call him a pseudo-apostle? Why did the Christian Church base itself on Paul's theology instead of the message of Jesus? Why does it deny the historical Jesus the Messiah, in favour of the mystical 'Chrestos' of Paul?

Evidently Paul did not have plans for establishing a new religion for future generations. A religion that the Church subsequently called 'Christianity'. Paul was merely warning 'humanity' ahead of the impending doom, the 'End of History' that he expected to befall the world in his own lifetime. Undoubtedly, Paul would have been dismayed at our present state of affairs not only in regard to the continuation of history for two millennia after his time, but more so because of the Church perpetuating Christianity to eternity! Paul envisaged nothing of the sort.

Few people are prepared to face the reality of biblical scholarship and its recent findings. Among those who do, many find it impossible to disentangle themselves from inherited preconceptions and emotional burdens: 'But they say "Behold, we found our forefathers agreed on what to believe – and verily, it is in their footsteps that we find our guidance"' (Qur'an 43: 22). Challenging creeds brought along from childhood requires intellectual courage that few possess (Funk 1996 pp. 11–13, 47–56: Parrinder 1992 p. 95).

Nevertheless, the majority is not aware of the vast gap between Pauline Christianity and the religion of Jesus; the gap between the 'Chrestos' of Paul, and Jesus the Messiah: 'And We caused Jesus, the son of Mary, to follow in the footsteps of those – earlier prophets – confirming the truth of whatever there still remained of the –Torah –Taurah, and We vouchsafed unto him the Evangel, wherein there was guidance and light' (Qur'an 5: 46). The Church maintains the pretence that the missionary activities of Paul plus the decisions of ecumenical councils are but a continuation of the message of Jesus. As a result, the majority is not aware of the difference between the New Testament and the Gospel of Jesus, the Evangel, the *enjil* mentioned in the Qur'an.

Towards the end of Jesus's mission, and subsequent to the conspiracy to kill him, he appeared to Mary Magdalene at the sepulchre where he is said to have told her, 'Touch me not, for I am not yet ascended to my Father, but go to my brethren, and say unto them, I ascend unto my Father, and your Father; my God and your God' (John 20: 17). That Jesus made this statement, towards the end of his prophetic mission, is very significant in two respects:

First, he assured Mary that he was the real earthly Jesus, not coming back from the dead – not yet ascended unto the Father-; meaning he did not die on the cross, but was going to be raised to the Father. Raising Jesus to the Father was the natural outcome of his people rejecting his mission, and their conspiring to kill him. 'God raised him up unto Himself, and God is exalted in Power, wise' (Qur'an 4: 158).

Second, before being raised to the Father, Jesus in his prophetic capacity must have anticipated in advance the future tendency of Christians to deify him, making him God incarnate, or Son of God. Thus he was warning mankind in advance that he was very much human like them. He emphasized that he was no Son of God in any special or unique sense, which is the meaning of 'my Father and your Father'. Furthermore, he was no god because 'He – God – is my God and your God'. 'But the Messiah said: "O childen of Israel! Worship God – alone – who is my Lord and your Lord"; behold, whoever ascribes divinity to any being besides God, unto him God will deny paradise' (Qur'an 5: 72).

Mythical Jesus of the Kerygma

Substantial theological and political developments took place from the time that Jesus died, *c.*37 CE, till the council of Nicaea in 325 CE. The process resulted in the transformation of Jesus the Messiah, the historical Jesus, into the

'Chrestos' of Pauline persuasion, Jesus of the kerygma, or the Christ of today's Christianity. The kerygmatic Jesus corresponds to the Hellenistic myth of a dying/rising god of some Hellenistic mystery cults. The kerygma concept is the basis of what was to become the Christian 'gospel'. Kerygma is a Greek term meaning 'proclamation' or 'message' or 'preaching'; in this case it is the preaching of a Christian 'gospel' involving the myth of a dying/rising god as in Greek and ancient mythology (Kelber 1997 p. 5; Funk 1996 pp. 39, 257; Mack 1995 pp. 79ff.; Dawes 1999 p. 277). Gospel authors under such 'cultural' influence resorted to inventing a history of the life of Jesus, for example, 'crucifixion and resurrection' to match their own kerygma. Conversely, they may have believed that the history they invented must have been in fact at the basis of Jesus's life (Dawes 1999 p. 278). In any case the net result was to superimpose the Hellenistic Christ myth on the reality of Jesus the Messiah, or in the least, merge the two together.

In ancient Egypt, the great god-man Osiris, incarnation of the sun-god Ra', was both human and divine. His human side was able to take upon himself all people's sorrow. He died, was buried, and rose from the grave. To all who joined his mystical cult, he gave of his mystical body his flesh to eat and his blood to drink so that this divine sacrament would transform his believers into celestial beings. The cult of Osiris was exported to Syria through Byblus on the eastern Mediterranean, which was then an Egyptian colony. In Byblus, Osiris became known as Adonis. In Phoenician, Adonis is Adon meaning Lord – similar to Jewish Adonai. According to the Phoenicians, Adonis was the saviour who ascended each spring from Hades, the realm of death, that mankind may have abundant life. In Babylon Osiris was known as Tammuz.

In the Greek religion, Osiris became Dionysus, the saviour-god who died for mankind and whose body and blood were symbolically eaten and drunk in the eucharist. Dionysus had many characters, one of which was a nature god of fruitfulness and vegetation who died each winter and was reborn in the spring. The Dionysian mystery cult became most popular in Greek religion. Dionysus was the only deity who penetrated many nations to become an international saviour-god (Larson 1977 pp. 23, 27–29, 37–49; Freke and Gandy 1999 p. 23; Laidler 2000 p. 56). In Graeco-Roman religion he was known as Bacchus.

The Hellenistic Age, which followed the conquests of Alexander the Great, had in due course extended its cultural influence through the establishment of Roman supremacy in the Mediterranean and the Middle East. It is called Hellenistic (Greek Hellas i.e. Greece) to distinguish it from the Hellenic culture of classical Greece. The religion of the Hellenistic Age combined Greek gods with local eastern deities. The majority of Romans were Hellenists in the sense that they had adopted the Greek way of life. However the term Hellenist was specifically applied to Jews of the Empire who had adopted the Greek culture as they came in close contact with Greek thought, religion, and literature, and eventually spoke Greek as their native tongue. Hellenists, also called Greeks in a cultural not a racial sense, were contrasted with Jews in Acts 11: 20, 18: 4, Romans 1: 16, Galatians 3: 28, and Colossians 3: 11. Jews who resisted Hellenistic influence were labelled Hebrews. The Hellenistic culture had made significant inroads into Jewish thought and life. The break-up of Alexander's empire following his death delayed the universalization tendency of the old world – 'globalization' in today's jargon – until the Romans fulfilled it.

Dionysus figured prominently in the play *The Bacchae* by the Greek dramatist Euripides. The play recounts the story of King Pentheus of Thebes and the god Dionysus who was in the habit of shedding his 'divinity' and walking in human disguise. Dionysus, disguised as a holy man, arrived at Greece from Asia Minor, accompanied by his women votaries, to introduce his orgiastic worship. But he was rejected by the Thebans and the young king Pentheus ordered his arrest. Dionysus, the god in disguise, told the king that his efforts to resist the Dionysian movement were in vain: 'You are mortal, he is a god. If I were you I would control my rage and sacrifice to him, rather than kick against the pricks'. It is significant that Luke, in Acts 26:14, while recounting for the third time the story of Paul's conversion, has Paul put this very phrase in the mouth of Jesus, when Paul was defending himself before the Roman prefect Festus, and the Jewish King Agrippa (Wilson, A.N. 1997 p. 76; Larson 1977 pp. 44–45; Freke and Gandy 1999 p. 28).

Turning to Paul's conversion, one should be aware that the whole Christian picture would be grossly distorted, if we thought of Paul as a convert to a pre-existent Christianity. Christianity was yet to be formed and fashioned by Paul, after he was 'converted' (Wilson A.N. 1997 pp. 61, 78). It is no less important that Paul maintained most of his pagan/mystical doctrines after his conversion. Later on, and over some twenty years of his preaching, he gradually replaced Jesus the Messiah, with a mythical 'Christ' of his own making conforming to his own convictions. He also succeeded, inadvertently, in setting up a Hellenistic Christ cult that had nothing to do with the historical religion of Jesus the Messiah. A most obvious analogy between the Pauline 'Christ', and Dionysus, is eloquently expressed by Paul's own words: 'Who [Jesus] being *in the form of God*, thought it not robbery to be equal with God, but made himself of no reputation, and took the form of a servant, and was made in *the likeness of* men. And being found in *fashion* as a man' (Philippians 2: 6–8).

The 'Apostle' Paul

Paul of Tarsus, an urbanite cultured educated Jew, was born and brought up in the Hellenistic world of the Roman Empire. His mastery of the Greek language, plus his knowledge of Aramaic facilitated his movement and communication in the Graeco-Roman world and put him at a great advantage. As a Roman citizen he may also have known Latin. Roman historian Dio Cassius recounts that Emperor Claudius used to revoke the citizenship of those who did not know Latin (Ferguson 1993 p. 59). But Greek, in any case, was more important as the one common language of the Roman Empire (Sanders 1996 pp. 10, 20, 25).

No one believes that Paul was an eyewitness to the life of Jesus, much less a disciple of Jesus. Paul wrote about his past: 'how that beyond measure I persecuted the Church of God and wasted it' (Galatians 1: 13). Indeed he was one of Jesus's dedicated enemies as documented by Luke's story that described Paul's conversion three times in Acts. While Luke, in his Acts, recounted the story of Paul's 'apocalypse' when the latter was on his way to Damascus, it is very peculiar that Paul himself, in his many letters, never mentioned the story (Sanders 1996 p. 9). Nor did he mention anything about Ananias, who is supposed to have baptized him and restored his sight in Damascus. For all this information we have to believe Luke, who wrote the book of Acts some twenty-five years after Paul's death; that is assuming Luke was the real author of Acts. Mack (1995 p. 103) contends that Acts was written some 80 years after the events.

In contrast to Luke's claims about Paul's 'apocalypse', Paul merely states about himself that: 'Paul, an apostle, not of men, neither by man, but by Jesus Christ, and God the father, who raised him from the dead' (Galatians 1: 1). The emphasis of Paul is that his apostleship does not derive from authority invested in him by any of the disciples, nor for that matter from Jesus himself on earth, whom he never knew anyway, but from the heavenly Jesus after his death, and from God himself. This was a very subtle and convenient claim indeed, putting himself above any temporal authority and having to report to no one. He claimed appointment exclusively from the supernatural Jesus, for which his testimony alone should have been sufficient. He added 'But when it pleased God, who separated me from my mother's womb ... to reveal His Son in me, that I might preach Him among the heathen, immediately I conferred not with flesh and blood' (Galatians 1: 15–16), meaning he had no need to consult Jesus's disciples, nor recognize their authority, since his authority was derived directly from heaven. 'Nor went I up to Jerusalem to them which were apostles before me, but I went into Arabia, and returned again unto Damascus' (Galatians 1: 17). The insinuation is that he stood to learn nothing from Jesus's disciples and companions who had known the Master throughout his life on earth. Thus from the outset Paul had distanced himself from the disciples whom he later called 'false apostles' (II Corinthians 11: 13) and 'false brethren' (II Corinthians 11: 26).

In sharp contrast to Paul's own story on his leaving Damascus for Arabia and then back to Damascus, Luke in his Acts explicitly contradicts Paul and states that the latter returned from Damascus to Jerusalem where he spent some time with the apostles, thereafter leaving for Caesarea and then for Tarsus (Acts 9: 20–30). As usual, Luke is at pains to create some affinity, through fabricated contacts, between Paul and the Nazarenes in Jerusalem.

Paul – as it seems from the story of his conversion – was a member of the police force of the Jewish high priest in Jerusalem. It must have been in Paul's capacity as member of the police force to arrest and imprison Jesus's followers, even cast votes against those of them who were condemned to death! It was apparently in this same capacity that Paul went to Damascus to arrest some of Jesus's followers, although it is not clear what authority the Jewish high priest of Jerusalem could have had in Damascus, which was clearly outside his jurisdiction. Damascus at the time was under Aretas IV, the Arab king of the Nabateans (9 BCE – 40 CE) (Maccoby 1998 pp. 10, 59, 81, 86–87, 99; Acts Ch. 26).

Some argue that Paul, in his capacity as member of the high priest's police force, could have been a participant in the arrest and crucifixion of Jesus (Wilson, A.N. 1997 p. 53). If that were true, this would have been the only instance where Paul could have actually known Jesus in his lifetime.

The Ebionites, another name for Nazarenes (Eisenman 1997; Baigent and Leight 1993 pp. 173–74), recount another aspect of Paul's life. They state that Paul –or Saul as he was then known – was a convert to Judaism in his native city of Tarsus, and that he came to Palestine during his adulthood and found employment as member of the police force serving the Jewish high priest (Maccoby 1998 p. 60).

In any case, the self-appointed 'apostle' Paul had been, from the start, a very controversial figure among the church community of his lifetime. Not only was he a self-appointed apostle, but also the one and only self-appointed spokesman for the heavenly Jesus. In this manner he made himself quite influential. Paul's own letter to Galatians, together with the book of Acts, testifies to this fact. He had been at odds with Peter and other leaders of the Jesus movement in Jerusalem whom he labelled 'false brethren' (II Corinthians 11: 26). In due course Paul had evolved into an imaginative, definitely confused, self-appointed missionary. He was able to extract a mystical significance from the 'crucifixion' of a great Jewish Prophet. Pagan myths of dying/resurrected deities, and myths of heavenly descended redeemers, dominated the mind of Paul. Thanks to his missionary effort, substantial damage to Jesus's prophetic mission took place, resulting into a fictitious Jesus embodying Paul's own formulations (Wilson, A.N. 1997 p. 27).

The term 'Christianity' was first devised in Syrian Antioch, some fifteen years after the death of Jesus. Subsequent to his conversion Paul was to become the pioneer missionary of the incipient Christian religion (Vermes 1998 p. 129). By Paul's own account, he had not been mixing with the disciples of Jesus during his missionary years to the extent that fourteen years had passed after his conversion before he visited Jerusalem to meet three of the disciples. To the exclusion of all disciples he seemed convinced that he alone knew the truth about Jesus. Indeed he began his letter to the Galatians by cursing anyone preaching a gospel different from his own, even an angel from heaven (Galatians 1: 8).

In actuality, Paul knew next to nothing about the prophetic mission, teachings, and life of Jesus, only that he was in direct contact with him through personal inspiration after his death. To Paul, the life and teachings of Jesus seemed irrelevant. Only the 'death' of Jesus, and his 'appearance' to Paul in 'visions', and what he construed of this claim, became the central points of Paul's gospel.

Paul's Hellenistic mentality and his imagination led him to squarely identify Jesus as a saviour figure of the Hellenistic type, a dying/rising god, such as the Greek god Dionysus, or Herakles – Roman Hercules. This was quite plausible for his contemporaries who were often aspiring for Herculean saviours. Their readiness to believe in and accept superstition facilitated Paul's task (Wilson, A.N. 1997 p. 26; Mack 1995 p. 13). Wilson described the masses of Paul contemporaries who would accept myth wholesale: 'The Roman Empire added to the huge and gullible slave class and allowed, by the trade routes it opened up for the commercial class to which Paul belonged to reach these masses of people.' (Wilson, A.N. 1997 p. 19).

In Paul's belief Jesus had to supersede all deified personalities of his Hellenistic age. It was customary in that age to accord divine honours to kings, heroes, and important leaders. Alexander the Great who initiated the Hellenistic age was called 'the new Herakles' (saviour), and after his death he became the object of a cult. Under the Romans, Greek cities accorded divine honours to Roman Emperors culminating in the Roman imperial cult. Imperial altars in honour of Roman emperors were erected around the empire.

Julius Caesar was voted divine by the senate during his lifetime. After his death he was admitted among the gods of Olympus, and a cult was organized in his name throughout Italy. His successor Augustus was decreed by the Roman senate as 'son of the deified'. Through Caesar, he became a descendent of Venus. Augustus was also regarded as a 'saviour' of the empire. In addition, he was the protégé of Apollo, the god of order. On the other end of the political spectrum, the patron of his rival Mark Antony was depicted as Dionysus, god of orgiastic excess (Le Glay 1997 p. 153). Emperor Caligula, the fourth of the Caesars, was so obsessed with the notion of his own divinity that he ordered the heads of Greek god-images to be removed and replaced with his own head. He also attempted to install a statue of Zeus, with his own personal features, at the temple in Jerusalem as a divine object of worship. Even Poppaea, Emperor Nero's wife, was declared divine after her death. Emperor Domitian insisted that his officials address him with the title 'our Lord and our God'. Some twenty-five years later, the author of the gospel of John chose this exact phrase and put it on the mouth of the disciple Thomas making him address Jesus as 'my Lord and my God' (John 20: 28).

Elevating mortals to godhead was plausible and commonplace. In such a cultural setting, Paul found no difficulty in elevating Jesus to godhead transforming him into a Herculean saviour. In Tarsus, Paul's native city, the demi-god Hercules, with one human parent, was believed to have vanquished death and thus became a saviour for his people (Wilson, A.N. 1997 pp. 26, 71).

For the pagan mentality of the Graeco-Roman world it was imperative that Jesus be held at least equal, certainly not inferior, to the dignity of Caesars. One story in the book of Acts testifies to the popular mentality of the time. When Paul and Barnabas went on their missionary journey to the city of Lystra, a few miles south of Iconium in Pisidia, they came upon a crippled man. Paul seemed to have performed faith healing and the people shouted: 'The gods are come down to us in the likeness of men. And they called Barnabas, Jupiter; and Paul, Mercurius' (Acts 14: 11–12). In another instance, the Greek populace of Caesarea, upon hearing the last speech of King Agrippa, shouted: 'It is the voice of a god, and not of a man' (Acts 12: 23). It was a tendency underlying people's behaviour in the Hellenistic world that kings and leaders should be divine. Bringing the unperceivable closer to one's limited perception by thinking of him as 'incarnate' in different forms, or at least material things that could be conceived as his 'emanation'.

This cultural environment was quite ripe for the kind of missionary endeavours that Paul took upon himself. On top of that, Paul was a gifted activist, administrator, and correspondent judging from his letters, which later formed a substantial part of the Christian Bible. His literary and rhetorical skills must have been quite effective benefiting his missionary activities. It was very important that Paul was a fluent Greek speaker and writer. In the eastern part of the Roman Empire, Greek, not Latin, was the common language of the populace. Paul's mastery of the Greek language was essential for effective communication with his converts (Wilson, A.N. 1997 p. 28).

In the Graeco-Roman culture in which Paul undertook his missionary activity, Jesus's message outside of Palestine underwent drastic changes resulting in catastrophic consequences. It was turned into a cult of a new Hellenistic god called Chrestos – Christ. It parted completely from the message of Jesus in that it focused on the significance of Jesus's 'martyrdom', his pre-existence, post-existence, and his transformation into a 'divine' being. The Christ myth spiralled out of control, and attention was completely shifted away from Jesus's message on earth. It did not take long for those familiar with Greek mythology and Hellenistic mystery cults to appreciate the new Chrestos cult. The creation of such a myth was standard practice in the Graeco-Roman age so that people found no difficulty in accepting Paul's ideas. Mack calls the Christ myth an overreaction that was uncalled for (Mack 1995 pp. 79, 123).

During the second and third centuries, Jesus as godhead was gradually accepted in the ecclesiastical world. Eventually in 325 CE the Byzantine Emperor Constantine convened the Council of Nicaea which formalized the 'divinity' of Jesus. Pauline Christianity took its definitive 'orthodox' form through the decisions of Nicaea and successive ecumenical councils which assembled – in theory – bishops from the 'whole world', thus the word: ecumenical. In short, Christianity was formulated and became successful primarily as the result of the work of two very different persons, at two different epochs, in two different manners, the first mystical, and the second political: Paul until the year 62 CE, and Emperor Constantine, 313–25 CE.

From Nazarenes to Christians

Jesus and his early followers, the Nazarenes (see Acts 24: 5 for this term), did not seek to detach themselves from Judaism. Christianity, a Greek term for a Hellenistic concept (Wilson, A.N. 1997 p. 113), was a post-Jesus invention in Syrian Antioch (Acts 11: 26). Pauline Christians appeared long after Jesus had left the scene. This is clear from the vast gap separating the message of Jesus the Messiah, and the kerygmatic Chrestos of Paul. Paul's faith in what he believed was Jesus's 'redemption of the sins of humanity' resulted in a new Jesus in a drastically new perspective previously unknown to the disciples and the Nazarenes.

The early Jesus followers in Palestine – the Nazarenes – must have been dismayed to learn that a new religion, unknown to them, was being preached in the synagogues of the Diaspora in the name of Jesus (Mack 1995 p. 103). They found out that Paul, a self-appointed apostle, whom most of them had never met, was preaching a mystical doctrine totally alien to the mission and teachings of Jesus. It was particularly shocking that Paul was teaching his doctrine in the name of the Messiah Jesus, whom he transformed into a Hellenistic Chrestos. He was claiming 'inspiration' from a 'risen heavenly'

Jesus, with whom he alone had direct contact. This was the sole justification of his authority that 'emanated' directly from the heavenly Master. Based on this 'authority' Paul was gradually establishing, in the Hellenistic world, a new religion with the doctrines of 'Christ atoning death', and 'salvation by faith only'.

This transformation from Palestinian 'Nazarism' to Hellenistic 'Christianity' constituted a drastic setback for the message of Jesus. Paul made the utmost of the pagan mentality of the Graeco-Roman world dealing an almost fatal blow to Jesus's message while in its infancy. Jesus came to destroy idolatry and icons but was made himself an icon (Funk 1996 p. 295; Kelber 1997 p. 3). It was a theological setback of a kind and magnitude rarely if ever before witnessed in history. Through confirming popular beliefs of the time on Hellenistic saviour man-gods, Paul took advantage of a new 'saviour' that had appeared on the scene. Ironically, an idolatrous worship of a new 'Chrestos' was born of a strict and monotheistic religion. Chrestos is a proper name in Greek meaning 'useful' or 'beneficial' (Schonfield 1997 p. 8; Maccoby 1998 p. 176). Paul managed to downgrade Jesus's message to the 'Romanism' of his time (Maccoby 1998 p. 181). This would readily explain the spectacular success of his missionary activity.

Not only was the Messiah transformed into a Hellenistic Chrestos but, in time, his mother too was gradually venerated with the Greek title 'Theotokos', meaning 'Mother of God' or 'God-Bearer'. The Council of Ephesus, 431 CE, solemnly affirmed Mary as the 'Mother of God', a title used, since then, by Orthodox and Roman Catholic churches. The Syrian monk Nestorius (d. 451) contested this title insisting that it compromised the reality of Christ's human nature, and stating that Mary was only the mother of Jesus, but he was anathematized at the Council of Ephesus.

Some scholars have seen the deification of Mary as an easy transference of the Hellenistic populace from worship of the Greek goddess Artemis, Roman Diana, to the cult of the Virgin Mary (Parrinder 1992 pp. 103, 106; Parrinder 1979 p. 135; Wilson, A.N. 1997 p. 183). Others have compared the Madonna and her Christ-child with the cult of the Egyptian Isis and her son Horus. In ancient Egypt, Isis was looked upon as the eternal protective mother and symbol of motherhood. Images of her and her son Horus were sacred objects displayed in Egyptian temples and households (Larson 1977 p. 9). In Babylonian-Assyrian religions, the Mother of Gods appeared under other names such as Ishtar, Aphrodite, and Venus. In the religions of ancient Greece, Demeter was the Hellenic recreation of the Egyptian Isis (Larson 1977 pp. 25, 37).

The limited and temporary success of Jesus's prophetic mission among the Palestinian Nazarenes, is conspicuously contrasted not only by its rejection by the majority of his own people, the Jews, to whom Jesus's mission was primarily addressed, but by the counter-effect it had inadvertently produced among the Graeco-Romans. The memory of Jesus the Messiah was gradually replaced by the mystical belief in a man-god, not unlike Dionysus, who walked on earth incognito.

Not until the advent of Islam some six centuries later – three centuries after Nicaea – was the situation redressed in favour of monotheism, and in favour of the historical Jesus the Messiah. In this respect, Islam was some fourteen centuries ahead of biblical scholars in revealing the reality of Jesus's Messianic message.

The Council of Nicaea

The missionary efforts of Paul culminated less than three centuries later, when Emperor Constantine issued the edict of tolerance in 313 CE. For the first time, Pauline Christianity was acknowledged as a legitimate religion in the Roman Empire. In 325 CE, Emperor Constantine moved to avert civil war by trying to end friction between Pauline Christians and the Nazarenes – or their heirs the Arians. He summoned religious leaders to the first ecumenical council at Nicaea, now Iznik in modern Turkey, presiding over the council himself, although not yet a Christian but a Hellenistic pagan. His objective was to formalize Pauline Christianity as the official religion of the Empire. For Constantine this was a pragmatic necessity predicated by political expediency. To reach a unanimous vote he had to banish from the council those who would not agree to the henceforth called 'Nicene Creed' embodying Pauline formulations. In this manner the religion of Paul was officially declared a Graeco-Roman religion. The emperor himself had been a follower of the Roman sun-god Sol Invictus, the invincible sun – the Greek Helios (Rubenstein 1999 pp. 44, 75). His understanding of Christianity was no doubt conforming to his pagan frame of mind. Even after his conversion Constantine had his own head put on the statue of the sun-god Helios in Rome. He also maintained the title of Pontifex Maximus, the high priest of the pagan world, as did all Christian Emperors until 382 CE (Freke and Gandy 1999 p. 235).

But there was undoubtedly a more important motive behind Constantine's conversion, having to do with consolidating the Emperor's grip on power. Eusebius (260–339 CE), bishop of Caesaria, and author of *The History of the Church*, proclaimed that the Christian Emperor was God's representative on earth. Eusebius explained that as the Word of God guided and governed the heavens, so the Roman Emperor, being the word of God on earth, expressed the will of God in the government of the civilized world (the oikoumene), and fulfilled this role by his imitation of the Word (Logos). Such an expression of the Emperor's role, in relation to the Word, tremendously enhanced the religious aura which Roman Emperors had had before. A.N. Whitehead wrote: 'When the Western world accepted Christianity, Caesar conquered. The deeper idolatry of fashioning God in the image of the Egyptian, Persian, and Roman Imperial rulers, was retained. The Church gave unto God the attributes which belonged exclusively to Caesar' (Eusebius 1989 p. xii; Rubenstein 1999 pp. 44, 46, 193).

The Council of Nicaea produced an official statement of 'orthodox' beliefs, to which everyone was obliged to agree. As usual, the search for uniformity resulted in creating heretics on the other side of the religion spectrum. Not only could people outside the orthodox church not aspire for salvation, but they were also vehemently persecuted.

The Council of Nicaea declared Arianism a heresy. Arians, ascribed to Bishop Arius, were closer to the early Nazarenes in their beliefs. As they opposed the imperial edict, they were deemed to be heretics, to be brutally suppressed, with their books and literature banned and burned, and their places of worship destroyed (Mack 1995 p. 277; Rubenstein 1999 p. 29). Hellenization, in the form of Christianity, had finally triumphed over monotheism.

The Christian Paradox

The paradox of a dying/rising god of the pagan mentality of the Graeco-Roman world, triumphed over the monotheistic Jewish faith. For the monotheistic descendants of Abraham, God could neither be seen nor pictured. But for the Greeks, to invent gods, depict them in statues, and worship them, was commonplace. In classical Greek literature one encounters gods, goddesses, man-gods, and sons and daughters of gods in countless numbers. Images were made of every imaginable deity. In their turn, Christians of the Hellenistic world replaced Jesus the Iconoclast by Christ the Icon. In line with Hellenistic culture, Christianity was growing predominantly iconic, a complete antithesis of Jesus's preaching. Because of the Greek heritage of Christianity on the one hand, and the refusal of the Jews to accept Jesus's mission on the other, Jesus's message had been marred, for centuries to come.

At the root of the failure of Jesus's mission was the confusion, in the mind of the Jewish masses, of the person of the Messiah with that of the Deliverer Prophet-King. A confusion that precipitated calamitous results. In Jewish thought, it was impossible that the awaited Deliverer Prophet-King should meet the pathetic end that Jesus is portrayed as having met. The Deliverer, the Anointed Warrior-King, far from dying on a cross was required to defeat Rome, and establish the Kingdom of God on earth. Ironically it was the 'crucifixion' of Jesus that initiated the Pauline faith. The purported 'crucifixion', the exact opposite of Jewish aspirations, was so horrible that it gave birth to a Pauline movement which was to mythologize, spiritualize, and account for the 'tragedy'. Something that was acceptable within a Hellenistic context. The fabricated miserable ending was easily counterbalanced by another fabrication: that Jesus had actually triumphed as Son of God and seated at the right hand of Power. Thus was born the cult of Chrestos.

Conspicuously, the Pauline creed did not require the believer to affirm anything positive about the earthly mission of Jesus. Only his 'suffering', his 'crucifixion', and 'resurrection' seemed to matter. It is a creed with no practical consequence. In such a creed Jesus does not appear to convey any useful message to humanity. The narrative gospels appear to take this point for granted by portraying Jesus mostly as a passive figure, taking a passive role in events, always waiting for things to happen to him, expecting his end, with no initiative whatsoever taken on his part (Funk 1996 p. 43).

Paul's Christianity made a convenient merger with the Graeco-Roman frame of mind, and from there onwards the Christian Church consolidated this pagan trend. The Hellenistic masses, thirsting for a human embodiment of deity, were more than happy with a 'Herculean' saviour who descended to earth incognito, and performed a redemptive task. This must have had a great appeal not only to the Graeco-Roman masses at large, but also to the pagan Emperor Constantine. It also largely explains the success of Paul's religion among the gentiles.

The Islamic View

Paul, who obscured the humanity of Jesus by elevating him to godhead, had in effect ignored Jesus's earthly mission and deprived it of any useful significance. This may be ascribed in part to one central belief of Paul, that the end of time was imminent in his own lifetime. As a result, he saw no practical value in Jesus's life on earth, but saw instead substantial theological significance in Jesus's divinity, suffering, crucifixion, post-existence, and expected return. The question remains as to why the Pauline Church persisted in such theological elaboration, having discovered the bitter fact, that Paul's prophecies about the end of history and the imminent return of Jesus were grossly in error.

On this very issue, the Qur'an restored to Jesus his humanity and highlighted the value of his historical prophetic mission. In other words, Islam stressed the mission of the Jesus of history while rejecting the mythical Jesus of Paul and the theology of the Pauline Church. For example, the Qur'an urges

Christians not to overstep bounds by raising Jesus to godhead, and not to ascribe to him beliefs that he did not preach:

> O followers of the Gospel! Do not overstep the bounds – of truth – in your religious beliefs – [i.e. by raising Jesus to the rank of divinity], and do not say of God anything but the truth. The Messiah Jesus, son of Mary, was but God's apostle – the fulfilment of – His promise which He had conveyed unto Mary, and a soul created by Him. Believe then in God and His apostles, and do not say, "– God is – a trinity". Desist from this assertion for your own good. God is but one God; utterly remote is He in His glory, from having a son. (Qur'an 4: 171)

The following verse sheds light on the essence of the message of Jesus while negating developments that occurred after him: 'Indeed, the truth deny they who say, "Behold, God is the Christ, son of Mary", seeing that the Messiah himself said, "O children of Israel! Worship God – alone – who is my Lord as well as your Lord", behold, whoever ascribes divinity to any being besides God, unto him God will deny paradise.' (Qur'an 5: 72)

The Messiah and his mother were humans who used to eat food like other mortals: 'The Messiah, son of Mary, was but an apostle, many other apostles had passed away before him; and his mother was one who never deviated from the truth, and they both ate food – like other mortals –; Behold how clear We make these messages unto them, and then behold how perverted are their minds' (Qur'an 5: 75). Those of primitive mentality would wonder: 'What sort of Apostle is this who eats food and goes about in the markets?' (Qur'an 25: 7) i.e. like other mortals.

The transformation of Jesus's message occurred after his death, while he knew nothing about Christianity later established in his name:

> And behold! God said [i.e. after Jesus's death]: 'O Jesus, son of Mary! Did thou say unto men, "Worship me and my mother as deities besides God"?' – Jesus – answered, 'Limitless are Thou in Thy glory! It would not have been possible for me to say what I have no right to – say –! Had I said this, Thou would indeed have known it! Thou knowest all that is within myself, whereas I know not what is in Thy Self. Verily, Thou alone who fully knowest all the things that are beyond the reach of a created being's perception. Nothing did I tell them beyond what Thou didst bid me – to say – "Worship God, who is my Lord as well as your Lord".' (Qur'an 5: 116–17)

Not surprisingly, Professor Funk, founder of the Jesus Seminar, unknowingly elaborated this very point:

> We must begin by giving Jesus a demotion. He asked for it, he deserves it, we owe him no less. A demoted Jesus then becomes available as the real founder of the Christian movement. With his new status, he will no longer be its mythical icon, embedded in the myth of the descending/ascending, dying/rising lord of the pagan mystery cults, but of one substance with us all. We might begin by turning the icon back into an iconoclast.
>
> ...
>
> Jesus' functions as the Christ were assigned to him by his admirers in the first few centuries. But the real vocation of Jesus was assigned to him by his vision. He was not calling on God, as God was calling on him. He was not making claims; he was being claimed. What interest me about Jesus is not so much what Peter and Paul thought of him, or even what Jesus thought about himself, but the call to which he was responding. To what divine manifesto did he succumb? (Funk 1996 pp.306, 309)

There is no doubt that the divine manifesto to which the Messiah had succumbed, was similar to what the Prophet, six centuries later, succumbed to, as it emanated from one and the same source.

The following Qur'anic verse states two of the three objectives of Jesus's mission. The first was to confirm whatever truth remained in the Book of Moses, the Torah, Taurah, with a view to separating the truth from human accretions and superstitions. The second was the tidings on the coming of the last and final Prophet to mankind.

> And when Jesus the son of Mary said, 'O children of Israel! Behold, I am an apostle of God unto you, – sent – to confirm the truth of whatever there still remains of the Torah, and to give – you – the glad tiding of an apostle who shall come after me, whose name shall be Ahmad.' But when he – whose coming Jesus had foretold – came unto them with all evidence of the truth, they said, 'This – alleged message of his – is – nothing but – spellbinding eloquence!' (Qur'an 61: 6)

Elaborating the common truth in monotheistic religions the Qur'an urges Muslims to say to Jews and Christians:

> Say: 'O followers of earlier revelation! Come unto that tenet – divine manifesto – which we and you hold in common: that we shall worship none but God, and that we shall not ascribe divinity to aught beside Him, and

that we shall not take human beings for our lords beside God.' And if they turn away, then say, 'Bear witness that it is we who have surrendered ourselves unto Him.' (Qur'an 3: 64)

Those who genuinely comprehend the Bible must of necessity believe in the Qur'an:

> For it is thus that We have bestowed this divine writ – the Qur'an – from on high upon thee – O Muhammad – And they to whom We have vouchsafed – the understanding of – the Bible believe in it – in the Qur'an –, just as among those pagan –Arabs – there are those who believe in it. And none could knowingly reject Our messages unless it be such as would deny – an obvious – truth. (Qur'an 29: 47)

It is a fact that the vast majority of the Jewish and Christian peoples of the seventh century, in Arabia, north Africa, eastern Mediterranean, and Asia Minor, have generally, though gradually, accepted Islam (Ali 1992 p. 999).

FOUR

The Nazarenes and the Christians

Say: 'O God! Originator of the heavens and the earth! Knower of all that is beyond the reach of a created being's perception, as well of all that can be witnessed by a creature's senses or mind! It is Thou who will judge between Thy servants – on resurrection day – with regard to all on which they were wont to differ.' (Qur'an 39: 46)

Who Were the Nazarenes?

Who were the Nazarenes? What were their beliefs? Why did the 'orthodox Church' suppress their opinions and writings? Why did they denounce Paul? Why did they believe that he was a false apostle, a pretender? Why did they believe in Jesus as the Messiah, but not as God? What did their name derive from?

All followers of Jesus were first called Nazarenes, including his disciples and companions. This is contrasted with Paul's converts who, at a later stage in Antioch, began to be called 'Christians'. 'Christianity' was not known during Jesus's lifetime, nor did Jesus know anything about the Pauline Christian doctrines later devised in his name. The term 'Christianity', which we have seen to be a Greek word for a Hellenistic concept, was a late invention in Syrian Antioch some quarter of a century after Jesus's departure (Acts 11: 26). Pauline Christian communities became operative long after Jesus had left the scene. They believed in a mythical heavenly Jesus with whom Paul alone was 'communicating' after Jesus's death. In contrast, the Nazarenes believed in the message of the historical Jesus the Messiah whom they, unlike Paul, had known during his lifetime on this earth.

The book of Acts explicitly states that the first followers of Jesus were called Nazarenes (Acts 24: 5). Ananias, the Jewish high priest in Jerusalem, in his effort to incriminate Paul in front of the Roman prefect Felix, made no distinction between the followers of Jesus and the followers of Paul, calling the latter 'a ringleader of the sect of the Nazarenes' (Acts 24: 5). In Jewish rabbinical writings they are referred to as '*notzerim*' (Parrinder 1992 p. 80; Maccoby 1998 p. 175; Eisenman 1997 p. 250). Geographically, and at the beginning of Jesus's mission, the followers of Jesus were also called Galileans (Luke 13: 2) because Jesus started to preach his mission among the inhabitants of Galilee.

To the Nazarenes is attributed the founding of the so-called 'Jerusalem Church', although the description 'church' is a misnomer if it is to be understood in a 'Christian' sense. The Nazarenes did not think of Jesus as a Hellenistic Chrestos, only as the awaited Messiah. Neither did they think of themselves as a Christian Church because they were not Christians in any sense that would be subsequently understood. The term 'Christians' started to be applied exclusively to Paul's followers at a late stage.

There are indications from the Qumran scrolls discovered near the Dead Sea after 1947 that the Jerusalem Church was indeed the 'Essene' community. The Essenes were a Jewish ascetic sect who seem to have deposited their literature in the caves near Qumran for safe keeping following the first destruction of Jerusalem by the Romans in 70 CE, or even as late as 136 CE, the time of the second destruction of Jerusalem by the Romans. Some believe that Jesus himself may have belonged to the Essenes. It is possible to construe from their literature that Jesus himself was meant by their reference to the 'Teacher of Righteousness' who was clearly not depicted as divine. Simultaneously Paul may have been indicated by their reference to the 'Liar'. According to Professor Golb of the University of Chicago, the scrolls did not originate in Qumran but were brought there from Jerusalem – possibly from the Jerusalem Church community – for protection (Baigent and Leigh 1993 pp. 130–37, 148–49, 158, 160).

The Nazarenes had acknowledged Jesus as the promised Messiah but did not believe that he was a divine person. They believed that he was the awaited Messiah-prophet who had come to reform and purify the Jewish religion from human accretions and superstitions that had adhered to it over the centuries. They held that the Jews falsified the Law of Moses and succumbed to pagan Hellenistic influences, and that the Jewish religion absorbed much from the idol worship of neighbouring Phoenicians. For example, at one stage of history, many Jews had adopted the native Canaanite religion of Baal, with its worship of fertility gods and goddesses, its human sacrifice and practice of 'sacred' prostitution (Rhymer 1996 pp. 39, 49; Jeremiah 7: 9–11).

As such, Jesus and the Nazarenes did not seek to detach themselves from Judaism because they were no more than a reformist movement within Jewry. At a late stage they were cut off from the main body of Jews who refused to acknowledge the prophetic mission of Jesus and his title as the Messiah. The

Nazarenes' belief in Jesus as the Messiah, and their belief in his teachings and prophetic mission, had led the Jewish religious establishment, perhaps as late as 135 CE, to declare the Nazarenes as heretics, meaning a 'heretic Jewish sect'. It is noteworthy that Pauline Christianity, repugnant as it was to all Jewish beliefs, was never declared heretical, because it was too far removed from Judaism to be regarded as a Jewish offshoot (Maccoby 1998 p. 179).

The Jerusalem Church

The early followers of Jesus did form a separate group, but not a 'church' in the present sense or the word. The usual expression 'Jerusalem Church' was borrowed from later Christian terminology. Only outside Palestine, and for that matter at a late stage, was a 'Christian Church' set up under the influence of Pauline ideas and innovations. Unknown to the disciples of Jesus and the Nazarenes, the priesthood was instituted within the late Pauline Christian Church, with its awesome authority and hierarchy.

But the gospels, written under Pauline influence, like to give the impression that Jesus had founded a 'church', although this flatly contradicts the fact that Jesus and the Nazarenes did not seek to detach themselves from Judaism. On the contrary, early followers of Jesus used to pray in the Jerusalem Temple, side by side with the Jews (Acts 21: 26). Jesus had come to reform the Jewish religion, not to set up a new one.

It follows that leaders and members of the so-called Jerusalem Church, were Nazarenes, but not Christians in the sense understood by Christians of a later date. They did not regard the death of Jesus as atoning for their sins, nor did they have any notion on the deification of Jesus. Neither the 'suffering' of the Messiah, nor his 'crucifixion' appear to have been part of the faith of the Nazarenes (Vermes 1998 p. 38). They opposed Paul as a false prophet and pretender. In short they believed in the mission of the real historical Jesus, and vehemently denied anything having to do with Paul's invention: the mythical Jesus.

It seems clear from the book of Acts that the Nazarenes in Palestine were taken aback by the news of Paul's missionary activity in the Hellenistic world of Greece and Asia Minor. The more so since Paul was a self-appointed apostle whom most of the disciples had never met, and was preaching a purely Hellenistic Chrestos cult while ascribing it squarely to Jesus. On the strength of alleged collaboration/communication between himself and a 'heavenly' Jesus, he was promoting new doctrines of Christ's divinity, Christ's atoning death, and of justification by faith only (Wilson, A.N. 1992 pp. 171–72).

Paul never met Jesus in his lifetime, yet he became a self-appointed 'apostle' on the authority 'invested' in him by a 'heavenly' Jesus, from whom he claimed personal inspiration. He claimed to have surpassed the disciples of Jesus in that he had a direct contact with the Master, something which all of them lacked. Paul therefore dared the disciples to preach Jesus's historical mission: 'For if he that comes preaches *another* Jesus whom we have not preached' (II Corinthians 11: 4). In that case Paul describes the disciples as 'Satans': 'For such are false apostles, deceitful workers, transforming themselves into the apostles of Christ' (II Corinthians 11: 13–14; see Sanders 1996 pp. 6–7). This is clearly an obvious acknowledgement by Paul that what he was promulgating was *another* Jesus, a Hellenistic Chrestos (Maccoby 1998 p. 176; Schonfield 1997 p. 8), having nothing to do with the historical Jesus known to the disciples and the Nazarenes in Palestine.

The Chrestos cult innovated by Paul was strikingly different from the message of Jesus in many distinctive features. The new cult had first and foremost focused on Jesus's 'crucifixion'. All the emphasis centred on Jesus's 'martyrdom', 'resurrection', and deification as a dying/rising god, in line with predominant Hellenistic myths of the time. Personal salvation was the theme of the new cult. Christ had died for the sins of humanity (I Corinthians 15: 3–5). Graeco-Roman myths were borrowed wholesale, and merged with the reality of the prophetic mission of Jesus. Not only had Jesus's mission been obscured, but it was also stripped of any meaningful content. Attention was shifted away completely from the teachings of the earthly Jesus the Messiah while retaining him as a symbol of the Pauline Chrestos faith.

The Nazarene–Christian Dilemma

Paul's missionary activities resulted in the gradual alienation of the message of Jesus from Judaism towards paganism so deeply embedded in Paul's conscience since his childhood. Therefore, from the outset there resulted serious conflict between the Nazarenes and Paul, a natural consequence of the vast gap between the Prophetic mission of Jesus and the innovative mind of Paul. Contrary to the claims and attempts of the book of Acts, there could have been no room for compromise between the two positions, diametrically opposed to one another.

The book of Acts describes Paul's last visit to Jerusalem and his encounter with the disciples of Jesus as they said to him: 'You see, brother, how many thousands of Jews there are which believe [in Jesus], and they are all zealous of the Law. And [now] they are informed of you, that you teach all the Jews which are among the gentiles to forsake Moses' (Acts 21: 18–21). This means that the

The Nazarenes and the Christians

Nazarenes including the disciples, were Jews who had acknowledged the coming of the Messiah in the person of Jesus, and that they had accepted his reformist prophetic mission.

But Paul, having been obsessed with Hellenistic 'wisdom' about dying/rising gods, and myths of heaven-descended redeemers, had advocated doctrines that were in line with pagan Greek myths instead of the message of Jesus, while ascribing such alien concepts, squarely, to the mission of Jesus the Messiah.

As for the message of Jesus himself, it is imperative that the beliefs of the Nazarenes must have shed valuable light on them. If the Nazarenes, including the disciples of Jesus, had never heard of the doctrines of later Christianity such as the deification of Jesus, the Trinity, the Atonement of sins, the Eucharist, the Saviour, then it is obvious that Jesus himself never preached them. Simultaneously, it is impossible to believe that Jesus the Messiah, a monotheistic Jew and a great Jewish Prophet, could have believed himself to be divine, or that he was the second person of a Trinity, or God incarnate, or Son of God in a unique sense. It would have been a gross contradiction to Jewish beliefs and monotheism; an inherent impossibility for any monotheistic Jew to contemplate or to believe in. Even in the New Testament itself, with all its Pauline influence, there is not the slightest evidence of Jesus believing himself to be divine, or approaching divinity, or preaching that he was divine. Consequently Jesus can *not* be considered as the founder of Christianity. It was obviously Paul who, almost single-handed, fulfilled this role. There is an obvious and absolute gulf between Jesus and Christianity.

But Christians believe the Pauline claim that Jesus himself had founded Christianity, a claim on which Christianity became totally dependent. The Christian Church chose to base itself solely on Paul's innovations, irrespective of how alien it was to the message of Jesus. Consequently, the average Christian is oblivious to the differences and huge gap between the Christ he believes in and Jesus the Messiah. Indeed he believes that both are identical. Biblical scholars in the last thirty years have argued that this is not the case, and that Christianity is based on the 'mythical Christ' of Paul, the one 'revealed' to him in his apocalypse, not on the historical Jesus who had no inkling of the Christian myth.

Christian theologians, on the other hand, have been at pains to argue that Paul's doctrines about 'Christ' and 'divine sufferings' are a continuation of Judaism as it appears in the Jewish Bible, whereas in reality it represents their lack of faith in the historical Jesus the Messiah. Since most Christians are unaware of the difference between the historical Messiah and the mythical Christ, such arguments will undoubtedly seem too obscure, too sophisticated, or too disturbing to the average Christian. Obviously one likes to feel that one's belief in Christianity is emanating from the real Jesus, not from a Pauline fabrication advocated by the priesthood (Maccoby 1997 pp. 127–28).

Paul and the Heavenly Jesus

The information we have on Paul is derived not only from his own epistles, which later became 'Holy Scripture', but also from the book of Acts, which was intended by its author Luke as a biography of Paul. Luke, one of Paul's converts, was the author not only of Acts, but he was also supposed to have authored the gospel bearing his name, the Gospel According to St Luke, notwithstanding that by his own account, he was no disciple of Jesus, nor an eyewitness to the events that he describes (Luke 1: 2). Through his book of Acts, Luke also intended to bridge the vast gap between Paul's theology and the message of Jesus, in order to create some link or continuity between the two.

The Pauline Christian Church likes to pretend that Paul was the sole interpreter of Jesus's mission. The Church deems that Paul had understood and explained – in ways that Jesus himself never thought of – how the death of Jesus fitted into a universal scheme of salvation for humanity. But the disciples of Jesus, who knew him best and were quite familiar with his prophetic mission, did not accept such Pauline innovations. On the other side, Paul conveniently claimed that his interpretations of Jesus's mission were not his own but had come to him through inspiration from the heavenly Jesus. He claimed personal acquaintance with a resurrected Jesus even though, or because, he never met him in his lifetime. Such a claim entitled Paul to a unique and much higher authority than that of the disciples of Jesus whose contact with Jesus came to an end after his death.

The central myth of Paul's religion was that of an atoning death of a divine saviour. The mere belief in this sacrifice, and a mystical sharing in the eating of the body of the dead deity and drinking from his blood, was the only way to salvation according to Paul. Obviously, Jesus had no inkling of Paul's doctrines and would have been shocked at the role assigned to him as a suffering deity. The Nazarenes, thus, had no recourse but to reject Paul's doctrines and break irrevocably with him. Ignorant as Paul was about Jesus's earthly career, and lacking incentive or interest to learn about it, he concentrated, instead, on evolving mystical doctrines such as atonement, vicarious suffering, and salvation by faith.

Trying to Bridge the Gap

Pauline authors dedicated to writing gospels some 50 to 90 years after Jesus's death had to face the bitter fact that the Nazarenes were strongly opposed to Pauline doctrines. At the heart of the problem is Pauline Christianity's ascription of its own views to Jesus, something which was rejected by the Nazarenes, the leaders of the Jerusalem movement who were the disciples and companions of Jesus. To counteract the Nazarene influence, Pauline Christians resorted to inserting into their Gospels unfavourable material about the disciples of Jesus. The disciples were often portrayed as stupid and failing to understand their Master (Mark 8: 33). They were also depicted as cowards deserting Jesus and going into hiding at the time of his ordeal (Mark 14: 27–31). The climax of discrediting the disciples culminates in the story of Peter's denial of Jesus during the latter's trial (Mark 14: 66–71).

The disciples are even portrayed as lazy, perhaps drunk, falling asleep three times and unable to remain awake at the garden of Gethsemane, at the most critical hour, in spite of Jesus's repeated exhortation. 'And he came unto the disciples and found them asleep, and said unto Peter: "What, could you not watch with me for one hour?"' 'And he came, and found them asleep again, for their eyes were heavy', perhaps from drunkenness! And he returned for the third time: 'are you still sleeping and resting?' (Matthew 26: 40–45; Mark 14: 37–41). And when the police came to arrest the Master he delivered a moving speech to his followers but all the disciples 'forsook him and fled' (Matthew 26: 56; Mark 14: 50). Thus all disciples were slandered en masse without any exception.

Discrediting the disciples served another important purpose. It was necessary to justify why Paul alone was chosen to receive inspiration from the heavenly Master to the exclusion of all his disciples. Since the disciples were stupid, lazy, cowards, and even traitors – as in the case of Judas – none of them was worthy of receiving inspiration from the 'heavenly' Jesus!

In addition to this, the gospels have almost totally ignored the role of James during Jesus's lifetime even though Paul acknowledged him as one of the disciples of Jesus (Galatians 1: 20). Surprisingly, James is depicted to have suddenly emerged on the scene as leader of the Nazarenes after Jesus's death (see Maccoby 1998 p. 5; Eisenman 1997). James's role, too important to be completely excised from the narrative in Acts, must have been drastically played down. Instead of defending the Nazarene view, as Paul's main ideological adversary, James is depicted as a somewhat conciliatory figure.

Simultaneously, gospel authors in their attempt to disguise the vast gulf between their own beliefs and those of the Nazarenes, put great effort into fictitiously linking the two. Attempts were also made to by-pass the Nazarenes by inventing a tradition linking Jesus directly to Paul (see Maccoby 1998 pp. 11–13, 73, 105–06).

The ideological differences between Paul and the Nazarenes were so drastic that it proved impossible for Luke to ignore them in his Acts, although he did his best to downplay such differences. He tried to portray the Jerusalem movement, guided by Peter, as gradually accepting Pauline views (Sanders 1996 p. 18; Maccoby 1998 pp. 4, 130–33, 139). For propaganda purposes, Luke tried to give the impression of compromise and eventual unity evolving between Pauline Christianity and the Nazarenes in spite of the deep divide between the two. This he did to the extent that Peter and James were portrayed as defending Paul's missionary activities in the Hellenistic world (Acts 15: 7, 13–21), something on which one authority commented, 'That Peter and James should defend Paul's mission is a marvellous piece of fiction [on the part of Luke], for every earlier scrap of evidence speaks to the contrary.' (Mack 1995 pp. 230, 232)

Luke's major contribution to Pauline Christianity was in rescuing it from the bitter fact that it was nothing more than Paul's own ideology. In his book of Acts, Luke created a seeming continuity between the Jerusalem Church, and the Pauline Church, with Peter as a natural link between the two. He was keen to show only minimal opposition of the Nazarenes to Paul while portraying them as gradually accepting Pauline doctrines (Maccoby 1998 pp. 4, 130, 139–47). At a later date, and on this basis, the Christian Church was able to disguise the Nazarene ideology of the Jesus movement.

But Paul, in his letters, particularly Galatians, was quite blunt. He had no room for compromise with Peter who was representing the mainstream Nazarene movement in Jerusalem. Yet in later generations the Christian Church depicted both Peter and Paul as twin saints completely in harmony, although they were in fact ideologically bitter opponents (Maccoby 1998 p. 139).

In the first half of the second century, Clement, the bishop of Rome, wrote letters vigorously attacking Paul as a misguided heretic. These letters described Peter as vehemently denying the 'apostleship' of Paul. Paul's vision on the road to Damascus is described as a revelation from an evil demon. And Jesus is reported to have been angry at Paul because what Paul taught was contrary to Jesus's message. Paul was accused of creating a heretical gospel in contrast to Jesus's true gospel (Freke and Gandy 1999 pp. 161–62). According to one tradition, Clement was thereafter banished to the Crimea and forced to work in the mines. He was later bound to an anchor and thrown into the Black Sea (Livingstone 2000 p. 124).

The Nazarene Legacy

The Christian Church stigmatized the Nazarenes as heretics, although they were the immediate disciples and authentic followers of Jesus, whose views and doctrines they faithfully held and preached. Indeed they were the mainstream of the Jesus movement until the destruction of Jerusalem in the year 70 CE. But the Pauline Church was keen to suppress their ideas by rewriting their history. However, some of their views and beliefs had been preserved in the writings of their opponents, such as the treatise on 'Heresies' by Epiphanius, a fourth-century Roman historian (315–403 CE). From Epiphanius, we also learn that the Nazarene 'sect' was still flourishing in his own time in Perea, the east side of the Jordan valley (Maccoby 1998 p. 17).

The letter ascribed to James in the New Testament also describes some of their beliefs. They had represented the views of the Jesus movement before the appearance of Pauline Christianity on the scene. Snatches of their teachings survive in the book of Acts which refers to them as forming the Jerusalem Church, (Acts Ch. 15). Their leader James, is depicted by Matthew and Mark as the 'brother' of Jesus. Paul also, in his letter to the Galatians, referred to James as 'the brother of the lord' (Galatians 1: 19). This 'brotherhood' although taken literally by many writers, was undoubtedly symbolic, meaning a brother on account of James's piety. James became leader of the Jerusalem Nazarenes after the death of Jesus, making him worthy of the title 'brother of Jesus' in a spiritual religious sense. It is noteworthy that the famous Essene movement, to which John the Baptist and possibly Jesus himself belonged, was called a 'brotherhood', in the sense of its members being religious brethren. As to James, he was obviously no blood brother of Jesus, but could have been one of his disciples deliberately ignored by the four gospels but acknowledged by Paul (Galatians 1: 20). He may have been either James, son of the Galilean fisherman Zebedee, or James, son of Alphaeus, or more probably James, son of the other Mary (see Mark 16: 1; Luke 24: 10).

The destruction of Jerusalem in 70 CE, was a triumph in disguise for Pauline Christianity. After the Jewish insurrection against Rome, 66–70 CE, most of the Nazarenes had either perished in the war or were dispersed to other cities and places (Mack 1995 pp. 150–51). Their power and influence as the 'Mother Church' and centre of the Jesus movement came to an end. It is ironic that the Pauline Christian movement, which up to 70 CE had been struggling against the disapproval of the stronger Jerusalem Nazarenes, now began to thrive freely, especially as it did not participate in the insurrection against Rome. Nevertheless, Nazarene ideas remained dominant in the East until the second Jewish insurrection with the final devastation of Jerusalem in the year 135 CE.

Eventually, Rome replaced Jerusalem, and became the centre of the Pauline Christian Church, just as Jerusalem was the centre of the Nazarene Jesus movement. Simultaneously, the descendants of the Nazarenes, the former Jerusalem Church, were scattered and despised as heretics having rejected the doctrines of Paul.

But in spite of their hardship, the Nazarenes survived into the Christian centuries having continually to confront Pauline Christians who were preaching a totally different religion: that Jesus was a saviour-god who had descended to earth to redeem humanity. This distortion of the original message of Jesus by the Christian Church was something for which the Nazarenes directly blamed Paul.

In later generations, a group known as 'Ebionites' evolved from the Nazarenes. Although most of the Ebionite beliefs appear to be similar to those of the Nazarenes, much confusion remains as to the differences that may distinguish the two. It is certain that both rejected the epistles of Paul calling him a renegade. Ebionites in Hebrew means 'poor people' to which Eusebius (260–339 CE), in his well-known hostility towards them, commented: 'Ebionites they were appropriately named by the first Christians, in view of the poor and mean opinion they held about Christ' (Eusebius 1989 p. 90; see also Eisenman 1997 p. 156). By this, Eusebius meant that they considered Jesus neither 'divine', nor 'semi-divine', nor 'Son of God', only the Messiah chosen by God! It is therefore possible that the Nazarenes themselves, at some point, were nicknamed Ebionites as a derogatory name, which they on the other hand accepted with pride being a reminder of Jesus's saying 'Blessed are the poor' (Matthew 5: 3,5; Luke 6: 20) (Maccoby 1998 p. 175; Ferguson 1993 p. 577). It is conspicuous that the Essene community in Qumran described itself as the 'Congregation of the Poor' (or the meek) (Baigent and Leigh 1993 pp. 134, 174). This strongly supports the view that the Essenes at some point became Nazarenes and that Jesus himself may have been one of their rank before his Prophetic mission.

Maccoby reports on a tenth-century manuscript, based on a fifth-century Nazarene source, discovered in Istanbul and written by a certain Abd al-Jabbar. The source describes the Ebionites' view towards Paul, calling him a falsifier of the message of Jesus. It describes Paul's Christianity as 'Romanism', and that instead of converting Romans into Christians, he converted Christians into Romans. The Nazarene source on which the manuscript is based strongly criticizes the gospels declaring them untrustworthy and self-contradictory. It refers to an original trustworthy gospel, written in Hebrew, without confirming whether it was still extant (Maccoby 1998 p. 181; Eisenman 1997 p. 249). It also describes the Messiah as a prophet insisting on his humanity. This source gives the impression of an underground Nazarene community descending from the original Jerusalem Nazarene movement of the disciples. Christian persecutions forced the Ebionites to remain underground except at times when the oppression was lifted for some reason (Maccoby 1998 pp. 181–83).

The Nicene Creed

The following are excerpts from the Nicene Creed issued by Constantine's Imperial decree (see Vermes 1998 p. 15):

> I believe ... in one Lord Jesus Christ, the only begotten Son of God, begotten of his Father before all worlds, God of God, Light of Light, Very God of Very God, begotten, not made, being of one substance with the Father, by whom all things were made. Who for us men, and for our salvation, came down from heaven, and was incarnate by the Holy Ghost of the Virgin Mary, and was made man, and was crucified also for us under Pontius Pilate. He suffered and was buried, and the third day he rose again according to the scriptures, and ascended into heaven, and sits at the right hand of the Father. And he shall come again in glory to judge both the quick and the dead: whose kingdom shall have no end.

Compare the Nicene Creed with what the Qur'an says on monotheism: 'Say: "He is the One God, God the Eternal, the Uncaused Cause of all that exists, He begets not, and neither is He begotten, and there is nothing that could be compared to Him"' (Qur'an 112: 1–4). Thus, the Qur'an puts an end to human theories and confusion about God's identity, emphasizing monotheism and that nothing can be compared to Him and denying son-ship. The following Qur'anic verse refutes the Nicene Creed: 'Indeed, the truth they deny who say: "behold, God is the Christ, son of Mary"' (Qur'an 5: 17). The Qur'an also refutes the Trinity concept devised towards the end of the fourth century as a development from the Nicene Creed: 'Indeed the truth they deny who say, "behold, God is the third of a trinity"' (Qur'an 5: 73).

John Shelby Spong, the Episcopal Bishop of Newark in New Jersey, wrote on the Nicene Creed:

> The words of the Apostle's Creed and its later expansion known as the Nicene Creed were fashioned inside a world view that no longer exists. Indeed it is quite alien to the world in which I live. The way reality was perceived when the Christian Creeds were formulated has been obliterated by the expansion of knowledge. That fact is so obvious that it hardly needs to be spoken. If the God I worship must be identified with these ancient

creedal words in any literal sense, God would become for me not just unbelievable, but in fact no longer worthy of being the subject of my devotion. (Spong 1998 p. 4)

The Nicene Creed obviously reflected the Church's keen and only interest in theology, such as Jesus's eternal pre-existence, his essence and substance, and whether he was God, man-god, demi-god, or begotten Son of God. The Church followed in the steps of Paul, showing no interest whatsoever in Jesus's prophetic mission on earth and its practical implications. As a result, the Christian faithful were left in the dark as to the message of Jesus the Messiah, the historical figure, whom the Church has totally replaced with the mystical Christ of Paul. In fact, the faithful were left with the impression that both are one and the same, while their knowledge was confined only to the replacement, Paul's Chrestos.

After Nicaea, those who did not subscribe to the Creed were branded as heretics and brutally suppressed. The oppressed became the oppressors. Bands of wondering monks attacked synagogues, heretics' meeting places, pagan temples, and the homes of wealthy 'unbelievers'. In Egypt local vigilantes incited by the Alexandrian Bishop Theophilus destroyed the Temple of Serapis, one of the largest and most beautiful buildings in the ancient world, with a library donated by Cleopatra. It was a violent and fanatical campaign to enforce a new order and beliefs on everyone (Mack 1995 p. 277; Allegro 1992 p. xxv; Rubenstein 1999 p. 226).

Among the most prominent opponents to the Nicene Creed at the Council of Nicaea was Bishop Arius of Alexandria (250–336 CE). Arius and his followers appeared to be a genuine historical continuation of the Nazarenes, and were much closer to the teachings of Jesus than the official Church that had based itself on the doctrines of Paul. Bishop Arius rejected the Nicene Creed, which embodied Paul's theology, and was therefore exiled by Emperor Constantine. Nevertheless, debate over the Arian creed engulfed the church for another half a century until 381 when it was again outlawed. Thanks to the efforts of Arian bishops, the Arian influence continued for some centuries in central and northern Europe, in Gaul and in Spain among Gothic and other tribes (Le Glay 1997 p. 525; Rubenstein 1999 p. 170).

Despite persecution of the Nazarenes – later Arians – by the Church, they used to come out of hiding and resume open existence whenever religious oppression was removed for some reason. This had been the case, for example, when the orient transferred from Byzantine to Muslim rule, starting in 635 CE. The Muslim state had been famous as a guarantor of religious freedom. In contrast, the seventh century saw the last of the Arian tribes in western Europe forcibly converted to Catholicism.

Unitarianism in the Modern Age

Conspicuously, about a thousand years after the extinction of the last Arians in Western Europe, Arian beliefs were revived anew during the sixteenth century following the Protestant Reformation and the new tendency towards free exercise of reason in religion. The Reformation made it possible for new religious ideas to emerge. 'Unitarianism' developed as a new type of Christian thought which rejects both the doctrines of the Trinity and the divinity of Jesus, holds that God exists only in one person, and stresses the role of reason in religion. We have already seen that the theological foundations for the view of God as a unity and for the humanity of Jesus are found in the teachings of the Nazarenes, Ebionites, and of Arius and his followers the Arians, in all such early groups of Christians whose doctrines were eventually declared heretical by the church. Following the Reformation, Unitarianism as an organized religious movement emerged in Poland, Transylvania, and England, and later in North America in the New England Puritan churches. In each country Unitarian leaders found no warrant in the scriptures for the doctrine of the Trinity.

On the European continent, certain liberal, radical, and rationalist reformers managed to revive the Platonic emphasis on reason and the unity of God, though many such thinkers had to flee Italy during the Inquisition. Michael Servetus, a Spanish physician and theologian, and a leading Unitarian, was burned at the stake for heresy by Calvinists in 1553 when he fled to Geneva, having written 'On the Errors of the Trinity', and 'The Restitution of Christianity'. But by then, he had provided important stimulus for the emergence of Unitarianism. Some Italian Unitarians found refuge in Poland. Chief among them was Faustus Socinus (1539–1604). In 1579 Socinus settled in Poland to become the leader of the Polish Unitarian movement. The Socinians taught a rationalist interpretation of the Scriptures, and accepted Jesus as God's revelation but a mere man, completely human, divine by office rather than by nature. Socinians thus rejected the doctrine of the Trinity. Having proliferated, the Socinians met their end in 1658 when the Polish Diet gave them the choice of either conformity to Roman Catholic doctrine, or forced exile, or death. Most of them chose to emigrate. Faustus Socinus and Michael Servetus both became pioneers of modern Unitarianism. They believed that the doctrine of the Trinity was an abstraction without basis in the scriptures, and that simple monotheism could best be protected if Christ was not defined as an expression of the Godhead.

In Transylvania, now part of Romania an important early Unitarian figure was David Ferenc (1510–79), a Unitarian preacher, writer, and theologian who in 1566 rejected Roman Catholicism and Lutheranism and became influential in promoting religious tolerance in Hungary. He advocated the unity rather than the trinity of the Godhead. Ferenc's followers were also known as Nonadorantes because they did not believe that worship should be addressed to Jesus, since Jesus was merely human. Ferenc was therefore charged with introducing Judaizing tendencies, partly because his refusal to offer adoration to Jesus was confused with the rejection of Jesus as the Messiah by Judaism. In 1579 he was brought to trial as a blasphemous innovator and was convicted as a heretic. He died in prison the same year. The church that Dávid Ferenc founded in Transylvania is the world's oldest extant Unitarian body.

In England, some unorthodox thinkers drew upon Socinus and other Unitarians, but the mainstream of British Unitarianism, like that of the USA, evolved out of Calvinist Puritanism. The Calvinist doctrine of providence, coupled with an increasingly scientific view of the universe, led to a decline in religious orthodoxy and an increased emphasis on reason and morals among the more liberal Calvinist clergy. Joseph Priestley, an English scientist and dissenting minister, was among those who began preaching Unitarian Christianity emphasizing Jesus's humanity, God's omnipotence, and the rational faculty of man. The English Unitarians became strong in Parliament and in the professions. The name 'Free Christian' was adopted by some groups who thought the name 'Unitarian' to be sectarian and divisive.

In America, Unitarianism developed more slowly out of New England Congregationalist churches that rejected the eighteenth-century revivalist religious movement called the 'Great Awakening'. Congregational autonomy provided protection from controversy for those ministers who stressed moderation, reason, and morals over spiritual revivalism. By the early nineteenth century, Unitarianism replaced Calvinism as the faith of a large part of the New England population. Channing (1780–1842), known as the 'Apostle of Unitarianism', author, moralist, Congregationalist and Unitarian clergyman, was a leading figure in the development of New England Transcendentalism. Transcendentalists, like other ancient and modern Platonists, trusted to insights transcending logic and experience for revelations of the deepest truths. Channing described his faith of Unitarian Christianity to be 'a rational and amiable system, against which no man's understanding, or conscience, or charity, or piety revolts'. He affirmed the divine unity, and the authority of Scripture rationally interpreted. In 1820, he formed a conference of liberal Congregational ministers, later reorganized as the American Unitarian Association (AUA) in 1825.

By the end of the nineteenth century American Unitarianism had adopted a rational liberal view recognizing the truth of non-Christian religions. In 1961 the American Unitarian Association joined with the Universal Church of America, with whom they shared a history of liberal idealism, forming the

Unitarian Universalist Association (UUA) (Livingstone 2000 p. 595), the strongest organization on a global scale. Universalists argue that Scripture does not teach eternal torment in hell and, with Origen, the third-century Alexandrian theologian, they affirmed a universal restoration of all to God. Unitarian Universalists deny the authority of dogmas promulgated by church councils. Their teachings historically have included the unity of God, the humanity of Jesus, mankind's religious and ethical responsibility, and the possibility of attaining religious salvation through differing religious traditions. They emphasize reason and experience as appropriate bases for formulating religious beliefs.

The Islamic Perspective and the Gospel of Jesus

The period of a thousand years, extending from the extinction of Arianism in western Europe in the seventh century to the reappearance of Unitarianism in the sixteenth, was conspicuously marked by the rise in the seventh century of Islam, a strict Unitarian monotheistic religion. Remarkably, Islam and Unitarianism have many themes in common. These include the belief in the unity of God, the rejection of the Trinity doctrine, the humanity of Jesus – that Jesus although divinely inspired as the Messiah was a mere human, the use of reason in arriving at religious belief, tolerance of differing religious views, rejection of dogma, and mankind's religious and ethical responsibility.

This natural affinity between Islam and Unitarianism was readily recognized at the beginning of the twentieth century by no less a personality than the late Reverend David Benjamin Keldani, the Roman Catholic Arch-Priest of Urmia, Persia, who towards the end of his career joined the Unitarian Community in England before finally embracing Islam.

We have already noted that the theological foundations of Unitarian beliefs originate with the Nazarenes who were the first followers of Jesus (Acts 24: 5). According to Eisenman and others, the Nazarene appellation had nothing to do with Nazareth, the supposed town, where Jesus was brought up. As for Jesus's purported origins in Nazareth, there may be some confusion between geographical connotation and ideological implication. The famous Jewish-Roman historian Flavius Josephus never mentioned Nazareth in any of his works, which were very detailed. Nor was Nazareth mentioned previously in any Biblical setting. The principal city of Galilee was rather Sepphoris. Nazareth, if it existed at all, may have been a little village not far from Sepphoris. On the other hand, Nazareth may have sprung into life to meet a later need. The first churches in Nazareth seem to be a product of the fifth century (Grant 1999 p. 72; Eisenman 1997 p. 251).

Matthew's gospel states: 'So was fulfilled what was said through the prophets: Jesus will be called a Nazarene' (Matthew 2: 23). There is good reason to believe Eisenman in that the appellation 'Nazarene' has nothing to do with geography, i.e. Nazareth, but rather with ideology. This opinion is shared by many (Schonfield 1994 p. 207; Maccoby 1998 p. 175). It is also remarkable that the word 'Nazarenes' is equivalent to the Arabic word '*nasara*'. Both seem to have the same root and are etymologically equivalent. The 'Nazarenes' are the '*nasara*', the word having the Arabic connotation of 'helpers', i.e. 'those who believed in Jesus and came to succour him'. It is significant that the Holy Qur'an specifically and *exclusively* uses the word '*nasara*' in reference to Jesus's followers. Concurrently and metaphorically, the Qur'an applies the term '*nasara*' to all Christians as they believe themselves to be genuine followers of Jesus. It is perhaps one of the biggest misconceptions, that many have thought the title of Jesus 'Nazarene' as denoting a geographical location, incognizant of its ideological implication.

The following Qur'anic verse is particularly significant in the semantics of the appellation 'Nazarenes' or '*nasara*':

O you who have attained to faith! Be helpers – in the cause of – God, as Jesus the son of Mary, said to the white-garbed ones – disciples – 'Who will be my helpers in God's cause?' – my *nasara* –, Whereupon the white-garbed ones – disciples – replied: 'We are – your – helpers–in the cause of – God!' And so it happened that a portion of the Children of Israel believed – in the prophetic mission of Jesus – whereas others denied the truth, but – now – We have given power to those who believed, against their foes, and they became the ones that shall prevail. (Qur'an 61: 14)

Significantly, those who believed in Jesus as God's Apostle and Messiah, and thus the forerunner of the last prophet Muhammad, were given the power to prevail, that is, through the advent of Islam.

The reference to 'white-garbed ones', the disciples, in the Qur'anic verse, is possibly a reference to members of the Essene brotherhood, to which probably Jesus himself belonged. The Essenes were a Jewish religious group in Palestine at the time of Jesus, besides the Pharisees and the Saducees. The evidence of the recently discovered Dead Sea scrolls lends support to this view. The Essenes having been characterized by their strong insistence on moral purity and unselfish conduct, always wore white garments as the outward mark of their convictions (Asad 1984 p. 75). According to some authors, the Essenes who always wore white are fully equated with the Nazarenes and the Jerusalem Church (Knight and Lomas 1998 pp. 22, 99; Baigent and Leigh 1993 p. 174).

Another Qur'an verse alludes to the Christians' conviction that they are Jesus's followers, i.e. Nazarenes.

> And from those who say, 'Behold we are Nazarenes', We have accepted a solemn pledge, and they too have forgotten much of what they had been told to bear in mind – wherefore We have given rise to enmity and hatred among them – to last – until Resurrection Day. And in time God will cause them to understand what they have contrived. (Qur'an 5: 14)

The phrase 'those who say, "Behold we are Nazarenes"' is an obvious allusion to the Christians' belief that they are followers of Jesus the Nazarene, whereas in fact they are of Pauline persuasion. In this manner the Qur'an elliptically rejects the Christians' claim of being the true followers of Jesus. Significantly, the Qur'an had brought the appellation 'Nazarenes' back to life insofar as it had perished from common knowledge and from common usage long before the advent of Islam. The same applies to the phrase 'the white-garbed ones', the Essenes.

While the phrase 'and they too have forgotten much of what they had been told to bear in mind' alludes to the corruption of the message of Jesus into Pauline Christianity. This in turn has led to 'wherefore We have given rise to enmity and hatred among them – to last – until Resurrection Day'. The consequence, although ascribed to God's act, is a natural outcome of their going astray from the message of Jesus. This consequence is manifested in recurrent enmities, warfare, and persecutions among Christian nations, not the least of which was the Thirty Years War (1618–48) in Germany between the Protestants and the Catholics whereby some seven million people perished. Significant also are the estimated 21,000 distinct Christian groups existing worldwide today. Many such groups treasure their differences as ultimate and of supreme importance as a matter of truth (Wilson, B. 1999 pp. 14–15). On this point, one contemporary historian, Ammianus, noted: 'no wild beasts are such enemies to mankind as are most Christians in their deadly hatred for one another'(Rubenstein 1999 p. 194).

So far as the person of Jesus and his prophetic mission are concerned, there are remarkable parallels between Muslim and Nazarene, and for that matter Unitarian beliefs. Muslims and Nazarenes acknowledge Jesus as the prophet-Messiah. They acknowledge the objective of his prophetic mission to reform the Jewish religion from the corruption it underwent over many centuries. They deny divinity concepts ascribed to Jesus by the Pauline Church. They reject other Pauline doctrines on atonement, heavenly sacrifice and redemption of sins. And they believe in the supernatural conception of Jesus. On this basis the following Qur'an verse becomes clear:

Thou will surely find that of all people, the most hostile to those who believe – in this divine writ – are the Jews, as well as those who are bent on ascribing divinity to aught beside God; and thou will surely find that of all people, they who say, 'we are Nazarenes', come closest to feeling affection for those who believe – in this divine writ –; this is because there are priests and monks among them, and because they are not given to arrogance. (Qur'an 5: 82)

Unlike the Jews, Christians – or those who claim to be Nazarenes – are not given to arrogance insofar as they do not claim to be God's chosen people, nor do they claim a tribal God of their own. Significantly the verse contrasted the Jews, and those who ascribe divinity to aught besides God, on one hand, with those who claim to be Nazarenes. This may be because the Christians do not consciously worship a plurality of deities but claim to be monotheistic in spite of the Trinity doctrine. Or the reference may be to the Nazarenes in particular who accepted Islam *en masse* after the Islamic conquests, as the following verse testifies – in effect foretelling the future:

For, when they come to understand what has been bestowed from on high upon this Apostle, thou can see their eyes overflow with tears, because they recognize the truth; – and – they say: 'O our Sustainer! We do believe; make us one, then, with all who bear witness to the truth'. (Qur'an 5: 83)

The Nazarenes had their own Gospel in Hebrew comprising the inspired sayings of Jesus. This Gospel of Jesus is referred to in Arabic as the '*Enjil*', from the Greek word 'Evangelion', meaning good tidings. The Gospel of Jesus finds its reference in the Qur'an. There is also a reference to such a gospel in the Nazarene source quoted by Abd al-Jabbar, mentioned earlier, and described as an original trustworthy gospel, written in Hebrew. The Gospel of Jesus, the '*Enjil*', is now lost having been suppressed out of existence by the Pauline Church. Still, there remain snatches of the sayings of Jesus in the re-constructed Q gospel and in the gospel of Thomas, and to a lesser extent in the later gospel narratives (see Chapter 2).

The Pauline Church had deliberately obscured Jesus's humanity, separating him from the human race and making his valuable prophetic mission seem irrelevant. In spite of its neglect of the message of Jesus, Pauline Christianity had gradually built up its own self-confidence and arrogance having become the world's foremost universal religion. It took six centuries after Jesus – three centuries after the Council of Nicaea – to partially overturn the fiasco of Jesus's mission into success. The advent of Islam through the mission of the last and seal of the Prophets, Muhammad, had redressed justice for Jesus's Messianic movement (Qur'an 61: 14). But the Christian Church still prefers to look the other way, avoiding the reality of Jesus and his true mission, in favour of a mythical Christ it has long cherished.

While the Church seems to be bent on holding on to Pauline dogma, many disgruntled clergy and Christian scholars are trying to rectify the situation in their own ways. Some resort to speculation about the real Jesus, others deny his historical reality altogether, while others reject his prophethood and Messiahship considering him a mere Jewish sage and preacher. Some are trying to devise a new religion calling for the formation of a *new* New Testament. Some would like to 'reshape' Christianity and invent a new religion (Spong 1998; Funk 1996 p. 314).

Not many scholars have chosen to research the truth about Jesus through the perspective of Islam. It is interesting that the Qur'an itself had predicted their attitude:

'Whenever there comes unto them a renewed message from their Sustainer, they but listen to it as in jest' (Qur'an 21: 2). And 'But there comes not to them a newly revealed message from – God – the Most Gracious but they turn away therefrom. Thus indeed, have they given the lie – to this message as well –, but in time they will come to understand what it was that they were wont to deride' (Qur'an 26: 5–6). In this manner, the Qur'an, many centuries in advance, portrayed the unbelievers receiving the message in amused self-superiority, later turning into active hostility or careless indifference.

Finally, it is interesting to summarize the beliefs of Jews, Christians, and Muslims on the issue of Jesus's mission. On the negative side there resulted a striking agreement between Jewish and Christian beliefs: neither acknowledged the mission of the historical Jesus the Messiah. However, while the Jews acknowledged neither Jesus the Messiah nor the Christ of Paul, Christians acknowledged only the Christ of Pauline persuasion. Only the Nazarenes who were in the minority acknowledged the historical Jesus the Messiah while rejecting the Christ of Paul.

It was then left to the Muslims, six centuries after Jesus, to acknowledge Jesus's historic Messianic mission. This is evidently the meaning of the Qur'an verse 61: 14 quoted earlier in this chapter. The rise of Islam in the early seventh century helped to support the cause of the Nazarenes who embraced the new religion *en masse*:

> Lo! God said 'O Jesus: Verily, I shall cause thee to die, and shall exalt thee unto Me, and cleanse thee – of the presence – of those who are bent on denying the truth; and I shall place those who follow thee – far – above those who are bent on denying the truth, unto the Day of Resurrection.' (Qur'an 3: 55)

The Muslims thus prevailed spiritually over those who are bent on denying the truth, and became far above them through logic and sound reason.

FIVE

Christianity or Paulinism?

> But God has full knowledge of the true believer – and of his despairing cry, 'O my Sustainer! Verily, these are people who will not believe!' Yet bear thou with them, and say, 'Peace – be upon you –' for in time they will come to know – the truth. (Qur'an 43: 88-89)

Cardinal Features

Any individual seeking to study the origin of Christianity ends up by necessity studying the career of Paul the 'apostle'; because, Paul alone, who was not a disciple of Jesus, nor an eyewitness to Jesus's mission, became the sole originator of Christianity. It is with good reason that Christianity is labelled 'Pauline', after its founder Paul, although a great misconception, arising from retaining Jesus as an icon of the Pauline faith, still prevails. It would be interesting to speculate what would have been the outcome of Jesus's mission had the Pauline phenomenon not erupted on the scene after the death of Jesus.

During his missionary years, Paul proved himself devoid of any interest in the human message of Jesus. This is because he believed in Jesus as a divine sacrifice and saviour whose objective was to redeem humanity before the imminent end of time. On this basis he distinguished himself by calling for the belief in three cardinal features of his own faith: (1) Jesus, having been a divine sacrifice, became a Saviour for mankind, (2) the institution of the Eucharist, (3) proclamation of the end of history.

In short, Christianity did not emanate from the mission of Jesus, but quite the contrary. For Paul, the history of Jesus starts at 'the *same* night in which he was betrayed' (I Corinthians 11: 23). The gospels, therefore, rewrote Christian history in accordance with the Pauline faith, side-stepping the historical Jesus.

The Saviour

According to Maccoby (1998 p. 184), Paul's faith in Jesus is summarized in one phrase: 'the descent of a divine saviour'. More clearly, it is the urgent descent of a divine saviour who was to redeem humanity before the imminent end of history. Paul, as shown by his writings, replaced the teachings of Jesus the Messiah, the historical Jesus, with a mythical 'Chrestos' of his own. His ignorance of Jesus himself had been compounded by his deliberate effort to avoid the disciples of Jesus during his missionary years. He remained at odds with them since his 'conversion', calling them 'false brethren' and 'false apostles' and 'Satans' (II Corinthians 11: 13, 26).

Contradicting Luke in Acts 9: 20–30, he denied having returned from Damascus to Jerusalem to join the disciples: 'nor went I to Jerusalem to them which were apostles before me; but I went into Arabia and returned again unto Damascus. Then after three years, I went up to Jerusalem to see Peter and abode with him fifteen days. But other of the apostles saw I none, save James' (Galatians 1: 17–19). The obvious insinuation is that he stood to learn nothing from the disciples of Jesus.

Paul's sole justification for his new faith was his own 'apocalypse'. A few years after his death, Jesus was 'revealed' to Paul, and through continuous 'revelations', Paul to the exclusion of all the disciples, was receiving instructions from the 'heavenly' Master. 'For if he that comes preaches *another Jesus*, whom we have not preached' (II Corinthians 11: 4), meaning that he – Paul – was the sole receiver of inspiration from his own mystical Chrestos. He was clearly denying the historical Jesus whom he was describing as 'another Jesus'. To this end he needed to scorn the disciples stating that those disciples who *seemed* to be important, whatever they were, made no difference to him (Galatians 2: 6). On another occasion he wrote, mocking the disciples: 'We dare not make ourselves of the number, or compare ourselves with some that commend themselves [i.e. the disciples]; but they, measuring themselves by themselves, and comparing themselves among themselves, are not wise' (II Corinthians 10: 12). Then he boasted: 'But we will not boast of things without *our* measure', and 'We are not boasting of things without *our* measure' (II Corinthians 10: 13–14). Paul was intent on solely appropriating the message of Jesus for himself and transforming it into a new faith of his own making.

Henceforth, Paul's Chrestos had replaced the Messiah. And the 'atonement' of Chrestos had 'delivered' the faithful from the 'bondage' of sin and its ramifications. 'For if righteousness comes by the Law, then Chrestos died in vain' (Galatians 2: 21). And: 'Be it be known unto you therefore, men and brethren, that through this man [Jesus], is preached unto you the forgiveness of sins, and by him all that believe are justified from all things, from which you could not be justified by the law of Moses" (Acts 13: 38–39).

This was the crux of the Pauline faith that was later to be known as Christianity. But clearly Paul was not intent on establishing a new religion for future society. Far from that, he had literally believed that the end of time was at hand, in his own days.

It did not matter to Paul that the 'inspiration' which he received from the 'heavenly' Jesus was completely at variance with the teachings of the historical Jesus. Indeed, it was this 'inspired' contradiction of the teachings of Jesus the Messiah that became the basis of Paul's appraisal of human behaviour, namely, independence of faith from deeds, and religion from morality. A faithful desiring to be saved needs a sole requirement: belief in Jesus as his 'saviour' by accepting the atoning death of the 'saviour' on the cross. Paul postulated a salvation through Jesus that anyone could obtain free of charge. According to Paul, this belief in itself is sufficient to make the believer superior to other human beings who did not share the same belief. At the same time, Paul preached next to nothing about Jesus's message on earth.

Paul decided that his own assessment on salvation should be sufficient, otherwise Christ would have died in vain (Galatians 2: 21). Was it possible that Jesus could sanction irresponsible behaviour among individuals, encourage social disorder, tolerate crime and corruption, give an open invitation and a free license to social chaos. James, leader of the Nazarenes, testifies to the contrary. But Paul put it bluntly: 'Because the law works wrath, for where no law is, there is no transgression' (Romans 4: 15), meaning that you cannot violate a law which does not exist. And 'Moreover the law entered, that the offence might abound; but where sin abounded, grace did much more abound' (Romans 5: 20), hence according to Paul, the net effect of the law was to create sin. 'Therefore we [Paul] conclude that a man is justified by faith without the deeds of the law' (Romans 3: 28).

How and why should anyone, believing in a saviour, be absolved of responsibility for his deeds? How can righteousness be achieved through mere faith in a Chrestos? How can society function in such fashion? What did Paul aspire to achieve by his attack on the law? Paul must have deemed such issues irrelevant in view of his concept of the end of time. There was no reason for the faithful to care about the law or organized society, since the appointed time was growing very short (I Corinthians 7: 29, 31). To make sense of what he wrote we must always remember that Paul was talking about a Chrestos (II Corinthians 11: 4), ahead of the imminent 'end'.

James, leader of the Nazarenes, who is much more likely to have represented Jesus's views on earth, wrote:

What does it profit, my brethren, though a man says he has faith, and has not works? Will thou know, O vain man, that faith without works is dead? You see then how that by works a man is justified, and not by faith only. For as the body without the spirit is dead, so faith without works is dead also. (James 2: 14, 20, 24, 26)

This flatly contradicts Paul's doctrine of salvation by faith only, and is therefore regarded by some as anti-Pauline. Not surprisingly, James was always seen as a threat by the Roman Catholic Church and from its earliest times the Church sought to control history by removing information about this highly important Nazarene figure. This has been uncovered by the discovery in 1947 of the Qumran documents (Knight and Lomas 1998 p. 3). Historically, Christian theologians have been at pains to grapple with the letter of James trying to harmonize it with Paul's creed of salvation by faith only. But from the beginning, it must have seemed necessary to incorporate at least James's letter within the canonical scriptures to preserve a semblance of continuity between Christianity and its Nazarene predecessor.

But in Paul's mind resided a totally different notion from that of James and the Nazarenes. It was not important to consider morals and codes of behaviour at this terminal stage of human history. The world was coming to an end. Therefore, belief alone was sufficient. In addition, Paul's conviction may have been reinforced by the 'ethical' atmosphere he lived in his time. His world was that of Greek gods, who themselves were devoid of any morality, and had no moral values to stand for. Readers of Greek drama are familiar with the outrageous immorality that Greek dramatists ascribed to their gods. By necessity, the societies of such pagan deities must have been as corrupt as their deities which they invented in the first place. Incestuous, sexually profligate, jealous, deceitful, bloodthirsty, and careless, Greek gods had no ethical lessons to teach their worshippers. On top, pagan gods were biased rather than fair and applied favouritism rather than justice. They took pleasure in driving people insane, wrecking human lives, and depriving life of any meaningful purpose (Wilson, A.N. 1992 pp. 9–10). Ironically, Jewish scriptures, had in their turn absorbed much pagan 'wisdom', see for example: Genesis 9: 21; 19: 30–38; 35: 22; 38: 15–30; II Samuel 11: 1–27; 13: 5–14; 16: 21–23; Proverbs 7: 7–22; Jeremiah 20: 7; Hosea 4: 12; 6: 10; 9: 1; Ezekiel 23: 2–49. (Kirsch 1997)

Paul was raised in an environment where the great statue of the Greek man-god Herakles – Roman Hercules – paraded annually through the streets of Tarsus, Paul's native city. Herakles was considered the son of the Greek god Zeus, and was worshipped for his gifts of good luck and as a 'saviour'. In Greek mythology the man-god Herakles went down into Hades, the realm of death, and was able to save Alcestis, the wife of his friend Admetus, from death.

Christianity or Paulinism?

Paul must have seen the mobs in the streets of Tarsus, calling the statue of their 'saviour' Herakles, hoping that he would wash away their sins. Under such pagan influence, the saviour concept seems to have left an indelible impression in Paul's mind. Eventually, in his adulthood, he appears to have developed his own conviction that people, irrespective of their sinfulness, would be saved or have their sins washed away by the blood of some 'divine saviour' whom they believed in (Wilson, A.N. 1997 pp. 26, 122).

Conditions were ripe for Paul's theology, even before his 'apocalypse' and his 'conversion', and long before he had developed his 'Christology'. The idea that Jesus must have been a man-god, a Herculean saviour type, would have been very plausible to the Hellenists of Syrian Antioch. Antioch was a most prominent Hellenistic city in the eastern Mediterranean so it is no wonder that it was the centre of the Hellenistic faith in Jesus. Paul, for whom the saviour concept was of prime importance, found it most convenient to direct his mission to the Hellenists of Antioch, rather than to attach himself to the disciples in Jerusalem. It was therefore Antioch where Paul came to prominence as a 'Christian' leader and where the followers of the Pauline faith were first called 'Christians' (Acts 11: 26), in contrast to the followers of Jesus in Jerusalem, the 'Nazarenes' (Acts 24: 5).

Ancient Greek poets portrayed their gods travelling incognito among humans, 'the gods in the guise of strangers from far apart, put on all manner of shapes, and visit the cities, beholding the violence and righteousness of men' (Homer's *Odyssey*). Plato had therefore banished poets from his *Republic* (Wilson, A.N. 1997 p. 127). Not surprisingly, this very concept of gods in disguise roaming around the country is found in the book of Acts (Acts 14: 11–12). According to Greek mythology, the god Dionysus – Roman Bacchus – concealed his own divinity and arrived in Greece disguised as a holy man, walking incognito among people (see Chapter 3). The Dionysian mystery cult became most popular in Greek religion. After the appearance of Paul on the scene, the figure of the Greek god Dionysus who walked the earth concealing his divinity had slowly replaced the historical fact of Jesus the Prophet. In Paul's own words: 'Who [Jesus] being *in the form of God*, thought it not robbery to be equal with God, but made himself of no reputation, and took the form of a servant, and was made in *the likeness of men*. And being found in *fashion* as a man' (Philippians 2: 6–8). Paul eventually succeeded in transforming Greek mythology into Christian theology.

While Greek mythology abounded with stories of gods, goddesses, sons and daughters of gods and man-gods, Hellenistic religions combined Greek gods with eastern deities. Paul too, combined the Greek mentality on dying/rising gods with a new 'deity': a Chrestos that just appeared on the scene. Chrestos was no longer synonymous with the Anointed Messiah. Hellenistically, Greek

'Chrestos' – meaning 'useful' or 'beneficial' – was an appellation of divine figures in mystery cults (Maccoby 1998 p. 176).

Paul, the Hellenist, having been imbued with much Greek culture, was in no mood to learn from the Nazarenes, the early followers of Jesus. He was particularly careful not to claim any earthly knowledge of Jesus. His letter to Galatians emphasizes this strategy: 'But I certify to you, brethren, that the gospel which was preached of me, is not after man. For I neither received it of man, neither was I taught it, but by the revelation of Jesus Christ' (Galatians 1: 11–13). Thus, not only did Paul turn his back to the disciples and the Nazarenes, but also entitled himself to a much higher authority than their own.

Paul was very keen to find significance, not for Jesus's mission, but for the mission of Chrestos: 'Wherefore henceforth, we know no man after the flesh; athough we have known Jesus after the flesh, yet, now henceforth, we know him no more' (II Corinthians 5: 16). In other words, Jesus's teaching and message on earth were not important. Paul was starting from zero establishing his own Chrestos.

The Eucharist

The Christian Eucharist is yet another innovation of Paul. The story of Jesus's 'Last Supper' with his disciples celebrating Passover is familiar in the synoptic gospels, which we must remember were written decades after the events, and certainly after Paul's time, yet John's gospel knows nothing about it. It was Paul who first wrote about the Eucharist. Later, the synoptic gospels followed suit under his influence. To Jesus were attributed words that a Jewish prophet should not and could not have said. Neither did such words fit the Passover that Jesus was supposed to be celebrating (Funk 1996 p. 226).

Paul imagined that Jesus in his passive anticipation of crucifixion had instructed his disciples to symbolically eat his flesh and drink his blood. At this point it must remembered that the drinking of blood was part of ceremonies of Hellenistic mystery cults symbolizing the conquest of death (Eisenman 1997 p. 284). This symbolism was a most striking Pauline Hellenistic analogy. Just like the Jews slaughter and eat lambs on Passover feast, in remembrance of their deliverance from Egypt's Pharaoh, so do the Christians 'eat the body of Jesus – the Lamb of God – and drink his blood' in remembrance of their deliverance from sin! Henceforth, a completely new Hellenistic deity, with the Hellenistic name and significance of Chrestos, Christ, having died for the sins of humanity, became its saviour (I Corinthians 15: 3). The net result: a transformation of the Messiah into a Hellenistic Chrestos.

Christianity or Paulinism?

Notwithstanding that the disciples and the Nazarenes in Jerusalem did not celebrate the Eucharist, Paul was the only source who first reported the Eucharist story and initiated its celebration. By his own account it was something that he learnt, not from the disciples, but received directly from the heavenly Jesus (I Corinthians 11: 23). This was something convenient and most necessary to acknowledge on the part of Paul, because it is impossible to believe that Jesus himself could have instituted the Eucharist. It was Paul who later initiated the analogy that Jesus, when 'crucified', became a new Passover Lamb, 'for even Christ, our Passover [Lamb],is sacrificed for us' (I Corinthians 5: 7). Some 70 years later, John, author of the fourth gospel – whoever he was – chose to put in the mouth of John the Baptist a most blasphemous phrase in the Jewish religion: 'Behold the Lamb of God, who takes away the sins of the world' (John 1: 29). The implication is that salvation was obtained by shedding the blood of a Chrestos, an obvious analogy with pagan concepts of atonement.

This Eucharist story provides a most prominent, sharp, and obvious contrast between the mythical Christ of Paul, and the historical Jesus the Messiah. The Eucharist, is further proof that Christianity is not based on factual history but derives from Pauline mythology. Even the most theologically developed of the gospels, John's gospel, provides no account of the institution of the Eucharist! As for the passage in John 6: 54: 'Whoso eats my flesh and drinks my blood has eternal life', it must be a late addition by a reviser who was embarrassed by the absence of the Eucharist from the John's gospel. In the words of A.N. Wilson (1992 p. 161): 'The truth is that even if we were to believe the fantastic claim that Jesus wished to found a new religion, with a sacramental order of bishops and deacons, we could not believe that he had instituted the Eucharist at Passover time as Paul and the [synoptic] Gospels aver.'

In the Egyptian Osiris cult, images of the saviour god Osiris were made of wheat paste and eaten as a holy sacrament. Power was believed to be derived from the flesh and blood of Osiris. Osiris was the grain, and the bread made from it was the sacred food, while the barley ale brewed from it was a divine drink. Both bread and ale were literally believed to be the body and blood of the god Osiris. The conviction that it was possible for humanity to achieve immortality by eating the body and drinking the blood of a god who had died, that mortals might have an everlasting life, was an obsession in the ancient world. It was literally believed that whosoever ate the flesh and drank the blood of Osiris had eternal life and that he dwelt in Osiris and Osiris dwelt in him. In one Pyramid Text dated 2600 BCE it is stated: 'all gods give thee their flesh and their blood ... thou shall not die', while the believer prayed for: 'thy bread of eternity, and thy beer of everlastingness'. About the god Horus, son of Osiris, it is also stated: 'Horus is both the divine food and the sacrifice'. In the

Greek religion, Osiris was identified with Dionysus who had a multiple of characters. One Dionysus character portrays him as the divine saviour god who died for mankind and whose body and blood were symbolically eaten and drunk in the Eucharist (Larson 1977 pp. 11, 20–23, 37).

Bishop John Shelby Spong (1998 p. 194) acknowledged that: 'in primitive practices of prehistory, worshippers tried to capture for themselves the strength of – first their enemies – and later their gods by eating their flesh and drinking their blood. These cannibalistic rites probably entered Christianity through the various cults of the Mediterranean mystery religions such as Mithraism'.

Paul nevertheless declared without ambiguity that it was the 'heavenly' Jesus who had instructed him to institute this major Christian sacrament.

> For I have received of the Lord that which also I delivered unto you, that the Lord Jesus, the same night in which he was betrayed, took bread, and when he had given thanks, he broke it and said, "Take, eat, this is my body, which is broken for you. This do in remembrance of me". In the same manner also he took the cup after supper saying: "This cup is the new testament in my blood. This do as often as you drink it in remembrance of me". (I Corinthians 11: 23–26)

In this fashion, Christians eat the body of Jesus and drink his blood! The analogy fitted perfectly with pagan mystery cults. Such a gesture, however symbolic, would have horrified Jesus, the Jewish Prophet and Messiah.

The celebration of the 'Eucharist' or 'Lord's Supper', which Paul derived from the Mithraic mystery cult, was another major step in alienating 'Christianity' from the message of Jesus (Wilson, A.N. 1997 pp. 165–66). The Nazarenes of Jerusalem, including the disciples who knew better, not only did not practise the Eucharist, but were totally unaware of it. Indeed, if the disciples of Jesus were already practising the Eucharist before Paul, as some may like to argue, it would have been absurd for Paul to claim personal inspiration for something already known and practised by the Nazarenes. Paul first used the term 'Lord's Supper', which the church later changed into 'Eucharist'. The term 'Lord's Supper' caused embarrassment to the early fathers of the church because, as we have seen, it was indicative of sacred meals dedicated to saviour-gods in mystery religions. To avoid embarrassment the Church replaced it with the name 'Eucharist', having Jewish rather than pagan connotations (Maccoby 1998 p. 116). 'The very phrase, borrowed from Mithraic mysteries, took Christianity far from the Palestinian world of Jesus' (Wilson, A.N. 1997 p. 165).

It was befitting Paul's mentality to use the term 'Lord' (Greek *kyrios*) as a title for a deified Jesus. The Greek Hebrew Bible, the Septuagint, uses the term 'Lord' to denote the Hebrew holy name of God, the 'Tetragrammaton', i.e. the

Christianity or Paulinism?

four-letter word 'YHWH' which, out of reverence, no Jew dare pronounce (Funk 1996 pp. 92, 207; Parrinder 1992 p. 113). For any devout Jew applying the title 'Lord' in a divine sense to a human being is outright blasphemy. But for Paul and the recipients of his letters in the Hellenistic world this must have been quite customary. They had been accustomed to this term used for deities and salvation gods of Hellenistic mystery cults all along.

But the embarrassment that the Eucharist caused to the early church fathers was so great that Justin Martyr, the Christian apologist-theologian (d. 165), was prompted to write: 'Which the wicked devils have imitated in the mysteries of Mithras, commanding the same thing to be done. For bread and a cup of water are placed with certain incantation in the mystery rites of one who is being initiated.' Justin was insinuating that the devils had anticipated this Christian rite long before Paul, and thus directed the Mithraic pagans to practise it ahead of him. Tertullian, the Christian theologian and apologist (d. 220) wrote similarly. That the Eucharist was practised by the cult of Mithras ahead of Christianity is well known and evident from the writing of Paul: 'You cannot drink the cup of the Lord, and the cup of devils; You cannot be partakers of the Lord's table, and the table of the devils' (I Corinthians 10: 21) (Larson 1977 pp. 182–83; Wells 1999 p. 100).

Mithras, in ancient Indo-Iranian mythology, was the god of light. After the defeat of the Persians by Alexander the Great, the Mithraic cult spread throughout the Hellenistic world as far west as Germany, Britain, and Spain. In the third and fourth centuries CE, the cult of Mithras, supported by the soldiers of the Roman Empire, was the chief rival to the newly developing Christianity. The Roman emperors Commodus and Julian were initiates of Mithraism, and in 305 CE Emperor Diocletian consecrated a temple on the Danube River to Mithras as 'Protector of the Empire.'

According to myth, Mithras, a saviour god, slew the life-giving cosmic bull, whose blood fertilizes all vegetation and brings it to life. The bull was sacrificed that mankind might have the bread of life, and Mithras drank his wine/blood eucharist. Mithras' slaying of the bull was a popular subject of Hellenistic art and became the prototype for a bull-slaying ritual in the Mithraic cult. Mithras as god of light was associated with the Greek sun god, Helios, and the Roman Sol Invictus.

Tarsus, Paul's native city, was a centre of Mithraic worship. A most prominent feature of the Mithraic cult was that the initiates had to drink from the blood of the slaughtered sacred bull, or drink wine as a symbol of the bull's blood. During initiation, the animal was ritually slain on a platform under which stood the initiate, who would drench himself with the blood dripping from above. This would have meant saving the initiate in the blood of the bull. Simultaneously, the faithful in the temple would share in drinking blood from the slaughtered bull. Paul as a child in Tarsus, could not have failed to notice the initiation rites of this mystery cult, although Jews in the Hellenistic world must have been disgusted by the cult of Mithras because drinking blood is strictly forbidden in the Jewish religion (Larson 1977 pp. 187–89; Wilson, A.N. 1997 pp. 25–26, 44, 71; Knight and Lomas 1998 p. 94).

In summary, the Eucharist, as it is called, is of pure Pauline origin. Paul himself did not in the least claim that it derived from any of Jesus's disciples, who were actually present with Jesus on the night of the Last Supper, the night of his betrayal, the Passover eve. He claimed that he received this information directly from the 'Lord', meaning the heavenly Jesus. Paul's claim is contradicted by the fact that blood is utterly forbidden, and later generations of the Church continued to prohibit it. The book of Acts itself testifies that the Jerusalem Church prohibited the drinking of blood (Acts 15: 29). The Nazarenes, Jesus's followers in Jerusalem, who were later led by Jesus's disciples, did not practise the Eucharist ceremony. Had Jesus himself established such a rite, the disciples and their followers would have been the first to celebrate it.

But Paul's letters overflow with innovations. For him the Eucharist analogy reflected part of his understanding of the death of Jesus. From the beginning, it was the death of Jesus that mattered for Paul. He did not present Jesus to his followers as an admirable moral teacher, but purely in mythological terms. Paul saw in the Eucharist what the followers of Mithras must have seen in the death of the sacrificial bull: Jesus was a dying demi-god whose blood was to be drunk from. Paul imagined that he could bathe in the blood of the 'crucified' and feel not only that the life of Christ had become his own, but that his sins had been washed off (Larson 1977 p. 189; Wilson, A.N. 1997 p. 71). 'For I delivered unto you first of all that which I also received, that Christ died for our sins' (I Corinthians 15: 3). Jesus was 'delivered [to death] for our offences' (Romans 4: 25). 'Whom God had set forth to be a propitiation through faith in his blood ... for the remission of sins that are past, through the forbearance of God' (Romans 3: 25). And 'He has made him to be sin for us, who knew no sin, that we might be made the righteousness of God in him" (II Corinthians 5: 21).

Such ideas must have strongly appealed to the pagans of the Roman Empire where the cult of Mithras strongly rivalled Christianity. One Mithraic hymn begins: 'Thou have redeemed us too, by shedding the eternal blood'. Paul found important parallels between the mystery cults and his Christianity. As such, pagans could retain beliefs they were used to, and yet embrace Christianity (Wilson, A.N. 1997 pp. 165–66, 174).

It is interesting that the adoption of Sundays, and of 25 December, as holy days, owes its origin to Mithraism. Sundays had always been sacred to the Mithraists, while the 25 December was Mithras' birthday. The ancient Mazdeans also glorified 25 December as the date when the sun-god was reborn.

On the official side, the Roman Emperor Aurelian in 274 CE officialized 25 December as the birthday of Helios, that is Mithras, god of light. Subsequent to the Council of Nicaea the Church accepted 25 December as Christmas day, although there is nothing in the New Testament that substantiates Jesus's birth in December, and if anything it must be to the contrary. Various dates are contemplated ranging from March to November. This is the time interval in the Palestinian climate, when Palestinian shepherds, who received the annunciation according to Luke (Luke 2: 14), would normally be out in the field.

Prior to the Council of Nicaea, and in some eastern churches until the sixth century, Christians celebrated Epiphany on 6 January as the date when Christ was born, baptized into Christ-hood, and shown himself to the Magis of Persia. This is the very day on which the cult of Persephone, queen of Hades the underworld, believed that she gave birth to Dionysus (Larson 1977 p. 184; Parrinder 1992 p. 34).

The End of History

Paul was haunted by the belief that the 'Day of the Lord' was about to happen, not for him alone, but for the world at large. This may have been the most fundamental of Paul's beliefs, the driving force behind his missionary work. Paul had expected this eventuality to occur literally, not symbolically, in his own lifetime and the lifetime of his contemporaries (Sanders 1996 pp. 4–5, 12, 17, 21, 33).

Paul figured that the suffering, death, resurrection, and rising into heaven of Jesus were all signs and preludes to the end of the world of his time. In his mind, time was growing short and he was convinced that he bore the unique task of forewarning the believers about what was going to happen. 'But this I say, brethren, the time is short ... the form of this world is passing away' (I Corinthians 7: 29, 31). Having completed, to his mind, his missionary duty in the east, he planned to travel as far as the end of the world of his time, i.e. Spain, in order to forewarn the gentiles on the impending calamity if they did not repent. 'But now having no more place in these regions ... I will come by you into Spain' (Romans 15: 23, 28). He was pressed for time and wanted to hasten to Spain to forewarn the Spanish before it was too late. And on his way to Spain he would pass by Rome to see his followers there.

It was clear that Paul never planned to establish a new religion for future humanity. For that matter the word 'Christianity' never once appeared in his writings, even though the New English Bible, for example, makes a point to intrude the word 'Christian' in Paul's letters. Forewarning the believers was the driving force behind his endeavours. It was the centre of all his actions and effort (Wilson, A.N. pp. 176, 177–78).

In this respect, Paul saw no need to reform or remake society, as he did not foresee the centuries that lay ahead. Ironically, and contrary to what Paul expected, his letters had a tremendous role in shaping future society that he did not foresee in the first place. He thought that as his world order came to an end, a glorious Christ was to reappear over the clouds in the likeness of the Son of Man in Daniel (Daniel 7), and a Kingdom of God established under Christ would then replace the Roman Empire. Paul expected most people living in his time to be still living to witness the return of Christ: 'then we which are alive and remain shall be caught up together with them in the clouds, to meet the Lord in the air' (I Thessalonians 4: 17). In the words of A.N. Wilson:

> Paul thought that Christ would be revealed to his chosen few in Jerusalem. The New Israel will thereby be established. It is not going to be the Christian Church, going on for Sunday after Sunday into eternity, with bishops, priests, and deacons, and a new Torah. Such an idea would have horrified Paul. That would be religion all over again. (Wilson, A.N. 1997 pp. 208–9).

Though events had challenged Paul's prediction, others after him were not discouraged from persisting in the same belief. A few years after Paul's death, John, whoever he may have been, repeated the same expectation, in his Revelation. Notwithstanding that such prophecies proved grossly in error, the church at later times decided to include the Revelation as part of the Christian Bible.

Decades after Paul's death, New Testament writers, compilers, editors, and theologians chose to maintain course. A Church establishment, committed to Paul's theology was already set in motion and had gathered momentum with no possibility of turning back. The only course to which the Church restricted itself was to look in vain for some logical conclusions of Paul's mission, and of course there were none (Wilson, A.N. 1997 p. 234).

The Christian apologist-theologian Justin Martyr (100–65) explained that God was delaying the End because He wished first to see Christianity proliferate on a world scale. Hippolytus (170–236), theologian and rival bishop of Rome, somehow fixed the End for the year 202. When history passed successfully beyond 202, the date was postponed to the year 500. Thereafter, and to avoid embarrassment, many Christian texts avoided any reference to the End. But there remained those who continued to warn, until today, that the End is near (Freke & Gandy 1999 p. 212; Wilson, A.N. 1997 p. 209). This in turn contributed to the complete erosion of whatever could have remained of Jesus's historical message. Only the advent of Islam, at the beginning of the seventh century, made it possible for the picture of the historical Jesus to re-emerge.

Paul's belief in the imminent end of time provides valuable insight into his social concepts such as preserving the political and social status quo of his time: 'I suppose therefore that this is good for the present distress, it is good for man to remain as is. Are you bound unto a wife? Seek not to be divorced. Are you unmarried? Do not seek a wife. Those who marry will face trouble in the flesh. I want to spare you. But this I say to you brethren, the time is short' (I Corinthians 7: 26–29). On this basis Paul justified unmarried status: 'It is good for a man not to touch a woman' (I Corinthians 7: 1).

Paul's conceptualization of Jesus's mission was concise. Having fulfilled his role on earth as a divine sacrifice, it was left for his Second Coming to end world history and establish the Kingdom of God, a belief that consumed all Paul's missionary effort!

Pauline Social Values

Paul's Letters the Only Valid Gospel

Paul insisted on assuring his audience, that he was preaching the only valid Gospel. He was convinced that he held a sole monopoly on the truth, to the exclusion of not only human beings, but also the angels in heaven. The angels in heaven, under the pain of being cursed, could not preach a gospel other than his own: 'But even if we, or an angel from heaven, preach any other gospel unto you, other than that which we have preached to you, let him be accursed. As we said before, so I say now again, if any man preach any other gospel unto you other than you have received, let him be accursed' (Galatians 1: 8–9). In this manner, Paul ensured that no disciple of Jesus could or should preach anything contrary to what he was preaching.

Submission to Governing Authority

> Let every soul be subject unto the higher powers. For there is no power but of God. The powers that be are ordained by God. Whosoever therefore resists the power, resists the ordinance of God, and they that resist shall receive to themselves damnation. For rulers are not a terror to good works, but to the evil. Do you want to be free from fear of power? Then do what is good, and you shall have praise of the same. For he [the ruler] is the minister of God to you, for good. He [the ruler] is the minister of God. (Romans 13: 1–4)

This Pauline concept of government authority has been used to justify, the 'divine' right of rulers, kings and emperors throughout Christian history. It has been used as a convenient legal and 'divine' means for exacting repression on a dissenting population, and muting criticism. The Roman emperor at the time of this Pauline writing was Nero (54–68 CE), 'the minister of God to you, for good'! More than two and half centuries after Paul, Eusebius the Bishop of Caesarea dedicated, at the Council of Nicaea, Paul's ideology on government authority declaring that the emperor represented the will of God in the government of the civilized world (the oikoumene).

The Status of Women

Paul considered women inferior to men. 'Let your women keep silence in the churches, for it is not permitted unto them to speak, but they are commanded to be under obedience, as also says the law. And if they will learn anything, let them ask their husbands at home, for it is a shame for women to speak in the church' (I Corinthians 14: 34–35). He also wrote, 'I permit no woman to teach, nor to usurp authority over man, but to be in silence. For Adam was first formed then Eve. And Adam was not deceived, but the woman being deceived was in the transgression' (I Timothy 2: 12–14). As a result of this Pauline view 'there has been almost institutionalized misogyny regarding women as inferior to men, or as a source of evil, and there has been a generally degrading attitude to sex' (Parrinder 1992 p. 117).

Slavery

Paul made no effort to abandon slavery. On the contrary, slavery is approved and condoned in his writings. 'Slaves, obey your earthly masters in everything according to the flesh, and whatsoever you do, do it heartily. For you serve the lord Christ' (Colossians 3: 22, 24). He only advocated kindness in the institution of slavery: 'Masters, give unto your slaves that which is just and equal' (Colossians 4: 1). On this 'Pauline' basis, slavery was justified in the Christian world for some nineteen centuries after Paul. The net result is that 'from the first days, and for nearly two thousand years, the church condoned slavery' (Parrinder 1992 p. 117).

Islam's Appeal to the Intellect

In sharp contrast to Pauline Church doctrines, which the believer is required to accept at face value notwithstanding man's gift of the intellect, the Qur'an repeatedly urges mankind to think and use his reason. 'And – so – whenever they commit an abomination they say, "we found our forefathers doing it"' implying they are followers of dogma. 'And God has enjoined it upon us' meaning had it been the will of God we could not have done it. 'Say: "never does God enjoin deeds of abomination". Would you attribute unto God something of which you have no knowledge?' (Qur'an 7: 28).

The principal cause of human suffering is shown to be due to blind imitation of absurd beliefs and customs of one's erring predecessors, with disregard of all evidence of truth supplied by both reason and divine guidance: 'For, behold, they found their forebears on a wrong way, and now, they make haste to follow in their footsteps!' (Qur'an 37: 69–70; Asad 1984 p. 686).

Warning against double standards, the Qur'an states 'Do you bid other people to be pious, the while you forget your own selves, and yet you recite the divine writ? Will you not, then, use your reason?' (Qur'an 2: 44).

The claim of Christians and Jews to salvation by virtue of their descent from 'their' father Abraham is refuted by reference to reason: 'O Followers of earlier revelation! Why do you argue about Abraham, seeing that the Torah – Tawrah – and the Evangel were not revealed till – long – after him? Will you not, then, use your reason?' (Qur'an 3: 65). Paul's doctrine of salvation by faith only and the 'vicarious atonement' are also contradicted: 'It may not accord with your wishful thinking – nor with the wishful thinking of the followers of earlier revelation – that he who does evil shall be requited for it, and shall find none to protect him from God, and none to bring him succour' (Qur'an 4: 123).

On the significance of our human life the Qur'an states: 'And nothing is the life of this world but a play and a passing delight; and the life in the hereafter is by far the better for all who are conscious of God. Will you not, then, use your reason?' (Qur'an 6: 32).

On the message of the Qur'an: 'We have bestowed upon you – O Men – from on high a divine writ in which is a message for you – containing all you ought to keep in mind – will you not, then, use your reason?' (Qur'an 21: 10).

On worshipping other than God: 'Fie upon you and upon all that you worship instead of God! Will you not, then, use your reason?' (Qur'an 21: 67).

Urging people to contemplate on the miracle of life: 'And He who grants life and deals death; and to Him is due the alteration of night and day. Will you not, then, use your reason?' (Qur'an 23: 80).

The Qur'an urges man's intellect to ponder on the miracle of re-creation: ' – But – know that God gives life to the earth after it has been lifeless! We have indeed made our messages clear unto you, so that you might use your reason' (Qur'an 57: 17).

Telling the Prophet that he could not be held responsible for the kind of man who chooses to follow his own whims and desires: 'Hast thou ever considered – the kind of man – who takes for his god his own desires? Could thou then – O Prophet – be responsible for him? Or dost thou think that most of them listen – to thy message – and use their reason? Nay, they are but like cattle – nay, they are even less conscious of the right way!' (Qur'an 25: 43–44).

Urging man to use reason before he is overcome by old age and possible senility, the Qur'an states: 'But – let them always remember that – if We lengthen a human being's days, We also cause him to decline in his powers – when he grows old –, will they not, then, use their reason – before it is late –?' (Qur'an 36: 68). Thus people are advised not to postpone the exercise of moral choice, given that one's lifetime is limited with not much time left at one's disposal. Humans are superior creatures inasmuch as they have been endowed with the faculty of discernment, and a wide measure of free will, but are soon liable to decline in old age (Asad 1984 p. 679).

As a result of Islam's appeal to the intellect and reason, the Islamic civilization flourished with the beginning of the seventh century. Within less than one and half centuries of the Prophet's death, Islamic civilization reached peaks unknown to the world of that time. Unlike Christian Europe of the time, in the Islamic world intellectualism was a highly admired quality and was encouraged in places where Islam spread (Knight and Lomas 1998 p. 239). In addition, Islam restored religious tolerance in those parts of the world long under repression by the Western Church.

In comparison, Rome fell to the barbarians a few decades after the Roman Empire decreed Christianity as the sole religion permitted for practice by individuals. The establishment of the Roman Church, six centuries before Islam, inaugurated an age of darkness and with it human advancement suffered a severe setback. Ironically, the kind of religious repression practised by the Church was a Christian innovation unknown before. As a result of Christian Church dominance, all learning in Europe went through a sharp decline while superstition replaced knowledge, a situation which continued until the Reformation in the sixteenth century. Describing this state of affairs, Knight and Lomas wrote:

> Intellectual and moral progress quickly ground to a halt. And Western Civilization regressed into a state of crude barbarism. The Church banned education on the basis that the spread of knowledge could only serve to encourage 'heresy'. Literacy rates across the Roman Empire quickly fell to almost zero, science gave way to superstition, and the engineering advances of the early empire were forgotten. All branches of human achievement were ignored in the name of Jesus Christ. Art, philosophy, secular literature,

astronomy, mathematics, medicine, and even sex became taboo subjects. (Knight and Lomas 1998 pp. 93–94; see also Freke and Gandy 1999 p. 246).

Only recently, Bishop John Shelby Spong (1998 p. 4) wrote: 'We are that silent majority of believers who find it increasingly difficult to remain members of the Church and still be thinking people'. In other words, Westerners became – and could become – intellectuals only when they rid themselves of Church hegemony and repression. This state of affairs explains to a large extent the fact that Western civilization was able to flourish only after the Reformation. Pope John Paul II emphasized this point on 7 March 2000, during his global apology to the world for what he termed as two thousand years of church mistakes. It is therefore not surprising that, in the modern West, human progress and civilized society are fully equated with secularism.

In sharp contrast Islam has an inherent secular aspect so often repeated in the Qur'an where the spiritual is not separated from the mundane. The Qur'an urges humanity to 'seek by means of what God has granted thee, – the good of – the life to come, without forgetting thy own –rightful – share in this world' (Qur'an 28: 77). According to the Qur'an, every Muslim intellectual can be a theologian and every theologian must be an intellectual. Muslim peoples fell into decadence when they abandoned the intellectual secular aspect of Islam and maintained only the dogmatic practice of religion merely fulfilling outward worship while becoming oblivious to Islam's secular ramifications.

SIX

Jesus, the Messiah

Say: 'Who is that provides for you sustenance out of the heavens and the earth?' Say: 'It is God. And, behold, either we – who believe in Him – or you – who deny His oneness – are on the right path, or have clearly gone astray!' Say: 'Neither shall you be called to account for whatever we may have become guilty of, nor shall we be called to account for whatever you are doing'. Say: 'Our sustainer will bring us all together – on judgement day – and then He will lay open the truth between us, in justice – for He alone is the One who opens all truth, the All-Knowing'. (Qur'an 34: 24–26)

The Titles of Jesus According to the Gospels

Gospel authors and editors managed to ascribe various, albeit contradictory titles to Jesus the Messiah. In turn, the Pauline church, throughout its history, appears to have been content to labour on defending such titles through theological elaboration. In the words of one renowned scholar:

The attitude of church leaders seems to be; don't rock the boat, or; say nothing for fear of offending the few. Often, indeed the clergy do not know, or do not want to know, what scholars have been writing for many years, and it does not get through to their congregation. And so the hungry sheep look up and are not fed. (Parrinder 1992 p. 120)

Jesus is acknowledged to be of Virgin birth by both Matthew (Matthew 1: 18) and Luke (Luke 1: 34), but they both find nothing wrong in stating that he was the son of Joseph (Matthew 1: 16; 13: 55; Luke 3: 23). In addition the synoptic gospels ascribe to Jesus, brothers and sisters (Matthew 13: 55–56; Mark 3: 31; Luke 8: 19). To assure Jesus's royal lineage, they also accept him as the son of David through Joseph, in spite of his virgin birth (Matthew 9: 27; 20: 30; Mark 10: 48;

Luke 1: 27; 18: 38). At the same time he is made to be the Son of God (Matthew 14: 33; 16: 16; John 11: 27). In stark contrast to the Son of God claim, the appellation Son of Man is ascribed to Jesus some 83 times in the gospels. He is also called the Lamb of God (John 1: 29). On top of all this he is acknowledged by all gospels to be simply a prophet (Matthew 13: 57; 21: 11, 46; Mark 6: 4; Luke 7: 16; 24: 19; John 6: 14).

Understandably, extravagant, divine, and contradictory titles of Jesus can only be explained in the light of the manner in which the gospels had evolved, together with the evolution of theological doctrines in a Hellenistic cultural context. But it is more difficult to understand why Christian theologians and clergy laboured throughout their history trying to accommodate and defend such contradictions.

It is of utmost importance to recognize that the New Testament uses the terms 'Christ' and 'Messiah' interchangeably and concurrently to denote various meanings, such as 'man-god', 'deliverer', 'saviour', 'son of God', 'son of man', 'prophet-king', 'son of David', all at the same time. This has resulted in obscuring important issues, as well as inverting beliefs that stand at the heart of Jesus's mission. The confusion has caused substantial harm to the faith of millions. Unless a clear distinction is made of the significance of each title, some scholarly research will, as a result, look with suspicion and sarcasm towards not only the historical mission of Jesus, but also towards the validity of divine revelation. In their writings, some scholars seem to give the impression that divine revelation cannot be reconciled with 'objective reality'. In addition, many Jewish scholars deny, implicitly or explicitly, the possibility of divine revelation to prophets other than those of the Old Testament.

Setting aside these two biased approaches, it appears that studying the subject from an Islamic point of view would assist in restoring to Jesus his historical status as a great prophet of a great monotheistic faith.

Titles of the Historical Jesus

Titles of the Jesus of history can safely be accepted as: Jesus the Prophet, Jesus the Messiah, Jesus of virgin birth – not son of Joseph and definitely not from the line of David. Each of these titles will be dealt with separately.

Jesus the Prophet

Aside from Pauline Christology and later ecumenical council decisions, it is clear from the gospels that Jesus contemporaries regarded him as a prophet. No authority can deny that Jesus is acknowledged in the four gospels as a prophet.

On many occasions, Jesus himself had declared that he was a prophet. When expressing the fact that prophets first encounter hardships and enmity among their kinsmen he stated: 'A prophet is not without honour, but in his own country, and among his own kin, and in his own house' (Mark 6: 4; Matthew 13: 57). In Luke, Jesus is reported to have said: 'Verily I say unto you, no prophet is accepted in his home country' (Luke 4: 24). Even the more theologically advanced gospel of John, acknowledged Jesus as a prophet.

Mark, Matthew and Luke narrate the story that the contemporaries of Jesus were confused about whether Jesus was a manifestation of John the Baptist, revived from the dead, or Elijah in his Second Coming, or a prophet. In all three alternatives he was considered as a prophet. Jesus once asked his disciples: 'Whom do men say that I am?' They replied: 'John the Baptist, but some say Elijah, and others say One of the prophets' (Mark 8: 28; Matthew 16: 14; Luke 9: 19). The entourage of Herod Antipas had doubted that Jesus could have been John the Baptist – whom they had killed in prison – risen from the dead, or Elijah, or 'a prophet, or as one of the [old] prophets' (Mark 6: 15).

After the famous miracle of the loaves fed to the 5,000 men assembled in Galilee, the crowd expressed the belief in Jesus as a prophet. 'Then those men, when they had seen the miracle that Jesus did, said: this is in truth that prophet that should come into the world' (John 6: 14). Admittedly, the aim of John was to portray Jesus as the Prophet foretold in Deuteronomy (Deuteronomy 18: 18). And when the Pharisees warned Jesus to leave, for fear that Herod might kill him, he said, 'It can not be that a prophet perish out of Jerusalem' (Luke 13: 33).

According to Matthew, 'when Jesus entered Jerusalem, all the city was moved saying: who is this? And the multitude said: this is Jesus, the prophet of Nazareth of Galilee' (Matthew 21: 10–11). The answer of the crowd reflected the popular view that Jesus was indeed a prophet whom the crowd deeply admired in view of his teachings and his miracles that they had witnessed. And in the story of the boy revived from the dead: 'They glorified God saying: A great prophet is risen up among us' (Luke 7: 16).

At the same time the chief priests were reluctant to arrest Jesus because the people believed in him as a prophet: 'When the chief priests and the Pharisees had heard his parables, they perceived that he spoke of them. But when they sought to arrest him they feared the multitude, because they took him for a prophet' (Matthew 21: 45–46). During Jesus's dialogue with the Samaritan woman she told him: 'Sir, I perceive that you are a prophet' (John 4: 19).

When Jesus allowed a prostitute to anoint him, the Pharisees expressed their shock while acknowledging the people's belief that Jesus was indeed a prophet. 'And she [the prostitute] stood at Jesus' feet behind him weeping, and began to wash his feet with tears, and did wipe them with her hair, and kissed his feet and anointed them with the ointment. When the Pharisee saw this he said to himself: if this man were a prophet, he would have known who and what kind of woman this is that touches him' (Luke 7: 38–39).

On the occasion of the reappearance of Jesus to two of his followers on the road to Emmaus – a village seven miles from Jerusalem – Cleopas, one of the two, commented on Jesus's mission. He said, 'Jesus was a prophet mighty in deed and word before God and all the people' (Luke 24: 19).

However, in the face of all this massive gospel evidence, the Christian Church had been keen, from the beginning, to discard the 'prophet' appellation of Jesus, in favour of Hellenistic 'divine' titles emanating from Pauline Church inventions and decisions of ecumenical councils.

The problem began with the Hellenistic theology of the time, which did not regard the 'prophet' title dignified enough for the Messiah. Competition was necessary with titles of great leaders and Roman Emperors of the epoch. Christian theologians had to compete with leaders such as Julius Caesar who was both a mortal and later became a man-god. His successor Augustus was proclaimed 'the son of the deified', and through Caesar was descended from Venus. Before them Alexander the Great had been called the 'new Heracles', a 'saviour' who deserved a cult worship after his death.

Jesus, the Messiah

The word '*masah*' in Aramaic, Arabic, and Hebrew means to rub with oil, to anoint; a ritual procedure used for installing someone in office, such as a king or a high priest (Vermes 1998 pp. 158, 159). Indeed the non-ritual significance is to appoint someone in office without necessarily rubbing him with oil. In the case of Jesus, he was the one chosen by God, the chosen Messiah 'anointed' by God. In particular, he was *the* Messiah awaited by the Jews, i.e. the Messiah *par excellence*, not just *any* Messiah. This is because the Old Testament uses the Messiah title freely and indiscriminately to the extent that Cyrus, the pagan Persian King is called a Messiah, (Isaiah 45: 1).

That the Jews were awaiting their expected Messiah, *the* awaited Messiah, is evident from the story mentioned in the fourth gospel (John 1: 19–25). The story is told about a Jewish deputation of priests and Levites sent to John the Baptist to confirm whether he was *the* awaited Messiah, which of course he denied.

It is worth remembering that the title 'Messiah' is *not* the same as the term 'Christ' that was translated from the Greek 'Chrestos'. The terms 'Christ' and 'Christian' were coined in Syrian Antioch where the 'Christ' of Paul started eclipsing Jesus the Messiah. At the beginning, all the followers of Jesus were called Nazarenes, whereas Paul's converts in Antioch began to be called Christians at a later stage. Syrian Antioch was a centre of Hellenistic culture where Paul conveniently chose to start his missionary activities. Paul's missionary activity had caused the significance of the term 'Anointed Messiah' to become that of 'Chrestos' – Christ. To the Hellenists of the Graeco-Roman world, Chrestos signified a mythical divine Hellenistic figure, not unlike Herakles and Dionysus (Maccoby 1998 p. 176; Schonfield 1997 p. 8).

Whereas Jesus proclaimed himself as the Messiah, he simultaneously denied any divine or militant associations with the title. He expressly declared that his title had nothing to do with a worldly kingdom. When asked by the Roman prefect Pontius Pilate: 'Are thou the king of the Jews? Jesus answered: 'My kingdom is not of this world, if my kingdom was of this world, then would my servants fight that I should not be delivered to the Jews, but now is my kingdom not from hence' (John 18: 33–36). On the other hand when he was asked by the high priest whether he was the Messiah he confirmed that he indeed was (Mark 14: 63–64; Matthew 26: 63; Luke 22: 67). This is also clear from Jesus's dialogue with the Samaritan women. 'The woman said "I know that the Messiah is coming, when he comes he will explain everything to us." Then Jesus declared, "I who speak to you am he"' (John 4: 25–26).

Undoubtedly, Jesus's notion of his 'Messiahship' differed considerably from popular expectations. This may account for his reluctance to emphasize his Messiah title which the masses confused with the Deliverer. In Matthew 16: 20, Mark 8: 30 and Luke 9: 21 Jesus had explicitly warned his disciples not to tell anyone that he was the Deliverer. It was a delicate point to avoid any popular view that would have equated his messianic title with any militant significance. He emphasized that the Messiah should not be confused with the Deliverer because his mission had nothing to do with deliverance from Rome. More on this point will be explained under the 'Son of Man' title.

Jesus of Virgin Birth

It is of utmost peculiarity that Paul, the originator of Christianity, either did not believe in the virgin birth of Jesus or he knew nothing about it! Contradicting the virgin birth, Paul wrote: 'Jesus was made of the seed of David according to the flesh' (Romans 1: 3), meaning literally, not metaphorically.

It is no less surprising that John, in his gospel, is completely silent about and perhaps oblivious to the virgin birth. Mark, alone among the four evangelists, refers to Jesus as the 'son of Mary'. In Nazareth, Jesus's hometown, his audience are reported to have said about him: 'Is not this the carpenter, the son of Mary?' (Mark 6: 3). Mark's unique use of the 'son of Mary' title is strengthened by the absence, in his gospel, of any reference to Joseph. And this 'son of Mary' title is the only reference by Mark to an implied virgin birth. The point is also strengthened by the fact that, among the four, Mark's gospel was the first to have been written. Significantly, the Qur'an uses the title 'son of Mary' for Jesus in the sense that he was miraculously born from the Virgin Mary.

On the other hand, the gospels of Matthew and Luke present Jesus at once as of virgin birth, as the son of Joseph, and as the descendant of David through Joseph. While Matthew and Luke referred to the virgin birth in a confused manner, both in their eagerness to prove that Jesus was in fact a descendent of David fell into grotesque contradictions. To both of them the virgin birth is proof of Jesus's Messiahship. But at the same time they wanted the Messiah to appear as the descendant of David – son of David – to 'fulfil' Old Testament prophecies. It is not clear why the Church decided to canonize such writings as 'sacred scripture' while it upheld belief both in Jesus's miraculous birth and in the perpetual virginity of Mary!

Both Matthew and Luke wrote that Jesus was born in Bethlehem, but that he was brought up in Nazareth. Apart from that, the two gospels have completely different and divergent stories about the circumstances surrounding Jesus's nativity. Matthew begins his gospel by detailing what he deems as the 'genealogy' of Jesus, starting from Abraham. The genealogy ends with the statement: 'and Jacob begot Joseph the husband of Mary, of whom was born Jesus, who is called Christ' (Matthew 1: 16). In Matthew's mind, this would assure the passing to Jesus of the royal blood of David. Two paragraphs later he states that Mary was betrothed to Joseph, while both were living in Bethlehem. Mary found herself unexpectedly pregnant, and an angel assured Joseph in his dream that Mary's conception is from the Holy Spirit (Matthew 1: 18-20).

Luke has a different, but no less vague story. Both Mary and Joseph lived in Nazareth, a town in Galilee. Virgin Mary was pledged for marriage to the man named Joseph, of the house of David. Contrary to Matthew, Joseph's father is reported as Heli, and not Jacob. The angel Gabriel appears to Mary and tells of her impending pregnancy through the Holy Spirit (Luke 1: 26-37). However, in Luke 3, Luke reminds his readers of Jesus's ancestry: 'Jesus being (as was supposed) the son of Joseph which was the son of Heli' (Luke 3: 23). In order to assure us of Jesus's royal blood, Luke continues detailing the genealogy of Jesus passing through David and ending with 'the son of Seth, which was the son of Adam, which was the son of God', (Luke 3: 38). In what sense Adam is made to be a son of God is incomprehensible!

In summary, Matthew and Luke presented two genealogies that are peculiar, meaningless, superficial, fictional, and so wildly divergent that they are impossible to reconcile. According to Matthew, Jesus had twenty-six ancestors from David to Joseph. Luke lists forty-one of them between the two. And the only common name to these two lists between David and Jesus is Joseph! And this one, too, was no more than a *supposed* father. What is extremely baffling, is what one is supposed to surmise of such meticulously fabricated genealogies given the fact that Jesus was of virgin birth in the first place!

If the genealogies were to have any significance, however marginal, one would have to presume that Joseph was the father of Jesus. What sense is to be made then, of Mary's virgin conception given that both Matthew and Luke allude in their stories to the 'father of Jesus'? Matthew flatly states that 'Joseph, the husband of Mary, of whom was born Jesus', (Matthew 1: 16). The unavoidable question remains as to why Matthew and Luke wasted time in fabricating genealogies that were pointless, needless, and irrelevant, given their belief that Jesus was of virgin birth? Or did their anxiety to prove the fulfilment of 'prophecy' that Jesus had to inherit the throne of his 'father' David (Luke 1: 32) mean that they did not care about stumbling into blunders of whatever magnitude. Some may argue that the intention of the genealogies was purely symbolic with the only intention of assuring readers of Jesus's royal lineage, but this endeavour had resulted in a wild delusion.

Ironically, the objective of the genealogy fabrication was null and void from the beginning. Jesus himself had, categorically and unequivocally, denied being descended from David. All three synoptic gospels report Jesus to have said: 'How say the scribes that the Messiah is the Son of David? David himself calls him "Lord". How then can he be his son?' (Mark 12: 35–37; Matthew 22: 41–45; Luke 20: 41). Claims of Davidic ancestry for Jesus have nevertheless persisted, propelled by theological influences desiring to fulfil 'prophecies' and satisfy popular expectations. This in turn resulted in blunders and awkwardness in the New Testament.

Adding to the confusion and peculiarity of Matthew's 'genealogy of Jesus', is the unnecessary inclusion of four women in Matthew's list, who not only had no bearing on the ancestry, but had all been either harlots or adulteresses (Parrinder 1992 p. 2ff)! The four women are Tamar, Rahab, Ruth, and Bathsheba. Tamar is narrated in (Genesis 38) to have performed the role of a harlot when she seduced her father-in-law Judah – son of Jacob son of Isaac son of Abraham – to sleep with her. The twins Pharez and Zerah were conceived from the fornication. One of the twins, Pharez passed on the succession to his great-grandson David. The story of Rahab the harlot, who was to become the great-grandmother of David, is mentioned in Joshua 2. Boaz, son of the harlot Rahab, is also reported to have been seduced by the Moabite woman Ruth before their marriage (Ruth 3: 9). Boaz became the great-grandfather of David. David was said to have had an adulterous relation with Bathsheba, the wife of Uriah, one of David's commanders. Out of the adulterous relation was born Solomon. David is supposed to have conspired to kill Uriah, Bathsheba's husband, in order to retain Bathsheba for himself. (2 Samuel 11: 2-15). Stories of harlotry and incest in the Old Testament can be dealt with as a separate subject (see Kirsch 1999), but for our purpose, we can only wonder what one is supposed to make of the intrusion of harlots and adulteresses on an, initially, fabricated and superfluous genealogy of Jesus?

Contrary to stories of harlotry and incest in the Bible, one nobility of the Qur'an is that it exonerates all prophets from any charges of grave sin. The Qur'an does not, for example, impute to David the double crime mentioned above – fornicating with Bathsheba, then killing her husband Uriah – as claimed in the Jewish Bible, both crimes according to the Law of Moses punishable by death. It is inconceivable that David a Prophet-King should commit such crimes.

Jesus Having No Blood Brothers and Sisters

The sayings of Jesus concerning the brotherhood of his followers and members of his religious community must have been misinterpreted, or misrepresented. In the gospels, certain individuals are insinuated to be Jesus's *blood* brothers and sisters (Matthew 13: 55–56; Mark 3: 31; Luke 8: 19). This would appear to contradict the belief in the virgin birth, and the church claim of Mary's perpetual virginity. Some church fathers speculated that such brothers and sisters could have been Joseph's elder children from a previous marriage. Others have suggested that the brothers and sisters were actually cousins from another Mary, the wife of Cleopas, sister to the mother of Jesus! This is because the Greek word 'adelphos' – remember that gospels were first written in Greek – used for brother, could also mean cousin, friend, or common nationality (Parrinder 1992 p. 42). But Jesus had made it clear beyond any doubt that this brotherhood was symbolic: 'For whosoever shall do the will of God, the same is my brother, and my sister, and mother' (Mark 3: 35). 'And Jesus answered and said to them: my mother and my brethren are those which hear the word of God and do it' (Luke 8: 21). Incidentally these sayings of Jesus are another proof of his virgin birth in that he did not mention a father, only his mother.

When the fourth gospel narrated the story of Jesus's brethren urging him to go to Judaea, the reference to the brethren was obviously symbolic (John 7: 3, 5). In Acts, the Nazarenes of Jerusalem are depicted as brethren (Acts 1: 16; 9: 30), in the sense of being members of one religious community, having the same religious beliefs. Jesus also referred to the disciples as his brethren. When he appeared to Mary Magdalene and the other Mary near the Sepulchre, his 'burial place', he told them: 'Be not afraid, go tell my brethren [the disciples] that they go into Galilee, and there shall they see me" (Matthew 28: 10). Jesus was obviously referring to the disciples as his religious brethren, as is evident from Matthew 28: 9. Also, in John 20: 17, Jesus told Mary Magdalene: 'Go to my brethren [the disciples] and say unto them I ascend unto my Father, and your Father; to my God, and your God'. In Corinthians, Paul clearly referred to 'the brethren of the Lord' in a symbolic fashion meaning co-religionists (I Corinthians 9: 5).

In particular, the gospels of Matthew and Mark – though not of Luke – depict the famous 'James' as being the brother of Jesus. After the death of Jesus, this James became leader of the Jerusalem Nazarenes (Thomas 12; Galatians 2: 12). Paul, in his letter to the Galatians, referred to James as 'the brother of the Lord' (Galatians 1: 19). But this brotherhood of James need not be taken literally to mean a *blood* brother of Jesus, but rather symbolically, meaning a brother on account of James' piety, virtues, and doctrine. James had the reputation of being the most righteous of men, and in this particular respect he was perfectly fitted for the title 'brother of Jesus'. This opinion is corroborated by Origen, the Christian theologian (185–254 CE) who in his 'Contra Celsus' commented on the 'brotherhood' of Jesus and James stating: 'not so much of their blood relationship or having been brought up together, as because of James' virtues and doctrine'; meaning that this brotherhood was symbolic. In the Apocalypse of James discovered in Nag Hammadi we also read that James is a brother of Jesus in a purely symbolic sense (Robinson, J. 1990 p. 262; Wells 1999 pp. 52–53, 69; Eisenman 1997 pp. 142, 396).

In support of this, Pope John Paul II issued a statement in 1996 declaring that Jesus was the only child of Virgin Mary, meaning that Jesus did not have blood brothers and sisters irrespective of what the gospels may aver (Knight and Lomas 1998 p. 3).

Titles of the Mythical Jesus

Late Pauline Christology produced extravagant titles for Jesus, such as 'Son of God', 'Lord', 'Son of Man', and the 'Lamb of God'. Such titles emanated from Paul's faith that grossly underestimated Jesus's message on earth. It was *another Jesus* Paul was talking about (2 Corinthians 11: 4). In his own words, he insisted on not regarding Jesus according to the 'flesh', meaning that the Jesus who walked on this earth was of no importance. Instead, he wanted to know who the 'real' Jesus was, only to 'discover' a mythical Jesus that 'existed in the form of God' (Philippians 2: 6).

Paul's quest for a 'divine' Jesus exhausted all his effort. The Pauline Church after Paul followed suit, and the issue of the works and message of Jesus on earth were never realized, only theories about Jesus's identity, atonement, vicarious suffering, sacrificial death, and how the blood of the 'crucified' wiped out the transgressions of the faithful, and that 'Christ died for our sins' (I Corinthians 15: 3).

The 'Son of God'

One must always bear in mind the appellation 'Pauline' whenever the word 'Christianity' is mentioned. This is necessary because 'Christianity' in the public mind is directly related to the mission of Jesus the Messiah. Few people are aware that the terms 'Christian' and 'Christianity' are not related to Jesus, but rather to Paul alone.

One should also keep in mind that the prophetic mission of Jesus was intended as a reformist religious movement within Jewry: 'And when Jesus came – to his people – with all evidence of the truth, he said: "I have now come unto you with wisdom, and to make clear unto you some of that on which you are at variance, hence, be conscious of God, and pay heed unto me"' (Qur'an 43: 63). It is impossible that the most unJewish doctrines of the Council of Nicaea on divine son-ship could have emanated from the teachings of a Jewish prophet.

Reimarus (1694–1768), a German philosopher and theologian, wrote that Christian doctrines such as the Incarnation and the Trinity are not found in the teaching of Jesus, and that Jesus himself did not claim divine status. On the contrary, his claims remained within the bounds of human nature. Reimarus compared and contrasted the original belief of Jesus and his disciples, with doctrines that arose after the death of Jesus. He concluded that the new doctrines are unreliable and contradictory to Jesus's message (Vermes 1998 p. 212; Dawes 1999 p. 67).

Despite its Pauline influence, the New Testament does not support any claim of divine son-ship on the part of Jesus, later claimed for him by Pauline theology. His immediate disciples and followers, the Nazarenes, did not use this terminology, and if they did, it was merely in the context of Old Testament usage. For example when Jesus addressed his audience: 'Jesus said to them: "If God were your father, you would love me, for I came from God ... He sent me"' (John 8: 42). Son-ship of God meant something very different to believing Jews from what it meant to Hellenistic Christians.

In Old Testament terminology, every believing Jew was considered metaphorically a 'son of God'. This of course would not give Jesus the distinction of being *the* 'Son of God' as intended by Hellenistic Christianity. Kings of Israel were supposed to be 'sons of God'. God's promise to David is related to have been: 'I will be his father, and he shall be my son' (II Samuel 7: 14). And 'You [David] are my son, this day I have begotten you' (Psalms 2: 7). And 'I will make him [David] my firstborn, higher than the kings of the earth'

(Psalms 89: 27). This was clearly to the extent of affecting David's royal office insofar as he became king, obviously without affecting his human nature. Needless to say, neither David, nor any of his contemporaries dared claim any divine status for themselves. It would have amounted to outright blasphemy. Son-ship of God did not imply deity among Jews.

But in the Hellenistic mentality of the gentile world, the term 'son of God' took a dangerous turn towards paganism, to mean something like 'man-god' having a divine nature. In the Graeco-Roman world, charismatic figures such as kings and emperors were called 'gods' or 'man-gods' or 'sons of Zeus'. This was true for the Roman emperors who were deified from Julius Caesar onwards. It was also true for the Ptolemaic kings of Egypt who were, like Pharaohs, the 'sons of Helios' the sun-god. In the same Hellenistic fashion, Jesus was transformed into 'the Son of God' in a unique and divine sense, instead of 'son of God' like any other Jew. The use of 'Son of God' by both Paul and John fashioned Christianity in a Greek frame of mind.

In any case, Jesus never alluded to himself as 'son of God', let alone '*the* Son of God'. Examples where such claims are put on the mouth of Jesus (e.g. Matthew 11: 27; 24: 36; Mark 13: 32; Luke 10: 22) are clearly artificial and can safely be accredited to late Pauline influence. When asked by the high priest during his trial whether he was the Messiah the son of God, Jesus denied the title saying: 'You say that I am' (Luke 22: 70). In a variant they made him reply: 'I am' (Mark 14: 62), possibly meaning 'I am the Messiah' with the word 'Messiah' struck out. In Matthew, his reply is dubious: 'You said it' (Matthew 26: 64), possibly meaning a son of God as every other Jew in a non-unique sense. It is also possible that gospel writers or editors had intentionally phrased the question in an equivocal fashion in order to give the false impression that the Messiah and 'son of God' are one and the same. But Jesus must have been well aware of the pagan association that the title 'son of God' could have carried among the public, and for this reason he was very careful to avoid it.

Yet three centuries later, pagan Hellenism in the Council of Nicaea insisted on acclaiming Jesus as 'the only begotten Son of God, God of God, being of one substance with the father'. On this point, Professor Funk (1996 p. 295) had the following to say: 'It is understandable that the bishops gathered at Nicaea in 325 CE insisted on the full equality of Christ with the Father: anything less would have put him on a par with other royal figures who could boast of one divine parent. Jesus as the Christ had to be made co-equal with God for political if not for theological reasons. In that process, the iconoclast was transformed into the icon.'

The Nicene Creed contrasted sharply with 'Arianism', which was condemned and declared heretical at Nicaea. Bishop Arius of Alexandria believed that only the Father was God, and Jesus merely a man subordinate to the Father. Arianism, having spread throughout central Europe to northern Italy, Gaul, and Spain, ultimately disappeared under persecution.

The 'Lord'

Another most dubious title that had been ascribed to Jesus, is Paul's use of the title 'Lord': Greek *kyrios*, in the sense of a deified Jesus (Vermes 1998 p. 106). This Greek word is used in the Septuagint, the Greek translation of the Hebrew Bible, as the name of the Almighty God (the Jewish Tetragrammaton, the four-letter word, YHWH) (Vermes 1998 pp. 109–12; Funk 1996 p. 207; Maccoby 1998 p. 63). *Kyrios* is originally derived from pagan Hellenistic culture that applies it to Hellenistic 'man-gods', Roman emperor cult, and Hellenistic deities. Its use as a sign of divinity for humans, could not have been valid except in a pagan Hellenistic environment. To understand the 'Lord' title in a divine sense applied to Jesus is clearly a late Pauline innovation. It is impossible that Jewish expectations could have identified the Messiah with God. Jewish monotheism is wholly at variance with such belief.

In the synoptic gospels Jesus never attributed the lordship title to himself, nor did he accept such 'dignity' in the manner claimed by Paul. In the gospel of John however, the matter is different because John's gospel is theologically the most developed of the gospels. It was written as a clear mixture of pagan Hellenism and Jewish elements reflecting the evolution of the use and significance of the title 'lord', from a casual title to a divine significance. This is made clear in the intentional phrase put in the mouth of Thomas when addressing Jesus: 'My lord and my God', (John 20: 28) (see Vermes 1998 p. 127).

In the Palestinian Aramaic-speaking environment, the obvious and very common usage of 'lord' was an expression of courtesy. Especially when addressing people of authority, for example when one addresses his king or ruler or judge, or even a wife addressing her husband, or a child his father, etc (Vermes 1998 pp. 114ff.). In this sense, the title 'lord' is clearly not equivalent to the Greek *kyrios* of the pagan Hellenistic mystery religions. Examples of the use of 'lord' in the gospels may have represented the manner in which the disciples and followers of Jesus addressed their Master as a sign of respect. But such use was later transformed into the sense fancied by Paul, although it originally carried no reference to any divine 'lordship'. It is impossible that a Jew could address his prophet with the title 'lord' in the Greek sense of *kyrios*, nor is it possible for a prophet to accept this title in the Greek sense.

This of course does not preclude the use of the title 'Lord' by worshippers, when addressing God in prayer. In this case, God is 'the *only* Lord' and not just 'lord'.

Jesus, the Messiah

The 'Son of Man'

When reading the gospels, one cannot miss the fact that the appellation 'Son of Man' was never used as a vocative title for Jesus. Jesus's audience did not use it to address the Master, nor was it used, in conversation, by anyone else other than Jesus, except in rare situations and never vocatively. It was, almost always, Jesus only who talked about 'the Son of Man'. Furthermore, it is noted that Jesus used this title exclusively in the third person, most certainly not a reference to himself. While the appellation 'Son of Man' has, for centuries, perplexed church commentators and theologians, it seems a fact that Jesus's audience were quite familiar with its significance, reference, and meaning. None of Jesus's audience, as recorded in the gospels, who heard him speak about the 'Son of Man' raised any question about the identity of this 'Son of Man'. They must have known whom Jesus was alluding to. Even the Pharisees who were in the habit of pressing Jesus with 'embarrassing' questions, had nothing to say or inquire about this 'Son of Man' (Vermes 1998 p. 161). More details on the subject are presented in Chapter 7.

The 'Lamb of God'

The Jewish exodus from Pharaoh's Egypt, c.1213 BCE, was a most important event in Jewish history. According to the story in Exodus Ch. 12, Moses ordered his people to mark their doors with the blood of slaughtered lambs – the paschal lamb. In this manner, divine punishment that was to befall the Egyptians, would spare the Jews from destruction by passing over the marked doors, hence the word 'Passover'. The Jewish 'Passover' was later commemorated every year by the Jews on the fourteenth day of the month of Nisan. Thereafter, in early Jewish history, each Jewish family would sacrifice a lamb, on this occasion, to commemorate the Jewish Escape from Egypt.

But the ingenious mind of Paul, himself a Hellenistic Jew, was capable of drawing a queer parallel between the sacrificed Jewish Passover Lamb and the 'crucifixion' of Jesus. For Paul's innovative imagination, Jesus became the 'Paschal Lamb' sacrificed by God: 'For even Christ, our Passover [Lamb] has been sacrificed for us' (I Corinthians 5: 7). Thus started the Pauline Christian view of Jesus as the Lamb of God, who by his 'crucifixion', freed mankind from the bonds of sin.

The gospel of John, which surpasses all other gospels in its high degree of Christology, obviously drawing from Pauline influence, puts in the lips of John the Baptist the following phrase: 'Look, [at Jesus] the Lamb of God, who takes away the sin of the world' (John 1: 29). Undoubtedly, this phrase was artificially ascribed to the Baptist who died some twenty years before Paul invented his doctrine of divine sacrifice. It seems that the author of the fourth gospel wanted to insinuate that the Baptist was ahead of Paul in discovering the 'Lamb of God' title. Although this flatly contradicts the story of Matthew's gospel, where John the Baptist was not even aware of the gift of prophecy in Jesus. In Matthew's gospel, we are told that the Baptist learned about Jesus's mission only after the former was imprisoned, shortly before his execution. It is related that the Baptist sent two of his disciples to ask Jesus: 'Are you *that* [Prophet] who is to come? Or do we look for another one?' (Matthew 11: 2–3).

Taking into consideration that John's gospel was the last of the canonical gospels to have been written, about 110–30 CE, i.e. some 60 years after the death of Paul, it was imbued with elaborate Pauline theology. It clearly represents late theological developments towards advanced Hellenistic Church views. If John the Baptist had indeed the audacity to declare to the Jews: 'the Lamb of God, who takes away the sin of the world', he would have made a mockery of himself, or this could be have been understood to mean a mockery of Jesus. Alternatively, and if taken seriously, this declaration would have been tantamount to outright blasphemy, or simply insulting the people of Israel. What could be more repugnant and absurd to a pious Jew than substituting the sacrificial Passover lamb with a 'crucified' Messiah?

The Pauline concept of the 'Lamb of God' became the basis of the Christian Eucharist celebration on Easter Holiday – Passover Eve. Just as the Jews celebrate their Passover by slaughtering a paschal lamb, the Christian faithful celebrate, on Easter, the crucifixion of their 'Lamb' Jesus, eat his body, and drink his blood! That this celebration is a totally Pauline fabrication is born by the fact that drinking blood, even symbolically, is absolutely prohibited in the Jewish religion.

The 'Lamb of God' terminology was the outcome of Paul's obsession with the death of a mythical saviour, with whom he was 'communicating' through the 'Holy Spirit'. The teachings of the historical Messiah were completely unknown to Paul, and irrelevant in any case in view of the End of History scenario. Jesus was to return victorious in his imminent Second Coming to inaugurate the Kingdom of God on earth. His First Coming having been significant only from the moment of his crucifixion as 'Lamb of God'!

It is noteworthy, that Paul, in his Greek wording, used the Greek term '*pascha*' in relation to both Passover and Easter, whereas, only in later times was the distinction made between the Jewish Passover and the Christian Easter.

The Islamic View

One of the most interesting points in the Muslim understanding of the mission of Jesus, is the meaning Islam attaches to the appellation 'Nazarenes', with an ideological connotation, rather than geographical. We have already seen that the early followers of Jesus in Palestine were called 'Nazarenes', in contrast to Paul's converts in Hellenistic Antioch who were called Christians. Substantial confusion ensued for many who were/are incognizant of the ideological implication of the terms: (a) 'Christian' in its pagan Hellenistic implication, and (b) 'Nazarene' as relating to the mission of Jesus the Messiah.

While Pauline Christianity had been able to succeed and proliferate basing itself on a mythical Jesus of Pauline and later Nicene persuasions, in effect Christianizing the historical Jesus, we note that Islam, three centuries after the council of Nicaea, put things back in the right historical and ideological perspectives. A distinction was made clear between the historical personality of Jesus on one hand, and the Pauline mythical Chrestos on the other. It is interesting that Bible scholars, only fairly recently, moved in their research to disentangle Jesus the Messiah from Paul's Chrestos (Funk 1993).

Islam has rescued Jesus's mission from oblivion, uncovering layers of Hellenistic dogma and accretions that the Christian Church made in his name. Islam acknowledged Jesus as *the* awaited Messiah, a great prophet to the Children of Israel to confirm whatever truth still remains of the Torah, and call for the worship of God alone (Qur'an 3: 49–51). At the same time it refuted extravagant pagan Hellenistic titles bestowed on Jesus such as 'Son of God', 'Lord', 'Lamb of God', all presumed 'dignities' which Jesus himself would have rejected. From this view it is remarkable that Islamic beliefs agree with the most coherent parts of the gospels, while rejecting the most dubious and self-contradictory parts. This, evidently, is the meaning of the Quran verse: 'and determining what is true therein' (Qur'an 5: 48).

Much scholarly research trying to disentangle the historical Jesus from the mythical did not make use of the Qur'an to this end. Those who see no need for such an approach are described in the Qur'an as saying: 'Our hearts are already full of knowledge' (Qur'an 4: 155).

The quest for the historical Jesus can be substantially aided when conducted through the light of the last and final divine revelation which, by its advent, the religion of mankind has been perfected: 'Today have I perfected your religious law for you, and have bestowed upon you the full measure of My blessings, and willed that self-surrender unto Me – God – shall be your religion' (Qur'an 5: 3).

But those who believe themselves to be 'self-sufficient' can never achieve the end of their overweening self-conceit: 'For those who call God's messages in question, without having any evidence therefore, in their hearts is nothing but overweening self-conceit, which they will never be able to satisfy; Seek thou, then, refuge with God for verily, He alone is all-hearing all-seeing' (Qur'an 40: 56).

And since this arrogant 'self-sufficiency' is entirely illusory, those who build their world view on it, will never be able to fulfil objectives that are based on their arrogant assumptions. 'For when their apostles came to them with all evidence of the truth, they arrogantly exulted in whatever knowledge they – already – possessed; and – so in the end – they were overwhelmed by the very thing which they were wont to deride' (Qur'an 40: 83), i.e. by the very truth of God's existence, His Oneness, and inescapable judgement. For 'It is in this way that God sets a seal on every arrogant, self exalting heart' (Qur'an 40: 35), i.e. one's own free choice, condemns him to spiritual blindness (Asad 1984 pp. 727–28).

SEVEN

The Son of Man: Who Was He?

Have they then never tried to understand this word – of God –? Or has there – now – come to them something that never came to their forefathers of old? Or is it perchance, that they have not recognized their Apostle, and so they disavow him? (Qur'an 23: 69–70)

So that the followers of earlier revelation – the Bible – should know that they have no power whatever over any of God's bounty – i.e. divine revelation –, seeing that all bounty is in God's hand – alone –; He grants it unto whomever He wills, for God is limitless in His great bounty. (Qur'an 57: 29)

Definitions

Any reader of the Christian Bible must be familiar with the term 'Son of Man' repeated some 83 times in the discourses of Jesus. The question is of course: who is this 'Son of Man' to whom Jesus was referring? The Book of Psalms (8: 4–8) defines the Son of Man as Adam, the progenitor of humankind, quite literally the offspring of Adam (McGinn 2000 pp. 36, 289; Funk 1996 pp. 90ff.; Funk 1993 pp. 76–77). In Aramaic, Arabic, and Hebrew he is *ben Adam*, a generic term for a human being, metaphorically the human race. Another definition explaining, more specifically, the identity of the 'Son of Man' is found in the Book of Daniel. The Son of Man in Daniel is the heavenly figure who comes over the clouds of heaven to be presented to the Almighty, and is given everlasting dominion, glory, and a kingdom that shall not be destroyed, that all people, nations, and languages, should serve him (Daniel 7: 13–14). The Book of Daniel is the key scripture on the 'Son of Man', the Deliverer, who was to come and change the order of things.

There is no shortage in Jewish teachings, prophecies, and sacred writings pointing to the divine event of the coming into the world of a Saviour-

Deliverer. Jews wished that he would be of royal descent, a descendent from the Prophet-King David, and that he would save the Jews from their Gentile – non-Jewish – oppressors, who at one stage in history were the Romans. The triumph of the Deliverer over the oppressors was to be both military and spiritual (Vermes 1998 pp. 131, 134; Freke and Gandy 1999 pp. 202–04).

Notwithstanding the above, Church commentators on the NT gospels like to give the impression that Jesus in his many discourses about the 'Son of Man', was making an oblique reference to himself. This is in spite of the understanding that on the arrival of the Son of Man, the order of things was to be dismantled and replaced completely with a new age in which the Son of Man, the Deliverer, would come as King, a Prophet-King, i.e. with worldly power combined with spiritual power. On his advent, secular powers with all their polytheistic idolatrous practices and their acceptance of moral and sexual licence will then be brought to an end. Obviously, and contrary to expectations, this age of deliverance did not come to pass in Jesus's lifetime, nor in the lifetime of his Apostles. The Jews who were, at the time, the sole surviving monotheistic people on earth, did not triumph over the pagans of Rome. They were hoping for a national deliverer to redeem them from of the Roman legions and the Roman Empire.

Yet, gospel authors, in their eagerness to portray Jesus as the triumphant Deliverer Son of Man, have innovated a most artificial and baffling title for the story of his last visit to Jerusalem: 'The Triumphal Entry into Jerusalem', (Mark 11: 1–11; Matthew 21: 1–11; Luke 19: 28–38; John 12: 12–19). Yet Jesus's visit had nothing to do with triumph, nor any notion or intention to lead his people against Rome, or establish a new order, or perform any of the deeds expected from the Son of Man.

As Jesus could not, in fact, be identified with the Deliverer-Son of Man, as prophesied in Daniel, the title in the minds of Bible authors lost its militant association. The Pauline Church then laboured to transform the connotation of this powerful and military title into a purely internal concept. It sought refuge in symbolizing and mythologizing. In Pauline theology the Son of Man became very different from the conventional scriptural Warrior-King described in Daniel. Instead, Paul sought refuge in the 'Second Coming' scenario. Only in his 'Second Coming' would Jesus fulfil the functions of Daniel's Son of Man! Paul added that the Second Coming would not be too far into the future, but would come to pass during his own lifetime. Indeed, Paul was the first to devise this 'Second Coming' concept.

Howevr, Jesus, in his discourses, was almost always talking about the Son of Man in the third person, that he must have been referring obliquely to someone else other than himself. This is the only way that his discourses could have made sense. The German NT scholar Rudolf Bultman believed that Jesus had used the title 'Son of Man' to refer to another figure, an eschatological judge. Many contemporary biblical scholars are not convinced that Jesus was claiming the title for himself (McGinn 2000 pp. 36, 289).

If Jesus's reference to the Son of Man was realistic and confined to the realm of this world, his reference could have only meant the last of the Prophets, who was to come after him: Muhammad. This would match exactly the description of the Son of Man, the powerful Prophet-King mentioned in the Book of Daniel. Only Muhammad has combined soldierly prowess, with prophethood, righteousness, and holiness.

The Messiah is Not the Deliverer

The title 'Messiah', in the Hebrew sense, is different from 'Deliverer'. Jews who sought deliverance from their enemies believed that the Prophet would bring this deliverance to pass. The Deliverer is the Prophet Warrior-King who would lead his people in war, crush his enemies, and defeat Roman legions. Jewish Scriptures abound with prophecies about the advent of the Deliverer. He would come in the likeness of the Son of Man in Daniel, restore the temple in Jerusalem, defeat his enemies, and establish the Kingdom of God on earth, in which – and this the most important point – only God would be worshipped.

An orthodox Jew can never be satisfied with the Christian idea that Jesus was the Saviour or Deliverer. He can always point to the fact that prophecies were not fulfilled in Jesus as a deliverer. Jesus did not deliver the Jews from their oppressors, and did not defeat their enemies. Thus, with good justification, they reject the Christian belief that Jesus was the Saviour. To Jews and Muslims alike, Jesus was not to be identified with the Deliverer. But the Jews alone go a step further. They reject the Christian–Muslim belief that Jesus was indeed the Messiah.

On the other hand, the word Messiah – not synonymous with the Deliverer – means the anointed, the one chosen by God, in reference to the Jewish belief that God would raise up and anoint a Chosen One, who was to restore the religion of Moses to its pristine form. In John 1: 19–21 the distinction is made clear between the Messiah, and the Prophet-Deliverer (Vermes 1998 p. 137).

The Jews' denial of Jesus as the Messiah, was a direct result of the confusion between the two distinct personalities: the Messiah, and the Deliverer. The two titles are definitely *not* applicable to one and the same person, but to two prophets at two different times. The first title belonged to Jesus the Messiah, and the second belonged to the Prophet who was to come six centuries later, Muhammad, the Deliverer.

Jesus the Messiah and the Hellenistic Chrestos

In contrast with the Aramaic appellation 'Messiah', the word 'Christ', wrongly considered as the equivalent of the Messiah, or equivalent to the Deliverer, is a Greek word 'Chrestos' expressing some mythical deity of the Hellenistic type, a Greek hero cult (Maccoby 1998 p. 176; Schonfield 1997 p. 8). From the start of Paul's missionary activity, the word Chrestos – rather than Messiah – ascribed to Jesus, meant god in human disguise, redeemer and saviour from sins. To the Hellenists of the Graeco-Roman world, Christ meant someone similar to the Greek man-god Herakles, who reclaimed human souls from death; and similar to Mithras where the blood of the slain sacred bull was to wash the sins of the faithful; and similar to the popular Greek god Dionysus who in Greek mythology discards his divine nature and walks disguised among humans. In the Hellenistic world, Jesus the Messiah was slowly transformed into a Chrestos, Christ, a man-god who had descended from heaven incognito to accomplish a redemptive task relieving people from the burden of sin.

The Messiah, Elias, and the Prophet

The distinction between the two titles, the Messiah and the Prophet, was made very clear through the questions put to John the Baptist by a Jewish deputation of priests and Levites. The story is told in the fourth gospel: 'And this is the record of John [the Baptist], when the Jews sent priests and Levites from Jerusalem to ask him: who are thou? And he confessed and denied not, saying, I am not the Messiah. And they asked him, what then? Are thou Elias? And he said I am not. And they asked him: are thou *that Prophet* [the awaited Prophet]? And he answered, No. ... And they asked him: Why do you baptize then, if you are not *that* Messiah, nor Elias, nor *that* Prophet?' (John 1: 19–21, 25). The obvious implication is their expectation of three distinct personalities different from one another. To summarize, the expected trio were: Elias (i.e. Elijah expected to return at the end of time), *the* Messiah, and *the* final prophet – the seal of the prophets – who was to be similar to Moses (Deuteronomy 18: 18).

Both Matthew and Luke narrate the very significant story of John the Baptist while he was in prison. Having heard about the miracles of Jesus, John sent two of his disciples to ask Jesus: 'Are you *that* Prophet who is to come? Or shall we expect another one?' (Matthew 11: 2–3; Luke 7: 20). Clearly there was confusion in John's mind as to whether Jesus was *the* Messiah or *the* Prophet-Deliverer? Besides this confusion, the Baptist must have known for sure that two distinct persons were expected by the prophecies, and that the mission and function of each was different and distinct from the other. In summary, it is impossible that Jesus could have been simultaneously the Messiah and the Prophet, irrespective of how much Church commentators like to ignore this fact.

Jesus Denies Being the Deliverer

Jesus answered John's disciples: 'Go and show John again those things which you hear and see: the blind receive their sight, and the lame walk, the lepers are cleansed, the deaf hear, and the dead are raised up' (Matthew 11: 4–5). John knew very well that this range of miracles, however impressive, is not what was expected of the awaited Prophet (Wilson, A.N. 1992 p. 107). John's question simply meant: 'Are you *that* Prophet or aren't you? Are you the Deliverer? Are you the Prophet-King?' Jesus's reply clearly implied: 'I am the Messiah. But I am not the Deliverer, I am not the Saviour, I am not the Prophet-King who is to come'. Jesus had effectively denied that he was the Saviour-Deliverer-Prophet-King. Indeed, had John believed Jesus to be the Deliverer, the Prophet-King, he would not have needed to ask the question. But John had hoped that Jesus was something more than the Messiah. He was hoping that Jesus was *the Prophet*.

John was not alone in this hope. Even the disciples seemed to be confused. But Jesus continually, obliquely and politely was implying to his followers, on many occasions, not to expect him to play a role that was reserved for someone else. Jesus was not going to play the role that they expected from the Deliverer, because he himself was not the Deliverer. Jesus taught that in accepting the persecution, in making peace, in meekness, in repentance, in righteousness, and in seeking, the Kingdom of God was to come. His time was not ripe for the promised Age in which God's Kingdom on earth can truly materialize, in which God alone will be worshipped, and in which idolatry and paganism will be wiped out. Jesus prayed to God: 'Thy Kingdom come'. The phrase 'Kingdom of God' is very familiar in the Old Testament. There is no doubt that Jesus did teach his followers that 'the Kingdom' would materialize as an actual eventuality as prophesied in the Book of Daniel, but not in Jesus's time.

Jesus knew that he, as the Messiah, could perform miracles, but the Prophet was expected to do something else. The Prophet-Son of Man would be the Prophet-King, the Deliverer, who would inaugurate the new age. He would defeat his enemies and establish the Kingdom of God on earth. A role reserved for the Prophet *par excellence*, whom Jesus prophesied by name (Qur'an 61: 6), and who was to come six centuries later: Muhammad.

Sit Down, O Men of Israel

Jesus, at the beginning of his ministry, took his headquarters at Capernaum, a village by the Sea of Galilee. Capernaum was a small commercial town with mixed population including Roman government officials (Schonfield 1994 p. 81). It was not the sort of place an insurgent or conspirator or disgruntled leader would want to use as a base against ruling authorities. On the contrary it was a good base for pacification and urging restraint.

Jesus never claimed to have been the Deliverer. He was not destined to deliver his people from Roman occupation nor was he destined to restore the Kingdom of David. During his short ministry, there had not been the slightest remark or hint in Jesus's discourses, nor in his planning or actions, that would lend any support whatsoever to the purported claim of his role as a Deliverer. For this reason Jesus never advocated confrontation. On the contrary most of his instructions were intended to pacify the zealots and the rebellious Galileans who were longing to evict the Romans from Palestine. Jesus was continually warning them against uprising or taking the law into their hands. He told them 'Love your enemies', 'Resist not evil, 'Whosoever smite you on the right cheek turn to him the other one. And whosoever shall force you to go a mile go with him two'. He had frankly and intentionally warned his people, the Jews, against violence, rebellion, and retaliation (Dawes 1999 p. 60).

In the discourses of Jesus, we cannot miss his repeated denials of being the Deliverer. On one significant occasion he restrained a crowd of five thousand. This was the occasion when he performed his famous miracle of the loaves (John 6: 5–14). 'Make the men sit down' Jesus told his disciples, referring to the five thousand men who, hoping that Jesus was the Deliverer, had followed him to Galilee. 'Now there was much grass in the place. So the men sat down, in number about five thousand' (John 6: 10). The clue to the meaning of this story is very significant. Jesus's message to his people the Jews was simply: 'Sit down, O men of Israel' (Wilson, A.N. 1992 pp.161–63). There was an obvious practical implication. Jesus had warned the men against thinking that the time was ripe for yet another military uprising against the Romans. Lest they think that Jesus was going to be their military leader, or their Deliverer and saviour from oppression, Jesus made them sit down and eat a miraculous meal. He wanted to impress upon the men that the time had not yet come for the advent of the Deliverer. He warned them against violence that would only bring self-ruin. While he preached to them a Kingdom that was yet to come after his age, a Kingdom he was not destined to lead, they were hoping that he would be their immediate Deliverer, a military leader against the Romans. They were under the illusion that he was the Prophet-Deliverer, something which Jesus tried to dissuade them off.

Jesus's message to the people of Israel was simple and concise: 'sit down'. Jesus was not the Deliverer, and he did not teach that he was the Deliverer. He emphasized that the Kingdom of God was yet to come. Only in this fashion, can his prayer: 'Thy Kingdom come' be comprehended. The group of men that Jesus addressed was representative of the rebellious people of Israel. They were adamant and unable to get the message. On the contrary, they may have confirmed their own delusion when they said: 'This is of truth *that* Prophet that should come into the world' (John 6: 14).

'When Jesus therefore perceived that they would come and take him by force, to make him a king, he departed again into a mountain himself alone' (John 6: 15). Unable to convince such self-serving mentality of his true mission, and lest they take him for a worldly king, Jesus had to flee them and go into hiding.

It was an alarming and catastrophic feature of Jesus's mission that his denial of any militant aspirations on his behalf, and his many attempts to counter such expectations on the popular level, failed to be accepted, both by his own people, and by the Pauline Hellenists of the Roman Empire after his death. There was persistent confusion between 'Deliverer' and 'Messiah'. Such confusion resulted in utter failure to appreciate the significance of Jesus's mission, and to accept it on its own merits, a failure that resulted in calamitous effects both in Palestine and in the Hellenistic world. Not only did the majority of Jews in Palestine reject Jesus's Messianic mission, but they also persisted in their insurgency culminating in the catastrophic results of the years 70 CE and 135 CE. In turn, the Nazarenes, the followers of Jesus, were dispersed and with time they lost control of events. Internationally, in the Graeco-Roman world, the messianic message of Jesus completely went off-course, and was replaced by a new mystical religion invented by Paul. Paul insisted that Jesus was indeed a deliverer and saviour, but only in a mystical and mythological sense. Pauline Hellenists continued to believe that he would very soon come back as a Deliverer to militarily prevail over his enemies as Paul himself prophesied. Such pattern of prophecies and expectations – although proved a failure by events – was repeated by John the Seer who wrote his Revelation a few years after Paul's death (Vermes 1998 p. 155). The world had to wait another six hundred years for the message of Jesus to prevail again with the advent of Islam.

The Coming of the Kingdom

Jesus's so-called 'triumphal entry' into Jerusalem occurred sometime after the miracle of the loaves. The point that is conspicuous in Jesus's 'triumphal entry' is twofold. First, Jesus had just fled the rebellious men of Israel who wanted to make him king. Second, Jesus, the supposed 'King', entered Jerusalem on a donkey, the obvious implication is that he was coming as a pacifist with no intention to establish a kingdom of power. He intentionally rode a donkey symbolizing to the people that his, was not a kingdom of worldly power, but a kingdom of conciliation and peace (Wilson, A.N. 1992 pp. 176–77). Nevertheless, the crowds maintained the illusion that he was coming as a Deliverer, a Prophet-King. People gathered around him shouting: 'Blessed be the kingdom of our father David that comes in the name of the Lord' (Mark 11: 10). 'Hosanna, the son of David' (Matthew 21: 9), meaning save us O son of David, even though he had explicitly denied being a descendent of David (Mark 12: 35–37; Matthew 22: 41–45; Luke 20: 41).

Jesus's entry on a donkey, was another attempt on his side to try to pacify the Jews, warning them that they were bringing destruction upon themselves. It was the same message he told them during the miracle of the loaves, demanding the fighting people of Israel to sit down. Having entered Jerusalem, Jesus did no more than go into the temple, look around, and then leave with the twelve (Mark 11: 11). The triumphal entry into Jerusalem was no more than a symbolic gesture implying a call to peace rather than military triumph.

The Jews were of the belief that the coming of the Kingdom of God on earth was at hand, and that it was going to be their own worldly kingdom. Moreover they believed that they could hasten its coming through their own efforts. But Jesus must have known for certain that the time was not ripe for the coming of the Kingdom. He had urged his people to pay tribute to Caesar (Mark 12: 17). He had overturned the money changers tables at the temple (Mark 11: 15), symbolizing that Jerusalem and the temple would be overturned if the Jews failed to abandon usury and mend their ways. For one thing, moneychangers in the temple were exploiting the poor by extracting exorbitant usury.

Jesus must have known for sure that any Jewish rebellion against the Romans would be not merely futile but disastrous. Unless the Jews abandoned their opposition to the Romans, Jerusalem and the temple would be destroyed. A nation infected with corruption can not hope to master its destiny. In an answer to a question by one of the disciples, Jesus replied: 'Do you see these great buildings [in Jerusalem]? There shall not be left one stone upon another that shall not be thrown down' (Mark 13: 2; Matthew 24: 2). There is no doubt that Jesus, in his prophetic vision, must have foreseen the failure of the Jews to accept his mission. Such a failure was to entail the devastation of Jerusalem and the dispersion of the Jewish people.

Jesus knew very well that the Jewish nation was worthy no more to play a role in the coming of the Kingdom: 'O faithless and perverse generation, how long shall I be with you, and suffer you?' (Luke 9: 41). 'Jesus said to them: "If

God were your father, you would love me, for I came from God; neither came I of myself but He sent me. Why do you not understand my speech? Because you are unable to hear what I say. You are of your father the devil, and the lusts of your father you will do'" (John 8: 42–44). 'O Jerusalem, thou that kills the prophets, and stones them which are sent unto thee' (Matthew 23: 37). 'O generation of vipers how can you, being evil, speak good things?' (Matthew 12: 34). Long before Jesus, Jeremiah stood at the gate of the temple and proclaimed to them: 'Will you steal, murder, and commit adultery, and swear falsely, and burn incense unto Baal, and walk after gods whom you know not ... is this house [temple] ... become a den of robbers' (Jeremiah 7: 9–11). Stephen the Martyr – a Nazarene from Jerusalem – told the Sanhedrin during his trial: 'You stiff necked and uncircumcised in heart and ears! As your fathers did so you do! Which of the Prophets have not your fathers persecuted? And they have slain them who predicted the coming of the Just One' (Acts 7: 51–52).

On this point the Qur'an states: 'Those of the Children of Israel who were bent on denying the truth have – already – been cursed by the tongue of David and of Jesus son of Mary, this, because they rebelled – against God – and persisted in transgressing the bounds of what is right' (Qur'an 5: 78). (See for example Psalms 78: 21–22, 31–33, and *passim*)

Another Qur'an verse on the same point: 'And indeed we vouchsafed the divine writ unto Moses, and some of his people set their own views against it, and had it not been for a decree that had already gone forth from thy Lord, judgement would indeed have been passed on them – then and there – for they were in grave doubt amounting to suspicion about it' (Qur'an 11: 110). One example of their grave doubt, amounting to suspicion about the divine writ, is the Saducees' disbelief in the hereafter (Matthew 22: 23; Mark 12: 18; Luke 20: 27; Acts 23: 8). Indeed the Hebrew Bible in its entirety, with the exception of Daniel (12: 2), lacks reference to life after death. The reference in the Qur'an to God's decree implies deferring punishment to the Day of Judgement, thus giving people a chance to repent in this world.

The failure of the Jews to accept the concept of immortality can be linked to its incompatibility with their purely materialistic outlook. Their religious belief therefore remained shallow because of their nationalistic chauvinist views and their earthbound interests (Izetbegovic 1989 p. 188; Sanders 1993 p. 44; Asad 1984 p. 763).

The objective of Jesus's mission was threefold. The Jews urgently needed religious, social, and moral reform. This was the first and most urgent objective of Jesus Messianic mission. On this point Thomas Jefferson, the third US President wrote: 'Jesus was sensible of the incorrectness of his forbears' ideas of the Deity, and of morality. He endeavored to bring them to the principles of a pure deism, and juster notions of the attributes of God, to reform their moral doctrines to the standard of reason, justice and philanthropy, and inculcate the belief of a future state.' (Jefferson Bible in Sanders 1993 p. 7; see also Dawes 1999 p. 68).

A Jewish scripture called II Maccabees records that the Jerusalem temple was transformed into a Greek temple to Zeus and festivals to Dionysus celebrated therein. The history of integration of Jewish and pagan practices went on for centuries. Ancient Jewish history is characterized by repeated relapses into idolatry (Rhymer 1996 pp. 39, 49; Freke and Gandy 1999 pp. 177–78). On this point the Qur'an quotes the Prophet Elijah addressing the Children of Israel: 'Will you invoke Baal and forsake – God – the Best of Creators' (Qur'an 37: 125). Baal in the OT has sometimes the generic connotation of idol worship, a sin into which according to the Bible the Israelites often relapsed (Asad 1984 p. 689).

Second, Jesus had to warn the Jews about the coming calamity that was to befall them if they persisted in their intransigence and armed rebellion. His third objective was to proclaim to them the Kingdom of God that was to come: 'Therefore I say unto you, The Kingdom of God shall be taken from you, and given to a nation bringing forth the fruits thereof' (Matthew 21: 43). Corruption had infected the Jews beyond reform and the burden of monotheism, the divine message, was to be taken away from them and given to their brethren the sons of Ishmael (Deuteronomy 18: 18–19). But they failed to comprehend Jesus, and they failed to respond to his message. They were so lost beyond reform that Jesus had to tell them: 'I have yet many things to say unto you, but you can not bear them now' (John 16: 12).

Jesus therefore ordered the Jews to sit down; sit down O men of Israel; with the divisions among yourselves, with your materialistic priestly hierarchy – the Sadducees – not believing in the hereafter, with the inroads idolatry had made within you, with your rejection and killing of the Prophets, with corruption infecting your society, armed rebellion will not do, you will only reap destruction upon yourselves (Wilson, A.N. 1992 pp. 187–88). To put it simply and clearly: they were neither destined nor fit to bring about the coming of the Kingdom. This was the essence of Jesus's message to them. Jesus had come as the last of the Jewish great prophets to reform the Jewish religion, and give his people their last chance. Thus the Qur'an states: 'For had We inflicted a penalty on them before a divine writ was revealed to them they would have said: "Our Lord! If only Thou had sent us an apostle, we should certainly have followed Thy signs before we were humbled and put to shame"' (Qur'an 20: 134).

But the three-fold message of Jesus fell on deaf ears. He was not the first Jewish prophet to have been rejected by his people. Moses had once told them: 'You have been rebellious against the Lord from the day I knew you' (Deuteronomy 9: 24). Not only did the Jewish majority reject Jesus, but they officially deemed his followers the Nazarenes as 'heretics'. 'He [Jesus] came unto his own [people], but his own received him not' (John 1: 11). Simultaneously, Paul's religion, which took root on the Hellenistic stage, was not declared heretical in spite of its Hellenistic beliefs.

The Son of Man

Churches commentators, almost without exception, like to pretend that Jesus, whom they believe to have been 'the Son of God', had taken the appellation 'Son of Man' out of humility and meekness. Although most of them know fully well that the Jewish apocalyptic scriptures foretold a 'Son of Man' who would be strong with tremendous power to protect his people and destroy his enemies; and not someone who would be meek, humble, with nowhere to lay his head, or delivered to his enemies to be 'killed'. Jesus was fully aware that he was not the expected 'Son of Man', and had he appropriated the title 'Son of Man' for himself, as church commentators pretend, his learned audience would have lost credibility in him. On the contrary, Jesus never contended for the royal throne of David, and never intended to lead his people the Jews against Rome. The learned Jews who heard Jesus speaking about 'the Son of Man' fully understood to whom he was alluding. Jesus did not invent this title but borrowed it from Jewish apocalyptic scriptures, and in particular from the Book of Daniel (Daniel: 7), and the Book of Ezekiel (1: 26; 10: 2). And for this reason his Jewish audience had no doubt about the identity of the Son of Man (Dawud 1990 p. 171; McGinn 2000 p. 289; Dawes 1999 p. 138).

When Jesus referred to his own 'lift up' to heaven, his Jewish audience asked him: 'Our Law teaches us that the Messiah abides *forever*, how do you say that the Son of Man must be lifted up? *What Son of Man is this?*' (John 12: 34). It is likely that this question was altered in favour of later Church views that the Messiah was the Son of Man. Or there may have been ambiguity in some minds confusing the identities of the Messiah and the Deliverer. The question of the audience can make sense only if the word 'Messiah' is replaced by the word 'Deliverer'. Furthermore, the question implies that the 'Deliverer' and 'the Son of Man' are one and the same. According to Jewish belief, the Deliverer, i.e. his message, shall continue and abide forever – being the final revelation to humankind. The audience were thus wondering what kind of 'Son of Man' is he, whose message is unable to continue 'intact' forever?

It is impossible that Jesus could have appropriated the title 'Son of Man' or 'Deliverer' to himself, simply because he was unable, in the least bit, to perform any of the functions the 'Son of Man' was supposed to have. Had Jesus claimed to be the 'Son of Man' and then urged his people to pay tribute to Caesar

(Mark 12: 17), and declare to them that he had nowhere to lay his head (Matthew 8: 20), and that deliverance would have to be postponed indefinitely, he would have fallen into grotesque contradictions.

A learned Jewish man, a scribe, followed Jesus and said to him 'Master, I will follow you wherever you go', to which Jesus replied: 'The foxes have holes, and the birds of the air have nests, but the Son of Man has nowhere to lay his head' (Matthew 8: 19–20). If Jesus had a place for thirteen heads – twelve disciples plus himself – he certainly could have found a place for the fourteenth. Or he could have allowed the scribe to join his 70 other followers (Luke 10: 1), especially since the new follower was a learned scribe whose sincerity was almost certain. But Jesus knew that the scribe was misled. He was led to believe that Jesus was the awaited 'Son of Man', the Deliverer, who at any time would mobilize his earthly and heavenly forces to defeat pagan Rome and establish the Kingdom of God on earth. But Jesus had obviously perceived the erroneous notion of the scribe and gently and subtly explained to him that he who had no place to lay his head, could not be the powerful 'Son of Man'. He did not want to be harsh with the scribe, but only to rid him kindly of his fanciful and futile hopes (Dawud 1990 pp. 175–76).

To literally understand that 'the Son of Man shall be betrayed unto the chief priests, and that they shall condemn him to death' (Matthew 20: 18), is to mock all Jewish aspirations. Alternatively, and more correctly, this statement is tantamount to confessing that Jesus himself was not the awaited Son of Man. It must be understood in the following sense: If I were the Son of Man, then how is it possible that I be betrayed unto the chief priests and scribes to be condemned to death? Jewish aspirations were for a 'Son of Man' who would be given everlasting 'dominion, glory, and a kingdom that shall not be destroyed, that all people, nations, and languages, should serve him' (Daniel 7: 13–14).

Jesus had explicitly warned his disciples not to tell anyone that he was the Deliverer. To make sure, he asked his disciples the question: 'Whom do men say that the Son of Man is?' (Matthew 16: 13; Mark 8: 27; Luke 9: 18). Of course Jesus's question about the 'Son of Man' was not an oblique reference to himself, as Christian theologians would like us to believe, but a reference to the Deliverer who was to come six centuries after him. 'Then he [Jesus] warned his disciples not to tell anyone that he was the Messiah' (Matthew 16: 20; Mark 8: 30; Luke 9: 21). This warning in the synoptic gospels can make sense only if the word 'Messiah' is replaced by the word 'Deliverer'. In other words, the Deliverer equals the Son of Man.

It is impossible that Jesus did not want his people to know that he was the Messiah, because he was indeed the Messiah. His whole mission was in his capacity as the awaited Messiah. But Jesus was keen that people should not mistake him for the Deliverer, because he was not the Prophet-King that many of his contemporaries hoped he would be. He was not a pretender for the royal throne of David, nor was he planning to lead an insurgency against Rome. He never said, directly or indirectly, that he was the Deliverer. Jesus was the Prophet-Messiah, but not the Prophet-King (Vermes 1998 p. 152ff.; Dawes 1999 p. 138).

When, in spite of Jesus's explaining his real identity to the disciples, Peter remained under the illusion that his Master was the awaited Prophet warrior-king, Jesus instantly rebuked him. 'He [Jesus] turned and said unto Peter, Get thee behind me, Satan: thou are an offence unto me', (Matthew 16: 23; Mark 8: 33) (Vermes 1998 p. 147; Halshell 1986 pp. 61–62). Once more at the garden of Gethsemane, when Jesus was about to be arrested, Peter struck out with his sword, cutting off the ear of the servant of the high priest, only to be rebuked by Jesus. 'Then Jesus said unto him, put up thy sword into its place, for all they that take the sword shall perish by the sword' (Matthew 26: 52). Thus, Jesus told Peter in plain words that it was not up to the Messiah to take the role of a military leader. During the trial of Jesus trial he was asked by the high priest about his Messianic title to which Jesus replied, 'I am [the Messiah], and you shall see the Son of Man sitting on the right hand of power, and coming in the clouds of heaven' (Mark 14: 62). Jesus was identifying himself clearly as the Messiah, but referring to the Son of Man in the third person – obviously not himself. He was telling the high priest that the Son of Man was to come after him so as to vindicate him from the charges of his enemies, and disentangle him from the mythical Christ of Paul.

On another significant occasion, Jesus called the Son of Man 'Lord of the Sabbath': 'For the Son of Man is Lord even of the Sabbath day' (Matthew 12: 8; Mark 2: 28). The sanctity of the seventh day is very important in the Law of Moses. The fourth Decalogue orders the people of Israel to 'Remember the Sabbath day to keep it holy' (Exodus 20: 8). But the priests took the Sabbath sanctity to extremes. Men, woman, children, and slaves, even domestic animals were to refrain from all labour under the penalty of death. No cooking, no walking, even charity was not allowed on the Sabbath. The Pharisees went to the extent of reproaching Jesus for miraculously healing a man's arm on the Sabbath (Matthew 12: 10). But Jesus did not adhere to literal interpretations of the draconian ordinances on the Sabbath. At the same time he never thought of abrogating it, nor could he have ventured to do so, had he desired, in the face of Jewish opposition. It was only in later generations that Hellenistic Christians gradually substituted Sunday instead of Saturday. Whereas the Nazarenes continued observing the Sabbath, the Eastern Churches observed both days until the end of the fourth century.

If Jesus was 'Lord of the Sabbath' he would have either modified its draconian laws, or abolished it in its entirety. He did neither one nor the other.

Indeed it was impossible for him to do that. There is no doubt that the Jews who heard him declare: 'the Son of Man is Lord even of the Sabbath day' (Matthew 12: 8), knew perfectly well that he was alluding to the awaited Prophet-Deliverer as Lord of the Sabbath. But editors of the gospels, here as elsewhere, had manipulated the text to make the reference to the Son of Man – in the third person – intentionally seem ambiguous, enigmatic and incomprehensible. When for example Jesus was speaking about priests who profane the Sabbath in the temple, he was reported to have said, 'But I say unto you, that in this place is *one* greater than the temple' (Matthew 12: 6). Whereas this phrase can only make sense if read as follows: 'in this place *there will be one* greater than the temple' alluding to the Son of Man who was to come. This is the only way that his audience could have understood and accepted what he said (Dawud 1990 p. 176).

The 'Son of Man' who was indeed greater than the temple, as prophesied by Jesus, visited the temple six hundred years after him: 'Limitless in His glory is He who transported His servant – Muhammad – by night from the Inviolable House of Worship – at Mecca – to the remote House of Worship – at Jerusalem –' (Qur'an 17: 1). Not only did the Prophet visit the Temple during his famous night journey to Jerusalem – Al-Isra'a – but this was also followed by the spectacular triumph of Islam after him. The Muslims liberated Jerusalem from the Roman yoke a mere four years after Muhammad's death, and established, physically not metonymically, the long-awaited Kingdom of God on earth. The Kingdom of God that Jesus had so often longed for in his prayers: 'Thy Kingdom come'. It was the Kingdom that has in fact materialized with the advent of Islam, in which God alone is worshipped.

The 'Son of Man' Foretold by Jesus: the Islamic Perspective

Jesus is reported to have said: 'Among them that are born of women there has not risen greater than John the Baptist, but the least in the Kingdom of God is greater than John' (Matthew 11: 11; Luke 7: 28). For centuries this saying has baffled Christian interpreters. Some have seen in it a contrast between the future of the elect, and the greatness of John on earth. Others have understood the kingdom as the spirits' realm of the followers of Jesus, compared with the earthly world of John. Others understood the least to be Jesus himself as the servant of God. But it is impossible that Jesus could have been referring to himself because the Kingdom of God on earth did not materialize during his lifetime. Even if it did, he could not have been the least in it, because he would have been its founder.

The Son of Man: Who Was He?

The key to interpreting this saying of Jesus should be the word 'least'. In Aramaic, Arabic, and Hebrew, the word 'least' or the 'smallest' carries a chronological significance, meaning: 'chronologically last', the youngest in a series, the junior of a group (Vermes 1998 pp. 32–33). The word *'z'eira'* in Aramaic, like the word *'zaghir'* in Arabic signifies 'small or young'. The Aramaic version of the Christian Bible – the Peshitta – uses the word *'z'eira'* for 'least'. Christians will admit that Jesus was not the 'last' prophet and therefore he could not have been the 'least'. Who, then, in the long series of prophets could the 'least' be, other than Muhammad? He is definitely and indisputably the last of the prophets, he is chronologically the youngest among them, yet he is the greatest compared to any one of them. He is the 'Benjamin' of the prophets, yet he is their greatest (Dawud 1998 p. 128). For the gigantic work accomplished by the last and seal of the prophets is greater than the work accomplished by all the prophets before him put together (Hart 1992).

The Sibylline Revelation, which was compiled after the collapse of Jerusalem in 70 CE, states that the Son of Man will appear and destroy the Roman Empire, and deliver the believers in the One and only God. This book was written at least 80 years after the death of Jesus. The Sibylline prophecy materialized six centuries later, with the advent of Muhammad the last of the prophets, the powerful Son of Man whose followers had indeed removed the Roman yoke from those who believed in the One and Only God. The Muslims had vindicated the Nazarenes, the early followers of Jesus, the believers in the One God, in the face of the artificial theology of the Pauline Church, the Nicene Creed, and other ecumenical councils' creeds. Later, the final blow to the last of the Romans, the Byzantines, came in 1453 CE, with the fall of Constantinople to the Ottoman Muslims led by Muhammad the conqueror (Schonfield 1997 pp. 59, 112–13; Dawud 1998 p. 173).

The importance of including the perspective of Islam in biblical research, with the Prophet Muhammad as the object of prophecies, can not be overemphasized. Otherwise, attempts to find the truth of the scriptures and arrive at a satisfactory conclusion on Jesus's mission can be in vain. Many research pursued by scholars, or 'neutral' writers, is cold or sceptical. Many do not appreciate the fact that whatever truth remains in ancient scriptures, can only be identified and understood in the light of the Qur'an. Research has so far concentrated on studying Jewish and Christian scriptures while for the most part ignoring the Qur'an, and therefore by necessity ending up with scepticism and bitterness. Scriptural contradictions and discrepancies can be reconciled only if one includes the Qur'an in one's studies. Only then is it possible to sift the genuine from the spurious, and only then can Jewish and Christian scriptures make sense in whatever truth remains in them, and only then will the true sayings of Jesus be seen in their proper perspective.

Jesus told his people that the burden of the divine message was to be taken from the line of David: 'And Jesus answered and said, while he taught in the temple: How say the scribes that the Deliverer is the son of David? for David himself [in spirit] calls him lord. How then is he his son?' (Mark 12: 35, 37; Matthew 22: 41–45; Luke 20: 41). This statement has a double meaning: first that the Deliverer will not be from the line of David, and second, that contrary to popular expectation, Jesus himself was not the Deliverer even though they hailed him as the son of David.

Without any ambiguity, Jesus said that the burden of carrying the divine message, the message of monotheism, was to be given to another nation (Matthew 21: 43). He had prophesied that the 'Son of Man' will be the Prophet who was to come from among their brethren as stated in Deuteronomy. God promised a Prophet like Moses: 'I will raise them up a Prophet from among their brethren, like unto thee, and will put my words in his mouth, and he shall speak unto them all that I shall command him. And it shall come to pass that whosoever will not hearken unto my words which he shall speak in my name, I will require it of him' (Deuteronomy 18: 18–19).

The Jews had been the chosen people of God until the advent of their last great prophet, Jesus the Messiah, who gave them their last chance for reform and repentance. Having rejected their last prophet they consequently lost this burden-privilege. The burden was therefore moved to their brethren the Arabs, descendants of Ishmael son of Abraham. The term 'chosen people' signifies those people chosen by God to receive and bear the burden of the divine message. It does not imply any superiority or any racial privileges over other nations. Only that the 'chosen people' were given a unique task to fulfil. Obviously, this would put them on a higher degree of responsibility, and therefore accountability. The term 'chosen people' does not imply any notion of nationality, race, or ethnic entity, but includes all people who accept Islam, of whatever origin they may be. Thus the Qur'an states: 'And thereupon We made you – O Muslims – their successors on earth, so that We might behold how you act' (Qur'an 10: 14), i.e. whether you act justly or not.

The task of carrying the message of God's Oneness and uniqueness to other nations was withdrawn from the Children of Israel as they came to believe that they were God's 'chosen people' in a preferential sense because of their descent from Abraham, Isaac and Jacob. They also came to believe the divine message to be theirs only, and not for other nations. One consequence was that they denied any possibility of prophethood bestowed on anyone not belonging to the children of Israel, irrespective of idolatry and corruption infecting the latter. They corrupted the divine writ bestowed on Moses, and were unable to derive benefit from it, nor to live up to its standard. 'The parable of those who were graced with the burden of the Torah, and thereafter failed to bear this burden, is that of an ass that carries a load of books – but clearly can not benefit therefrom –' (Qur'an 62: 5). Having rejected Jesus as *the Messiah*, they later rejected Muhammad *the Prophet*, despite clear predictions of his advent in their scriptures (Deuteronomy 18: 15–18).

The Qur'an clearly spells out the prophecy of Jesus about the advent of Muhammad: 'And remember, Jesus, the son of Mary, said: "O Children of Israel! I am the Messenger of Allah – sent – to you, confirming the Law – which came – before me, and giving Glad Tidings of a Messenger to come after me, whose name shall be Ahmad." But when he came to them with Clear Signs they said, "This is evident sorcery!"' (Qur'an 61: 6). The Glad Tidings on the coming of the Prophet is exactly the meaning of the term 'gospel' or the Evangel (Dawes 1999 p. 70). As for the names Ahmad and Muhammad, they are alike and have the same connotation, meaning 'the highly praised one'.

The Son of Man came six centuries after Jesus to reverse the failure of the latter's mission into success:

> O you who have attained to faith! Be helpers – in the cause of – God, as Jesus the son of Mary, said to the white-garbed ones – the disciples –: 'Who will be my helpers in God's cause? – my Nazarenes –, Whereupon the white-garbed ones – the disciples – replied: 'We are – your – helpers – in the cause of – God!' And so it happened that a portion of the Children of Israel believed – in the prophetic mission of Jesus –, whereas others denied the truth, but – now – We have given power to those who believed, against their foes, and they became the ones that shall prevail. (Qur'an 61: 14)

The implication is that the Muslims are the only people who acknowledged the truth of the prophetic mission of Jesus, and so the power to prevail had been given to them. Obviously, prevailing is understood in the context of the basic tenets of the Qur'an, that is through reason, logic, and free intellect, quite far from of rigid dogma, coercion and persecution.

The mission of the Son of Man was to be universal bearing the final Divine Revelation to all humankind: 'And thus We have willed you – Muslims – to be a community of the middle way, so that – through your lives – you might bear witness to the truth before all mankind, and that the Apostle might bear witness to it before you' (Qur'an 2: 143). Bearing witness to the truth is the sole justification for the presence of the Muslim community, devoid of any notion of chauvinism, hegemony, or intolerance.

Nevertheless, the People of the Book held on to the belief that divine revelation and prophecy is their prerogative alone to the exclusion of all other peoples. Something that the Qur'an refutes categorically: 'So that the followers of earlier revelation – the Bible – should know that they have no power whatever over any of God's bounty – divine revelation –, seeing that all bounty is in God's hand – alone –; He grants it unto whomever He wills, for God is limitless in His great bounty' (Qur'an 57: 29). This means that the People of the Book have no exclusive claim to the bestowal of divine revelation. The discourse is addressed in the first instance to the Jews who cling to the belief that the office of prophethood is their exclusive preserve as 'Children of Israel' and hence reject the Revelation granted to both Jesus and Muhammad. It is also addressed to the Christians who, as followers of the Bible, implicitly accept this unwarranted claim, thus rejecting the Last Prophet and the Qur'an Revelation (Asad 1984 p. 842).

EIGHT

The Crucifixion?

And never concern thyself with anything that thou have no knowledge thereof. Verily – thy – hearing and sight and heart – all of them – will be called to account for it – on Judgement Day. (Qur'an 17: 36)

And say: 'The truth – has now come – from your Sustainer, let him then who wills, believe in it, and let him who wills, reject it'. (Qur'an 18: 29)

The Evidence

Professor Robert Funk, founder of the Jesus Seminar, was not the first to cast doubt on the crucifixion of Jesus. He wrote (1996): 'The crucifixion of Jesus is not entirely beyond question' (p. 219); 'The story of Jesus' arrest, trial, and execution is largely fictional' (p. 127); 'Mark's account of the Passion, which reaches its climax, with Jesus' arrest, trial, and crucifixion are products of Mark's narrative imagination' (p. 131); and 'Jesus' crucifixion is a very unmessianic thing to happen' (p. 138).

A.N. Wilson (1992) wrote: 'No real evidence can be found for Jesus's arrest and execution' (p. 227); and 'The first three gospels claim that the Eucharist was instituted during or after the traditional Jewish Passover meal. If this is the case, then every single event that follows: the arrest of Jesus, his trial, his execution, must be a work of fiction. It is unthinkable that the Jews would have broken their most sacred religious observance in order to put a man on trial' (p. x).

Professor Burton L. Mack was more emphatic in his statement. He wrote:

As for the story of Jesus' crucifixion and resurrection, Mark took the basic idea from the Christ myth but dared imagine how the crucifixion and resurrection of the Christ might look if played out as a historical event in Jerusalem, something the Christ myth resisted. Thus Mark's story is best understood as a studied combination of Jesus traditions with the Christ myth ... All other narrative gospels start with Mark. None would change his basic plot ... Ever later, Christians would imagine Mark's fiction as history. (Mack 1995 p. 152)

Professor Geza Vermes wrote:

Neither the 'suffering' of the Messiah, nor his 'crucifixion' appear to have been part of the faith of the Nazarenes ... Whether there was a trial of Jesus by the supreme Jewish court in Jerusalem on a religious charge, and a subsequent capital sentence pronounced and forwarded for confirmation and execution by the secular arm, remains historically more than dubious. (Vermes 1998 pp. 38, 36).

On top of all evidence, or lack of it, it is conspicuous that both the Q gospel, and the gospel of Thomas, include no reference to Jesus's 'passion and execution'. They include no passion story, and lack any reference to the death of Jesus. Both are much closer to Jesus's time, having been written at least thirty years earlier than the earliest of the four canonical gospels.

The Qur'an for its part, fourteen centuries ago, categorically rejected the story of Jesus's crucifixion:

And they said – in boast–, we have slain the Messiah, Jesus son of Mary, – who claimed to be – an apostle of God. However they did not slay him, neither did they crucify him, but it only seemed to them – as if it had been – so. And verily, those who hold conflicting views thereon are indeed confused, having no – real – knowledge thereof, and following mere conjecture. For, of a certainty, they did not slay him. (Qur'an 4: 157– 58)

In sharp contrast, one gnostic document from the Nag Hammadi Library, the 'Second Treatise of the Great Seth', discovered in Egypt in 1945, relates Jesus saying the following:

It was another ... who drank the gall and vinegar, it was not I ... it was another, Simon, who bore the cross on his shoulder. It was another upon whom they placed the crown of thorns. But I was rejoicing in the height over ... their error ... And I was laughing at their ignorance. (Second Treatise of the Great Seth 56: 6–20 in Robinson, J. 1990 p. 365; and see also Freke and Gandy 1999 p. 120)

Another gnostic Nag Hammadi document, 'The Apocalypse of Peter', relates the following information on the lips of Peter:

> I saw him *apparently* seized by them. And I said, 'What am I seeing, O Lord! Is it really you whom they take? And are you holding on to me? And are they hammering the feet and hands of another? Who is this one above the cross, who is glad and laughing?' He said to me, 'He whom you see being glad and laughing above the cross is the living Jesus. But he into whose hands and feet they are driving the nails is the fleshy part of the substitute. They put to shame that which remained in his likeness. And look at him, and look at me.' (Apocalypse of Peter 81: 4–24 in Robinson, J. 1990 p. 377; and see also Freke and Gandy 1999 p. 120)

Such tales among the Gnostics seem to have, at some level, penetrated Muslim thought, creating stories that at the last moment God substituted for Jesus a person closely resembling him. Some specify Judas Iscariot having been crucified in his place. Clearly, such legends do not find the slightest support either in the Qur'an or in the authentic traditions of the Prophet. The Qur'an phrase 'but it only seemed to them – as if it had been – so' simply implies that after the time of Jesus a legend somehow grew up to the effect that Jesus died on the cross to atone for the 'original sin' of humankind. This may have been under the influence of Mithraic worship and in particular the slaying of the 'sacred' bull in Mithraic ceremonies. Professor Mack's comment above serves to strengthen this point. With the passage of time, even the Jews, Jesus's enemies, began to believe the story, although in a derogatory sense, since crucifixion was in those times a heinous form of death-penalty reserved for the lowest of criminals (Asad 1984 p. 134).

Passion Narratives

Even if the four gospel narratives on the arrest and crucifixion of Jesus, are taken at face value, many points in the story remain in question.

Jesus was supposed to be celebrating the Jewish Passover feast with his disciples on the night of his 'betrayal'. The passion narratives of the four gospels describe the agony and suffering of Jesus during the mocking, scourging and crucifixion. They included the events that began the evening prior to his death (Mark 14–15), or even prior to his arrest, beginning with his 'triumphal' entry into Jerusalem (Mark 11: 1–10). The defection of the followers of Jesus, including Peter, is stated in Mark 14: 27–31. In the garden of

Gethsemane, during and after the arrest, the disciples were supposed to have deserted Jesus and gone into hiding.

Contradicting the gospels, the Qur'an redresses the injustice done to the disciples, exonerating them from disgraceful behaviour:

> And when Jesus became aware of their – his people's – refusal to acknowledge the truth, he asked: 'Who will be my helpers in God's cause?' The white-garbed ones – the disciples – replied: 'We shall be – thy – helpers – in the cause – of God! We believe in God, and bear thou witness that we have surrendered ourselves to Him'. (Qur'an 3: 52)

> O you who have attained to faith! Be helpers – in the cause of – God, as Jesus the son of Mary, said to the white-garbed ones – the disciples –: 'Who will be my helpers in God's cause?' – my Nazarenes–, Whereupon the white-garbed ones – disciples – replied: 'We are – your – helpers–in the cause of – God!' And so it happened that a portion of the Children of Israel believed – in the prophetic mission of Jesus –, whereas others denied the truth, but – now – We have given power to those who believed, against their foes, and they became the ones that shall prevail. (Qur'an 61: 14)

This is one aspect of the nobility of the Qur'an, portraying the disciples as truly responding to Jesus and supporting him in the time of need.

The synoptic gospels claim that the 'Eucharist' that preceded Jesus's arrest and 'crucifixion' was instituted during the traditional Jewish Passover meal. However, John's gospel puts Jesus's meal with the disciples well before Passover, meaning it had nothing to do with Passover. In consequence, John's gospel is oblivious to the institution of the Eucharist and includes no account of it.

In the words of A.N. Wilson:

> The first three gospels claim that the Eucharist was instituted during or after the traditional Jewish Passover meal. If this is the case, then every single event which follows: the arrest of Jesus, his trial, his execution must be a work of fiction since it is unthinkable that the Jews would have broken their most sacred religious observances in order to put a man on trial. The fourth gospel tells us that the meal took place well before Passover. It was not a Passover meal, and in this account there is very conspicuously no institution of the Eucharist. This is perhaps the most glaring inconsistency in the Christian claim to be an historically based religion. The truth is that even if we were to believe the fantastic claim that Jesus wished to found a new religion, with a sacramental order of bishops and deacons, we could

not believe that he had instituted the Eucharist at Passover time as Paul and the Gospels aver. (Wilson, A.N. 1992 p. x)

Eyewitnesses

On the authority of Mark, all the followers of Jesus fled during his arrest. 'And they all forsook him and fled' (Mark 14: 50). None of Jesus's followers were present during his trial; and none of them spoke to him or saw him after he was arrested and convicted. We only have the story of the denial of Jesus by Peter, during Jesus's trial (Mark 14: 66–71), and that one too seems to have been designed by later generation Pauline scribes to discredit Peter.

The second gospel states that three women, Mary Magdalene, Mary the mother of James, and Salome the mother of James and John sons of Zebedee, had witnessed the crucifixion (Mark 15: 40). But even if those women had, we must face the problem that their recollections had to wait some half a century, obviously passing through intermediaries, before the authorship of a detailed passion narrative, if indeed that narrative reflects any reality or any eyewitnessing at all.

In the absence of eyewitnesses, and the half-century time gap before forming a passion story, and the need to explain the disappearance of Jesus and his subsequent reappearance, early Christian authors researched the ancient scriptures for 'evidence'. Such scriptural 'evidence' was used as a framework for the main themes and details of the story. Christian scribes put great effort into extracting clauses from the Greek Jewish Bible 'proving' that Jesus had 'died in accordance with the scriptures' (Funk 1996 pp. 230–33).

Old scriptures were conditioned to look like fulfilled prophecies. It seems to have been quite common and legitimate to extract scriptural texts, rewrite them, and reinterpret them to establish a future 'fact' or 'event'. It was a way of re-forming scriptures to make them 'predict' or dictate future conceptions. The net result was that historical reality had been totally obscured or masked. Thus, it became impossible to know, with any degree of certainty, which of the details in gospel narratives bear any relation to historical reality. Origen, the Christian theologian (185–254), wrote:

> He must be dull indeed who does not of his own accord observe that much which the scriptures represent as having happened never actually happened. The Scriptures wove together with history that which did not occur, in one place that which is not able to occur, in another that which is able to occur but certainly did not. And what more is it necessary to say? Those who are not altogether dull are able to infer a great number of things of this sort,

written down as if they occurred, but which have not occurred in the manner related. (Dawes 1999 p. 93)

In recent times, Bible scholars have established that so many details connected with the passion story were derived from ancient scriptures. That prompted one biblical authority to conclude: 'We know virtually nothing about the arrest, trial, and execution of Jesus' (John Dominic Crossan 1992, quoted in Funk 1996 pp. 232–33).

Roman Justice

Even if the passion narratives of the gospels are accepted at face value, they do not lend support to the belief that Jesus was indeed crucified, or that he had died on the cross. Pontius Pilate, the Roman prefect in Palestine, sensing that the matter was a purely Jewish internal dispute, had from the start dismissed Jewish charges against Jesus. Roman prefects in general were judicious when dealing with Jewish leaders, or with Jewish internal disputes, for fear of antagonizing the locals and because they were answerable to Rome on their performance in maintaining the peace in their areas of jurisdiction. For example, when Pilate learned that Jesus was from Galilee he saw an opportunity to do away with the problem by sending him to Herod Antipas, the Jewish client king of Galilee. In this manner he would let someone else take responsibility for resolving the issue. Herod Antipas happened to be in Jerusalem at the time and tried unsuccessfully to obtain incriminatory confessions from Jesus. Having failed, he sent Jesus back to Pilate (Luke 23: 7–11).

The charges brought against Jesus by the Jewish high priest included both sedition and blasphemy: 'We found this fellow perverting the nation, and forbidding to give tribute to Caesar, saying that he himself is Christ, a king' (Luke 23: 2). Thus, Jesus was accused of blasphemy because the Jewish religious hierarchy would not recognize him as the awaited Messiah. Clearly, Jesus had always been at odds with Jewish priests over their corruption. On their part the Jewish priesthood disliked the non-conformity that Jesus had preached. For example, they wanted him to refrain from healing on the Sabbath. They clearly enjoyed testing him with embarrassing questions, such as whether tax should be paid to Caesar, or whether a prostitute should be stoned. Jesus's mission was to bring about religious, moral and social reform in Jewish society. Among his objectives was purifying the temple from materialistic endeavours, the practice of usury by money-changers, and idolatrous practices that had prevailed among the Jews since the time of Jeremiah the Prophet (Jeremiah 7: 9–11). Obviously, such issues were of no interest to Pontius Pilate, and provided no grounds for him to arrest or condemn Jesus. It was a purely Jewish internal dispute.

During the trial, if indeed there had been one, Caiaphas the High Priest addressed the question to Jesus: 'Are you the Christ, the son of the Blessed? Jesus said, I am.' (Mark 14: 61–62). Jesus merely proclaimed that he was indeed the Messiah. As for the appellation 'Son of God', it did not mean 'more than human'. It was merely symbolic and applicable to any pious Jew. It provided no ground for a charge of blasphemy. According to the Jewish Mishnah, only the misuse of the Tetragrammaton, the four-letter name of God 'YHWH', constitutes blasphemy (Vermes 1998 p. 35).

In any case, for Pontius Pilate, the pagan, a charge of blasphemy against Jesus would have meant nothing. Pilate had his own Greek gods, man-gods, sons and daughters of god beyond count. One more, or one less, would not make any difference to him. The only thing that mattered for him was that Jesus posed no threat to peace or to Roman authority. Jesus was no political agitator. On the contrary, he had plainly told his followers: 'Render to Caesar the things that are Caesar's, and to God, the things that are God's' (Mark 12: 17).

A King's Triumphant Entry

The story of Jesus so-called 'triumphant entry' into Jerusalem (Matthew 21: 1–11), has been greatly embellished. The aim was to create a story to exactly mirror and fulfil the prophecy in Zechariah: 'Behold, your King comes to you, he is just, and bringing salvation, humble, and riding upon an ass, a colt the foal of an ass' (Zechariah 9: 9). Zechariah tried to paint a poetic picture of a saviour-king coming into Jerusalem, by simply saying that he was seated on a young ass, a colt, described as the son of a female ass. Obviously, he meant one male colt, a young donkey, not two! But Matthew was desperate to prove fulfilment of Old Testament prophecies, in Jesus, to the smallest detail. He wrote: 'Behold, your King comes to you, meek, and sitting upon an ass, and a colt the foal of an ass' (Matthew 21: 5). It is not certain whether Matthew really believed that Jesus on his entry into Jerusalem was sitting simultaneously on two beasts, the mother ass and her young colt! But it seems the majority of Christian fathers so believed (Dawud 1990 p. 67)! Other gospel authors, however, were more careful and did not fall into Matthew's trap.

After the return of the Jews from their Babylonian captivity in the sixth century BCE, Zechariah foretold the coming of a humble saviour king, who would come to rebuild Jerusalem, the temple, and the nation. His prophecy was made at a time when the Jews were striving to rebuild their temple and the city, waiting for permission from the king of Persia to start construction while they were surrounded by hostile nations. Clearly, Zechariah was yearning for material and immediate salvation, not a salvation that was to come more than five centuries later when Jesus, seated on two asses simultaneously, would enter an already rebuilt and wealthy Jerusalem, with its magnificent temple (Dawud 1990 p. 68), only to be betrayed, arrested, tried, and executed according to the gospel stories! Far from fulfilling the prophecy, this would have been no consolation to Zechariah who was hoping for immediate salvation!

The embellishment of the story was also designed to portray Jesus as the powerful Son of Man, the warrior Prophet-King predicted in Daniel Ch. 7! But had the exaggeration of the 'triumphal entry' into Jerusalem been true, Pilate would have had been prompted to arrest Jesus. However Pilate was not in the least disturbed and the 'triumphal entry' did not bother him.

Both Matthew and Luke, who referred to the 'crowds' or the 'multitude' hailing Jesus, greatly exaggerated the events of Palm Sunday. On the other hand, Mark merely says that 'many' participated in hailing Jesus. It is impossible that a major inflammatory demonstration with shouts of 'king' or 'kingdom' could have occurred. It would have resulted in Jesus's immediate arrest by Roman agents or by the police of the Jewish high priest who was accountable to the Romans for maintaining the peace. However Jesus remained free, which means that the demonstration was quite modest and perhaps symbolic. This is confirmed by Pilate's response to the chief priests: 'Why, what evil has he done?' (Mark 15: 14).

To make doubly sure Pilate asked Jesus: 'Are thou the king of the Jews? Jesus answered him: My kingdom is not of this world, if my kingdom were of this world, then would my servants fight that I should not be delivered … but now is my kingdom not from hence' (John 18: 33–36). Jesus assured Pilate that his kingdom was purely spiritual. He had no worldly designs or material ambitions. Pilate, in turn, was fully convinced. He therefore addressed the waiting Jews, delivering to them an unequivocal verdict: 'I find in him no fault at all' (John 18: 38). 'For he [Pilate] knew that the chief priests had delivered Jesus for envy' (Mark 15: 10). Adding to Pilate's conviction of Jesus's innocence, his wife sent him a message: 'Have thou nothing to do with that just man [Jesus], for I have suffered many things this day in a dream because of him' (Matthew 27: 19).

Reluctant as Pilate was to condemn an innocent and harmless subject, one must view with great suspicion the rest of the story on the summary 'execution–crucifixion' of Jesus. The book of Acts testifies that it was not Roman practice to summarily condemn and execute Jewish leaders, on the mere desire of mobs or the chief priests. Romans, if not actually keen to apply justice, did fear political repercussions. If the chief priests were asking Pilate to execute 'a King of the Jews', this amounted to asking Pilate to kill, perhaps, a popular figure. It could entail an uprising and bloodshed: the last thing a Roman prefect would want. In addition, Pilate knew that he was answerable to the Roman Emperor if trouble erupted in his region. The story of Paul in Jerusalem, three decades later, strongly supports this point.

Contrast with Paul's Trial

One cannot fail to notice a sharp contrast, between the very hasty trial and condemnation of Jesus, portrayed in the gospels, as compared with the very lengthy trial of Paul in similar circumstances and the prudence exercised by the Roman prefect. According to the gospels, Jesus was arrested in the garden of Gethsemane late Thursday night, and by Friday noon the next day he was put on the cross. Meaning that his trial by the Sanhedrin, his interrogation by Pontius Pilate, then by Herod Antiaps, and his condemnation, all happened in a matter of less than twelve hours, six of which were after midnight! For this we have to assume that the Sanhedrin court held an emergency trial after midnight in spite of the Jewish Passover celebration. We also have to assume that the matter was then brought to the attention of the Roman prefect Pilate in the very early hours of Friday morning, perhaps as early as six o'clock. This would leave less than six hours time for Jesus interrogation by Pilate, then by Herod Antipas, and then by Pilate again, plus the deliberations with the chief priests on whether Jesus or Barabbas the criminal should be released. The whole timeframe is impossible and dubious, considering that there was no urgency for the trial and the hasty condemnation. Add to this the fact that court hearings at night were illegal, and that members of the Sanhedrin should have been occupied by their Passover celebration on that night (Vermes 2000 p. 169).

Comparing the case of Paul three decades later, one will notice the prudence meticulously exercised, by both the Roman commander in Jerusalem and the Roman prefects – Felix and then Festus – in Caesarea, when Paul was arrested and charged in a similar situation.

The story is narrated in the book of Acts (Acts 21: 27–40; Chs. 22–26). Luke, author of Acts, recounts that Paul was accused of taking a gentile into the temple (Acts 21: 29). For the Jews, such an offence entailed a death penalty. Luke depicts the mob dragging Paul out of the temple clamouring for his death, then his arrest by Roman soldiers, with the crowds shouting: 'Away with such a fellow from the earth, for it is not fit that he should live' (Acts 22: 22). The Roman commander, fearing the mob would tear Paul to pieces, commanded his soldiers to rescue him from his Jewish co-religionists and bring him into the castle. The next day Jewish fanatics vowed to kill Paul (Acts 23: 14).

When the commander heard of their plan and foresaw more trouble he made the decision to send Paul out of Jerusalem.

The Roman commander took the additional trouble of assigning a cohort of 200 infantry and 70 cavalry to escort Paul by night out of Jerusalem (Acts 23: 23). Paul was then handed over to the Roman prefect Felix at Caesarea, with a letter from the Roman commander at Jerusalem explaining, 'whom [Paul] I perceived to be accused of questions of their Law, but to have nothing laid to his charge worthy of death' (Acts 23: 29), meaning there was no breach of Roman law. The acknowledgment that Paul's case involved no breach of the Roman law bears a marked similarity to that of Pontius Pilate some thirty years before declaring 'I find in him [Jesus] no fault at all' (John 18: 38).

The High Priest Ananias followed Paul to Caesarea to further press charges of sedition against him: 'For we have found this man a pestilent fellow and a mover of sedition among all the Jews throughout the world and a ringleader of the sect of the Nazarenes' (Acts 24: 5). Again, we are reminded of a similar charge brought against Jesus three decades earlier: 'We found this fellow [Jesus] perverting the nation, and forbidding to give tribute to Caesar, saying that he himself is Christ, a king' (Luke 23: 2). It is noteworthy that Ananias at that early time did not distinguish between Nazarenes and Christians.

To avoid trouble and be on the safe side, the Roman prefect Felix found it sufficient to incarcerate Paul in Caesarea. He remained in prison until, two years later, a new Roman prefect, Festus, replaced Felix. The story serves to show that, once the defendant was in the custody of the Roman authority, Roman prefects did not readily bend to the desire of the mob or chief priests to condemn suspects to death. In addition, suspects who were Roman citizens had the additional privilege of appealing to Caesar, just as Paul did. Festus, the new governor, sent Paul to Rome because of the his appeal unto Caesar.

Paul's ordeal provides a vivid contrast with the story of Jesus three decades earlier. Appearances of Jesus to his disciples after his 'crucifixion' strongly negate the story of his trial and execution. Most Roman prefects were judicious not to unnecessarily provoke local animosity. The Roman legate of Syria did sometimes send his Palestine prefect to Rome to answer charges of harshness against the local population. This indeed was the fate of Pontius Pilate when Vitellius, the legate of Syria, sent him to Rome in the year 37 CE.

On Roman justice Professor Michael Grant (1990 p. 260) wrote: 'For all the inadequacies and inequalities of ancient social structure, among free men at least a large measure of justice prevailed wherever the imperial writ ran.'

The Crucifixion?

Three Women at the Sepulchre

Mark narrates that three women: Mary Magdalene, Mary the mother of James, and Salome the mother of both James and John sons of Zebedee, came to Jesus's 'burial place' on Sunday morning, the third day after the 'crucifixion' to anoint him (Mark 16: 1), i.e to rub him with oil and sweet spices. The story raises suspicion as to whether Jews massage dead bodies after two days? In two days a dead body would be fermenting from within. Anyone rubbing such a decaying body might cause it to fall apart. Unless the women knew that Jesus was alive!

If Mary Magdalene, Mary the mother of James, and Salome, were witnesses to the 'crucifixion' (Mark 15: 40), then they must have known that Jesus had remained very much alive. Only a live Jesus would explain their desire to anoint him, in order, perhaps, to heal bruises on his body. One of two things could have happened. Either that Jesus was never crucified, and those women knew it, or, if he was indeed tied to a cross, he must have been taken down too soon before he was harmed, and those women were witness to it (see also Schonfield 1993 pp. 119–21).

Contradicting Mark on the identity of the three women, John in the fourth gospel lists them as: Mary Magdalene, Jesus's companion, Mary his mother, and Mary her sister the wife of Cleophas (John 19: 25). In either case the listing of the three women is conspicuous. Freke and Gandy (1999 p. 58) noted the following: 'the fact that we are given three Marys is a clear indication that we are in ancient mythological territory. The triple goddess was a familiar figure in the Pagan world. At Eleusis she appears as Demeter, Persephone, and Hecate. We find her appearing as the three fates, three charities, and three graces.'

According to John, the time was about the sixth hour – meaning 12 noon – when Pilate handed over Jesus to the Jews for crucifixion (John 19: 14). Mark, Matthew, and Luke agree that darkness fell over the land between the sixth hour and the ninth hour – meaning between 12 noon and 3 p.m. Darkness would have helped to disperse the crowd so there would be no witnesses.

Joseph of Arimathea, a sympathetic counsellor, helped by a sympathetic Roman centurion, came to Pilate and craved the body of Jesus. Pilate marvelled if Jesus was already dead (Mark 15: 43–45), and with good reason. From experience, he knew that it would take days for a person to die on a cross. Pilate expected that Jesus should be very much alive at this early time. But he had no special reason to ensure that Jesus was dead. From the beginning he was convinced of Jesus's innocence. So, if Jesus was still alive, good luck to him. Pilate granted permission for Joseph to take the body (Mark 15: 45–46). One authority noted that Joseph of Arimathea had asked for the *body* of Jesus (*soma*)

Christianity, Islam and Orientalism

– not for his corpse (*ptoma*) – betraying his knowledge that Jesus was not crucified (Schonfield 1994 p. 168).

Between the stories of Matthew, Luke, and John, the maximum time that Jesus was supposed to have been on the cross, if ever, was merely three hours, that is between the sixth hour – noontime – to the ninth hour – afternoon. It was definitely much less than that. If Jesus was handed over for crucifixion at the sixth hour, we have to deduct the time between handing him over and the supposed crucifixion, including the journey time to Calvary.

The 'burial place', the sepulchre, to which Jesus was taken, was no ordinary grave. It was a big roomy chamber. In other words it was a hiding place! For how else could Peter and other disciples go into the sepulchre? 'Then comes Simon Peter, and went into the sepulchre … Then went in also that other disciple' (John 20: 6, 8). 'And they [the three women] entered in [the sepulchre]' (Luke 24: 3). 'And entering into the sepulchre they [the three women] saw a man sitting on the right side' (Mark 16: 5).

As Mary Magdalene and the other women came to anoint Jesus at the burial place, they were perplexed on his disappearance from the site. Two men approached them: 'And they [the two men] were afraid and bowed down their faces to the earth, and said unto them [to the woman]: why do you seek the living among the dead?' (Luke 24: 5). The only sense that this statement could make is the hint that Jesus was alive. Both men 'were afraid and bowing down their faces' so that they would not be recognized, because one of them must have been Jesus. Jesus had reason to be afraid, because he did not want his enemies to know that he had escaped death. If he had indeed died and was resurrected from the dead, he would have no reason to be afraid anymore. A resurrected person cannot die again.

John in his narrative gives a better glimpse: 'Mary stood at the sepulchre weeping … And saw Jesus standing, and knew not that he was Jesus' (John 20: 11–14). Mary was weeping because she had failed to recognize the live Jesus she was looking for. Jesus consoled her saying 'woman, why do you weep? Whom do you seek? She supposing him to be the gardener' (John 20: 15), because, as a precautionary measure, Jesus disguised himself as a gardener. In Luke's story he was bowing down his face to the ground so that he would not be recognized. Then 'Jesus said unto her: Mary. She turned herself and said unto him, Master' (John 20: 16). She was overjoyed that the disguised gardener was Jesus himself. Elated, she apparently came forward to hug him, but he told her: 'Touch me not, for I am not yet ascended to my father' (John 20: 17).

Jesus apparently did not want her to touch him because he might have suffered some bruises which would hurt if hugged. He may have gone through a lot of pain. And he had not yet ascended to the Father, meaning that he was still alive, not resurrected from the dead. He was not a ghost. He was telling her in his own parabolic style, for which he was famous, that he had escaped death, as she knew very well anyway. Then, Jesus sent her to inform his disciples. 'And they, when they had heard *that he was alive* [not resurrected from the dead] and had been seen of her, believed not' (Mark 16: 11).

Jesus Reappears with the Disciples

On that very day, on the way to a village called Emmaus not far from Jerusalem, Jesus joined two of his disciples and discoursed with them for five miles. 'Jesus *himself* drew near and went with them ... And they said unto him concerning Jesus who was a Prophet mighty in deed and word' (Luke 24: 15, 19). 'Then he said unto them, Oh fools, and slow of heart to believe all that the prophets had spoken' (Luke 24: 25), meaning, can't you see, you fools, that it is me the live Jesus. 'And their eyes were open, and they knew *him*' (Luke 24: 31).

In Jerusalem, on that same day, Jesus met the eleven disciples – twelve minus Thomas:

and said unto them, Peace be unto you. But they were terrified and frightened, and supposed that they had seen a spirit. And he said unto them why are you troubled? And why do thoughts arise in your hearts? Behold my hands and my feet, *that it is I myself*, handle me and see [that I am not a resurrected spirit], for a spirit has not *flesh and bones*, as you see me have. And as he had thus spoken, he showed them *his* hands and *his* feet. (Luke 24: 36–40)

Jesus was saying clearly that he had not been killed, and he was proving it to the disciples beyond any doubt.

But the disciples were afraid because they had heard from hearsay that the Master was killed on the cross. All their knowledge was from hearsay. None of them was eyewitness to the 'crucifixion'. Because 'they *all* forsook him and fled' (Mark 14: 50). In contrast Mary Magdalene was not afraid when she saw him, because she was an eyewitness to the events, and therefore she was expecting to see a live Jesus. She had known very well from the start that Jesus was not killed.

In order to dispel any doubt, and assure the disciples further, that he was no resurrected spirit, that he was no ghost, Jesus asked them: 'Have you here any meat? And they gave him a piece of a broiled fish and of an honeycomb. And he took it, and did eat before them' (Luke 24: 41–43). To prove what? That spirits and ghosts eat? If Jesus had only eaten to show that he could eat, while he was a spirit with no need for nourishment, it would have been absurd (Deedat, Vol. 2 p. 213).

Thomas, the twelfth disciple, could not believe what the eleven had told him (John 20: 24–25). He was told it was the physical Jesus that they had seen; not a resurrected spirit. A Jesus that ate fish and honeycomb. Had they claimed that they had seen a resurrected Jesus, a spirit, there would have been nothing special about this; Thomas would have readily believed. In the disciple's teaching the resurrection of Jesus was not something particularly impossible. The rising of the dead was a sign of the beginning of the messianic age. Jesus would have been the first to rise (Wilson, A.N. 1997 p. 63). For example, Matthew claimed that at the moment of crucifixion 'the graves were opened and many bodies of the saints which slept arose' (Matthew 27: 52).

After eight days Jesus met the twelve disciples together, including Thomas, and said to them, 'Peace be unto you. Then he said to Thomas: Reach your finger and behold my hand' (John 20: 26–27), meaning, see for yourself that I am the physical Jesus, alive, not a spirit or ghost; what more proof do you need?

An additional point is worth noting. If the gospels' claim that Jesus indeed had so clearly predicted his crucifixion and resurrection in three days saying, 'after three days I will rise again' (Matthew 27: 63), and 'on the third day he shall rise again' (Matthew 20: 19), why is it that all the disciples were dazzled in disbelief to see their Master alive after the crucifixion? Or was this promise another fabrication similar to Jesus's anticipation of his 'suffering' passion? Not a single disciple seems to have heard or remembered the 'promise' of Jesus's resurrection on the third day. And if the promise of Jesus's resurrection in three days was true, why did not a single disciple go to the sepulchre on the third day to witness the fulfilment of the Master's 'promise'? On the contrary, they were all astonished and frightened at an event which they were all 'supposed' to have anticipated! (Dawes 1999 pp. 74–76).

Other Appearances

Luke stated in the book of Acts that Jesus was *alive* for forty days after his passion, 'To whom he also showed himself *alive* [not resurrected] after his passion, by many infallible proofs, being seen of them forty days, and speaking of things pertaining to the Kingdom of God' (Acts 1: 3).

A gospel of Secret James, discovered in 1945 among Nag Hammadi codices, describes Jesus continuing his instructions to the disciples for 550 days after his 'crucifixion' (Robinson, J. 1990 p. 29). Paul, in his letter to the Corinthians, documented that Jesus was seen by Peter, then by the twelve, then by some five hundred people (1 Corinthians 15: 5–8).

It is significant that in his reappearances Jesus never showed himself to his enemies, only to the faithful. As a live person he would have been afraid that his enemies might conspire again against him. Had he been a spirit, he would have no reason to fear anyone.

Jesus's Lifetime

One of the most intriguing features of the ministry of Jesus is that it should have lasted no more than one year, according to the synoptic gospels. This seems too short a duration considering the immense importance of the Messiah's mission. One explanation of this difficulty is that gospels cannot and should not be viewed as accurate historical records. One Bible authority suggested that the authors of the gospels did not order their material according to chronological events in the life of Jesus, but rather according to the Jewish liturgical year which covered Jesus's lifetime on an annual cycle (Spong 1996 p. 95). Consequently, a gospel reader might obtain the impression that Jesus journeyed to Jerusalem only once, at the end of his ministry, with the *false* impression that Jesus's mission was covered by its Galilean phase culminating and concluding in his journey to Jerusalem.

The exact years of Jesus's birth, his ministry, and his death are uncertain. The gospels depict Jesus's ministry as having followed shortly after that of John the Baptist, and in particular, shortly before the latter was executed in prison by the tetrarch Herod Antipas (4 BCE – 39 CE). According to Matthew's gospel, Jesus was born during Herod the Great's reign (37 BCE –4 BCE) (Matthew 2: 1). Knowing that Herod the Great died in 4 BCE, that would put Jesus's birth at 4 BCE at the latest. Luke, however, offers two contradictory dates for the birth of Jesus, one in the days of Herod the Great (Luke 1: 5, 26), and another at the time of the census of Cyrenius, 'a decree from Caesar Augustus (31 BCE–14 CE) that all the [Roman] world should be taxed, and this taxing was first made when Cyrenius was governor of Syria' (Luke 2: 2–3). This is contradictory with Luke 1: 5 because Cyrenius made the census in the year 6 CE, a full ten years after the death of Herod the Great (Freke and Gandy 1999 pp. 199–200). Cyrenius was not legate of Syria while Herod the Great was alive. But even if we accept that Jesus was born late in Herod the Great's reign we do not know the exact year. Dismissing the story of Cyrenius' census, scholars therefore speculate that the birth of Jesus was somewhere between 7 and 4 BCE, the year when Herod the Great died (Sanders 1993 p. 11). Sanders (1993 p. 12) offers an interesting analysis of why the birth of Jesus is a few years ahead of the beginning of the era that is supposed to start with his birth.

There is also conflict on Jesus's age at the start of his prophetic mission, its duration, and on the year of his death. Luke's story requires that Jesus was in his early thirties when he started his prophetic mission (Luke 3: 1, 23). Luke explicitly states that John the Baptist started his prophetic mission in the fifteenth year of Emperor Tiberius' reign. Since Tiberius' reign covered the years 14–37 CE, the fifteenth year should be 29 CE, and assuming that Jesus started his mission one year later than the Baptist, namely in 30 CE, Jesus would have been between 34 and 37 years of age. But John's gospel states that Jesus was in his forties during his ministry: 'not yet fifty years old' (John 8: 57).

Contradicting John, Luke explicitly stated that Jesus was about thirty years of age when he began his mission (Luke 3: 23). This Lukan piece of information requires that Jesus be born in the year 1, which is probably the reasoning behind our present calendar.

As to Jesus's death, the gospels assign the date to the period when Pontius Pilate was Roman prefect of Palestine (26–37 CE). If Jesus died when Pilate was prefect, and certainly after the martyrdom of John the Baptist, that would put his death *after* the year 35 CE, or at the year 37 CE at the latest. This notion is predicated by the date of John the Baptist's martyrdom, which is implied by Flavius Josephus to have been between 35 and 36 CE (Eisenman 1997 pp. 62, 106). This makes Jesus's age between 41 and 44 years at the time of his death, which would be closer to John's gospel: 'not yet fifty years old'. In this case, Jesus's ministry would have lasted 6–8 years, not including the duration of his reappearance after the 'crucifixion'.

In summary, all such records and dates make it extremely improbable that the duration of Jesus's prophetic mission could have been limited to merely one year as depicted by the synoptic gospels, nor three years as depicted by the fourth gospel. In the words of Eisenman (1997 p. 107): 'If Jesus died after John the Baptist, as Scripture seems to think, then by Josephus' chronology it must be around 37 CE or just a little time before. If Jesus died before John the Baptist, then what are we to make of these scriptural accounts at all?'

The Islamic Viewpoint

Illuminating snatches remaining in the New Testament point to the fact that Jesus was not crucified. It had proved awkward and impossible for authors and editors of the New Testament to superimpose, on factual history, fabricated stories invented 'in accordance with scriptures' matching their own preconceptions.

The Crucifixion?

Once more, the Qur'an is found in agreement only with the most coherent parts of the Scriptures. In turn, modern scholarly research seems to be arriving at conclusions clearly stated in the Qur'an fourteen centuries earlier. This is systematic with how the Qur'an describes itself: 'setting forth the truth, confirming the truth of whatever still remains of earlier revelations and determining what is true therein' (Qur'an 5: 48). More specifically: 'And upon thee have We bestowed from on high this divine writ for the express purpose that thou might make clear unto them all – questions of faith – on which they have come to hold divergent views, and – thus offer – guidance and grace unto people who believe' (Qur'an 16: 64).

Contrary to the Christian creed, Muslims believe all humans to be born sinless and therefore not in need of advance redemption. In consequence, religion and the feeling of guilt are not interconnected. The concept of vicarious atonement of the so-called 'original sin' is unnecessary and is rejected in Islam.

On the subject of Jesus having been raised to God, there seems agreement between the Qur'an verses (4: 157–158) and the dialogue reported in John's gospel, between Jesus and Mary Magdalene at the Sepulchre: 'Jesus said unto her, Touch me not, for I am *not yet* ascended to my father, but go to my brethren, and say unto them, *I ascend unto my father*, and your father; *my God and your God*' (John 20: 17). Having first assured Mary that he was not coming back from the dead – not yet ascended unto the father– he asked her to tell his brethren, the disciples, that *he was going to be ascended* – raised – to God. He also dissociated himself from any notion of divinity, while denying being a Son of God in any unique sense.

There is another instance of Jesus referring to his future 'lift up' into heaven: 'And I, if I be lifted up from the earth', to which John by way of explanation erroneously stated: 'This he said, signifying what death he should die' (John 12: 32–33). Obviously John added this explanation because of his preconception of the 'crucifixion'. In comparison, it is noteworthy that the Qur'an explicitly states that Jesus was raised by God, not crucified.

Events of the last days of Jesus's mission on earth are neatly summarized by the Qur'an as follows:

> And when Jesus became aware of their refusal to acknowledge the truth, he asked: 'Who will be my helpers in God's cause?' The white-garbed ones – the Disciples – replied: 'We shall be – thy – helpers – in the cause – of God! We believe in God, and bear thou witness that we have surrendered ourselves to Him: O our Sustainer! We believe in what Thou has bestowed from on high, and we follow this Apostle – Jesus–; make us one, then, with all who bear witness – to the truth –; And the unbelievers schemed – against Jesus – but

God brought their scheme to nought; for God is above all schemers; Lo! God said: 'O Jesus! I shall bring your term on earth to completion, and shall exalt thee to Me, and cleanse thee of – the presence of – those who are bent on denying the truth; and I shall place those who follow thee – far – above those who are bent on denying the truth, unto the Day of Resurrection. In the end unto Me you must all return, and I shall judge between you with regard to all on which you were wont to differ. (Qur'an 3: 52–55)

For one thing, the above verses honour the disciples for their performance in helping Jesus, and praise their surrender to God's will – in this sense becoming Muslims. This is in vivid contrast to the gospels, which slander the disciples accusing them of cowardliness, treason, and desertion. A second point of the verse is its emphasis on the utter failure of the scheme to kill Jesus. A third point is that Jesus was raised without being killed. The fourth point is the emphasis that those who followed Jesus, i.e. the Nazarenes, will eventually have the upper hand through the advent of Islam. And finally, the verse asserts that all will return to God whereby everyone will know the truth behind Jesus's mission, i.e. final judgement rests with God alone.

During the lifetime of the Prophet (570–632 CE), he could not have had access to the Christian Bible, nor to pertinent historical records, let alone objectively analysed them and reached such conclusions. At the time of the Prophet's mission there existed no Arabic translation of the New Testament, much less the Old Testament. We have already noted that the first Arabic translation of the Christian Bible, a scripture now present at St Petersburg library, dates back to the year 1060 CE, more than four centuries after the Prophet's death. And in any case, Muhammad was illiterate. As for the Qur'anic verse: 'Say – to the Children of Israel –: Come forward, then, with the Torah and recite it if what you say is true' (Qur'an 3: 93), this could possibly be an allusion to the fact that there was none among the Arabs who could read the Septuagint in Greek, nor the Hebrew version of the Old Testament. It could also constitute a challenge to the Jews in that they were unable to come forward with the Torah – Taurah – of Moses that they lost long ago. All that they possessed were scriptures that they themselves authored, possibly including snatches of the original divine revelation.

Conspicuously there was no religious cultural centre in Arabia that could have propagated the kind of Old Testament precepts that the Qur'an dealt with (Ben Nabi 1986 p. 246). On this point the Qur'an remarkably states: 'For – O Muhammad – thou has never been able to recite any divine writ before this one – was revealed–, nor did thou ever transcribe one with your own hands, or else, they who try to disprove the truth – of thy revelation – might indeed have had cause to doubt – it.' (Qur'an 29: 48)

Another verse alludes to the 'foreign' language of the Bible in Muhammad's Arabia: 'And indeed We know that they say, "It is but a human being that imparts – all – this to him" – notwithstanding that – the tongue to which they so maliciously point is wholly outlandish, whereas this is Arabic, clear – in itself – and clearly showing the truth – of its source –' (Qur'an 16: 103). Clearly, the outlandish language of the Bible at the time of the Prophet was either the Syriac of the Peshitta, the Latin of the Vulgate, or – in the case of the Old Testament – the Greek of the Septuagint.

NINE

The Book of Revelation, US Orientalism and Christian Fundamentalism

But whatever they may say or do – Repel the evil – which they commit – with something that is better; We are fully aware of what they attribute to Us. (Qur'an 23: 96)

And, whenever they hear frivolous talk they turn away therefrom, and say: 'Unto us shall be accounted our deeds, and unto you, your deeds. Peace be upon you, we do not seek out such as are ignorant'– of the meaning of right and wrong. (Qur'an 28: 55)

Orientalism

An Orientalist is one who studies and researches the Orient, tries to understand it, and perhaps writes about it. Orientalism, however, is not necessarily a purely academic endeavour. The academic interest of the West in the Orient has often been a prelude to practical application for the purpose of power and control over the Orient. It is usually an application in the way of how to deal with the Orient in order to further the West's political, imperialist, or economic interests. A problem clearly arises when the Orientalist embarks on his work with preconceptions carried forward from his cultural and religious background. An Orientalist may also start from the 'prerogative' of the West to dominate or manage the East. In this case Orientalism is paralleled or followed by concrete steps taken on the ground by the West's political structure to implement Western policy.

Edward Said sees in Orientalism an enormous system through which Western culture, since the post-enlightenment period, was able to manage the Orient not only politically, but also socially and scientifically. To the Orientalist, the Orient is not merely a field for academic learning and discovery but a field to be restructured and dominated. The academic interest of Orientalism is therefore coupled with practical implementation for the benefit of the West. Since the post-enlightment period Orientalists have been mostly Biblical scholars, students of Semitic languages, and students of Islamic studies, not to mention functionaries of Western governments. The wealth of Orientalist studies that the West accumulated prompted Victor Hugo to state in 1829: 'While we used to be Hellenists, we are now Orientalists.' Conspicuously, and perhaps sadly, it is noted that people of the Orient did not develop a reciprocal interest in Western biblical culture and orientation (Said 1979).

As early as the seventh century, the West found itself faced with the inevitability of having to deal with the new monotheistic religion of Islam that occupied a part of the world that had been traditionally until then the domain of Christianity. However, because of the Dark Ages the West was plunged into, the Christian Church was both unable and unwilling at the time to discover the truth behind the new religion or come to terms with it.

In the aftermath of the Council of Nicaea in 325 CE, Christianity became the official religion of the Roman Empire. In consequence, in 395 CE, the Empire first split into two. Then, in 410 CE, a mere 85 years after the Council of Nicaea, the Visigoths, a wandering nation of Germanic tribes from the north-east, sacked Rome. Christianity had proved itself a strong catalyst that resulted in the fall of Rome and the inauguration of the Dark Ages. Conspicuously, while the invention of the Christian Church ushered in the beginning of the Dark Ages of the West, the rise of Islam three centuries later, ushered in the East an age of enlightenment, religious tolerance, and the rise of a brilliant Muslim civilization that spread from China in the East to Spain in the West while Europe remained a backwater.

As a result, the West saw in Islam then, what Islam sees in the West today, namely a source of humiliation and injury to its self-esteem, the bitterness of which seems to persist to this day. Even the European enlightenment failed to free the West of its long-standing adverse attitude towards Islam. The West preferred to maintain a feeling of superiority emanating consciously or unconsciously from a church of rigid dogma.

Orientalists today are occupied in particular with the Muslim and Arab peoples. It is the religious and cultural background of the West that predicates today, as it did in the past, its political, economic, and military policies towards the Orient. From the start, Islam was looked at as a challenge to cope with, a new religion whose novelty and suggestiveness were to be brought under control. Orientalism as engrained in the Western mind, looks at Islam as the religion that replaced Christianity in the very biblical lands where Christianity first arose. American fundamentalists in particular believe that the destiny of the Orient must be tied to what America fundamentally stands for. This was a very important, indeed sufficient, reason for the West to create and sustain the state of Israel in Palestine. In consequence, we witness today the Western political structures, in particular the USA, mobilizing their civil societies in the face of the Orient in general and the Middle East in particular.

Revelation

There is little doubt that the book of Revelation – the last book of the New Testament – had captured the imagination of many Christians in the first centuries, and that it continues to fascinate many Christians in the Western Hemisphere, to some degree or another, to the present day. This is because Revelation, written in an aura of expectations and hope for salvation, upheld and nurtured Christian belief in two respects. First, it sustained the conviction in the imminent return of Christ, as Paul had once prophesied. Christians of the first and later centuries never despaired that the prophecy of Paul on the Second Coming would somehow, sometime materialize. Second, it sustained the conviction that Christ in his Second Coming would or should accomplish, according to Christian aspirations, what he was unable to fulfil during his first lifetime on earth.

The book of Revelation, a treatise written by John the Seer in the late sixties of the first century was not considered 'Holy Scripture' until the fourth century. Subsequent to the Council of Nicaea, Emperor Constantine assigned to Eusebius, Bishop of Caesarea, the task of preparing Holy Scriptures for the new church. Even at that time, it is not certain whether Eusebius included Revelation in the newly formed Christian Bible. This is because some authorities contended it was not authentic, but others did not agree. Thus, Revelation may have been added to the Holy Scriptures much later than the time of Eusebius. It is noteworthy that Revelation is not included in the Syriac Peshitta version of the Christian Bible adopted by the Eastern Syriac-speaking Churches.

Dionysius, Bishop of Alexandria, and a contemporary of Eusebius, wrote that John, author of Revelation, is most definitely *not* the disciple John, son of Zebedee. He added that Revelation was incomprehensible to him, and that some of his predecessors had rejected the book and pulled it entirely to pieces, saying that the author was not a disciple, not a saint, not even a member of the Church, but Cerinthus, the founder of the sect called Cerinthian after him (Eusebius 1989 pp. 88, 89, 240–43; Mack 1995 pp. 216, 288; Freke and Gandy 1999 p. 238; McGinn 2000 p. xiv).

Christianity, Islam and Orientalism

By way of introduction to the book of Revelation, the following excerpts are of particular interest to the subject of this chapter.

Only 144,000 to Be Saved

And I saw another angel ascending from the East, having the seal of the living God, and he cried with a loud voice to the four angels to whom it was given to hurt the earth and the sea. Saying, Hurt not the earth, neither the sea, nor the trees, till we have sealed the servants of our God in their foreheads. And I heard the number of them which were sealed … a hundred and forty four thousands of all the tribes of the children of Israel. Of the tribe of Judah were sealed twelve thousand. Of the tribe of Reuben were sealed twelve thousand. Of the tribe of Gad were sealed twelve thousand. Of the tribe of Asher were sealed twelve thousand. Of the tribe of Naftali were sealed twelve thousand. Of the tribe of Manasseh were sealed twelve thousand. Of the tribe of Simeon were sealed twelve thousand. Of the tribe of Levi were sealed twelve thousand. Of the tribe of Issachar were sealed twelve thousand. Of the tribe of Zebulon were sealed twelve thousand. Of the tribe of Joseph were sealed twelve thousand. Of the tribe of Benjamin were sealed twelve thousand. (Revelation 7: 2–8)

The 144,000 Not Defiled with Women

And I looked, and, lo, a Lamb stood on Mount Zion and with him a hundred and forty four thousand, having his Father's name written on their foreheads … the hundred and forty four thousand which were redeemed from the earth … These are they, which were not defiled with women; for they are virgins. They follow the Lamb wherever he goes … And there followed another angel saying, Babylon is fallen, is fallen, that great city, because she made all nations drink of the wine of the wrath of her fornication. (Revelation 14: 1, 3, 4, 8)

Vials of Wrath at the Euphrates and Armageddon

And the sixth angel poured out his vial upon the great river Euphrates; and the water thereof was dried up, that the way of the kings of the east may be prepared … and he gathered them together into a place called in the Hebrew tongue Armageddon … and great Babylon came in remembrance before God, to give unto her the cup of the wine of the fierceness of his wrath. (Revelation 16: 12, 16, 19)

The Book of Revelation, US Orientalism and Christian Fundamentalism

Babylon: the Great Harlot

And there came one of the seven angels which had the seven vials, and talked with me, saying unto me, Come hither; I will show unto thee the judgement of the great whore that sits upon many waters. With whom the kings of the earth have committed fornication, and the inhabitants of the earth have been made drunk with the wine of her fornication. ... Upon her forehead was a name written, Mystery, Babylon the Great, the Mother of Harlots and Abominations of the Earth. And I saw a woman drunken with the blood of saints, and with the blood of the martyrs of Jesus. (Revelation 17: 1, 2, 5, 6)

The Fall of Babylon

And after these things I saw another angel come down from heaven, having great power ... And he cried, Babylon the Great is fallen, is fallen, and has become the habitations of devils, and the hold of every foul spirit, and a cage of every unclean hateful bird. For all nations have drunk of the wrath of her fornication, and the kings of the earth have committed fornication with her ... For her sins have reached unto heaven ... Reward her even as she rewarded you ... so much torment and sorrow give her ... Therefore shall her plagues come in one day, death and mourning, and famine; and she shall be utterly burned with fire ... And a mighty angel took up a stone like a great millstone, and cast it into the sea, saying, Thus with violence shall that great city Babylon be thrown down, and shall be found no more at all. (Revelation 18: 1–3, 5–8, 21)

The Battle at Armageddon

for He has judged the great whore [Babylon], which did corrupt the earth with her fornication ... And I saw heaven opened and behold a white horse, and he that sat upon him was called Faithful and True ... and his name is called the Word of God. And the armies which were in heaven followed him upon white horses ... And he has on his vesture and on his thigh a name written, King of Kings, and Lord of Lords ... And I saw the beast, and the kings of the earth and their armies gathered together to make war against him that sat on the horse and against his army. And the beast was taken, and with him the false prophet ... These both were cast alive into a lake of fire burning with brimstone. And the remnant were slain with the sword of him that sat upon the horse, which sword proceeded out of his mouth. (Revelation 19: 2, 11, 13, 14, 16, 19, 20, 21)

The Happy 1,000 Years' Kingdom

And I saw an angel come down from heaven, having the key of the bottomless pit and a great chain in his hand. And he laid hand on the dragon, that old serpent, which is the devil, and Satan, and bound him a thousand years, And cast him into the bottomless pit, and shut him up, and set a seal upon him, that he should deceive the nations no more, till the thousand years should be fulfilled, and after that he must be loosed a little season ... And when the thousand years are expired, Satan shall be loosed out of his prison, And he shall go out to deceive the nations which are in the four corners of the earth, Gog and Magog ... And the devil that deceived them was cast into the lake of fire and brimstone, where the beast and the false prophet are, and shall be tormented for ever and ever. (Revelation 20: 1–3, 7, 8, 10)

The New Jerusalem

And I John saw the holy city, new Jerusalem, coming down from God out of heaven, prepared as a bride for her husband ... the bride, the Lamb's wife ... that great city, the holy Jerusalem, descending out of heaven from God ... had a wall great and high, and had twelve gates [with] the names of the twelve tribes of Israel written on them. (Revelation 21: 2, 9, 10, 12)

The book of Revelation, is attributed to John the Seer, known as divine, although it is far from certain who this John was. Any intelligent reader of Revelation would inevitably ask the question: Why did John – whoever he was – produce such writing? And what was the background behind it? A.N. Wilson, in his brilliant book, *Paul, the Mind of the Apostle* (1997 pp. 1–13), provides an excellent account on this point. (see also McGinn 2000, pp. 45–56)

Emperor Nero

The reign of the Roman Emperor Nero, who became emperor at the age of seventeen and was compelled to commit suicide at the age of thirty, was plagued by a series of setbacks making it remarkable that he survived in office as long as he did (54–68 CE). In the tenth year of his reign in July 64 CE, the famous fire of Rome erupted and raged for almost one month consuming three of the fourteen districts into which the city was divided. When the fire started, Nero was at the seaside resort of Antium, not too far from Rome. He returned hastily to Rome to be with his people, and to personally supervise fire fighting. Nero's move may well have been out of political shrewdness. He was later accused of deliberately starting the fire to provide land for his grandiose beautification and building projects, and specifically to make space for his own Golden House. Nero's capriciousness and ruthlessness, which he developed in the last decade of his reign, earned him the reputation, possibly fictitious, that he was on a tower above Rome gazing onto the inferno beneath, singing and fiddling, while Rome went in flames.

Rome at this time was populated with some two million people, roughly half of them slaves. There was public dismay at the catastrophe, as thousands were left homeless. Rumours that Nero himself may have been responsible for starting the fire increased security fears with the possibility of rioting. At such difficult times, demagogues find it typically expedient to placate the mobs by searching for scapegoats, and Nero was no exception. Thus loomed the political advantage of choosing for blame a barely known Christian minority, the followers of 'Chrestos' as they were known. Assigning blame squarely on Christians seemed a very attractive proposition at the time, as not many people would have sympathized with them. In addition to this, watching human torture was a favourite Roman entertainment. The Roman historian Tacitus (55–117 CE), in his Annals, described how Christians were punished:

> First, then, those of the sect who confessed were arrested. Next on their disclosures vast numbers were convicted, not so much on the count of arson, as for hatred of the human race. And ridicule accompanied their end: they were covered with wild beasts' skins and torn to death by dogs. Others were fastened to crosses as human torches, to serve as lights when daylight faded. Nero made his gardens available for the show and held games in the circus, mingling with the crowd or standing in his chariot in charioteer's uniform. (Tacitus 1996 p. 365)

Nero and Rome's population of the time found delight in such displays of savagery. But this does not mean that Nero was particularly anti-Christian, only that he was devoid of any religious feeling, and that he found it expedient, in that particular instance, to choose Christians as a means of distracting public attention.

Christian Persecutions

It should not, therefore, be inferred that Nero alone was the originator of anti-Christian persecution. The persecution of Christians which he initiated seems modest compared with what was to come. Large-scale persecutions of Christians started some two centuries after Nero. Even these were grossly overshadowed by later persecutions of Christian 'heretics' in the hands of the Christian Church itself. We have already noted that the Christian Church, in its pursuit of faith uniformity, was the one institution that invented religious persecution, something previously unknown to the pagans of the Graeco-Roman world (Wilson, A.N. 1997 pp. 9–10).

Alongside this search for uniformity, Victor, Bishop of Rome, in 190 CE demanded that Christians in Asia Minor abandon their traditional practice of celebrating Easter on 14 Nisan according to Jewish Passover and conform instead to the Roman custom of celebrating on the following Sunday. The stark alternative that he posed for them was to abandon their claim to be 'catholic Christians'. Victor threatened excommunication for dissenters, and when defied he went through the motions of carrying out the sentence. Victor's threat was reputedly the first papal act to enforce papal rigid authority.

After the council of Nicaea in 325 CE, Christianity became an official religion of the Empire. Tolerance for other faiths and religious freedom were not contemplated under official Christianity. Christian bishops previously brutalized by the police now led them. People who did not subscribe to the Nicene Creed were deemed heretical and ruthlessly eliminated. Advocacy of Arian views and possession of Arian literature were crimes punishable by death. Inquisitors were appointed to investigate the faith 'orthodoxy' of various groups even within the Christian Church.

Under Emperor Theodosius (378–95 CE), who was an enthusiastic persecutor, bands of roaming monks attacked and destroyed synagogues, Arian and pagan temples. In Alexandria, Egypt, they destroyed the temple of Serapis, one of the largest and most beautiful buildings in the ancient world, together with its library donated by Cleopatra. Illiterate monks wiped out thousands of years of accumulated wisdom and scientific knowledge.

Such was the novelty in 'religious' persecutions that the Nicene Church required in order to satisfy its need for the imposition of its 'catholic' (universal) and 'orthodox' doctrines. It was totally opposed to the Graeco-Roman 'pagan' practice of the age which, before Christianity, tolerated various cults throughout the Empire with the implicit acknowledgement that the 'truth' can be sought through more than one single course (Rubenstein 1999 pp. 223–27; Freke and Gandy 1999 pp. 243–51).

In later history, Christian Crusades inspired by popes were directed against 'heretics' in the Orient as well as in the West. Repression of heresy by force became standard Church practice. No Roman emperor, however ruthless, could have matched the brutality of the Crusades first incited by Pope Urban II against the Muslim Orient. One example was the horrible incident of cannibalism occurring at the Syrian city of Ma'arrah on 11 December 1098. The Frankish chronicler Radulph of Caen documented the butchery: 'In Ma'arrah our troops boiled pagan [i.e. Muslim] adults in cooking pots; they impaled children on spits and devoured them grilled.' Another Frankish chronicler Albert of Aix, who accompanied the Crusade and took part in the battle of Ma'arrah, confessed the horror: 'Not only did our troops not shrink from eating Turks and Saracens, they also ate dogs.' Finally on 15 July 1099 the Christian army entered Jerusalem only to massacre every man, woman, and child of the Muslim non-combatant population, amounting to some 40,000 people (Fuller 1995 p. 33; Maalouf 1984 pp. 39–40). A century later, the crusade of Pope Innocent III against the Albigensian 'heretics' in southern France (1209–13) ended with the slaughter of hundreds of thousands of innocent people, and much of southern France was left desolate. The reason was that they denied the sacraments and the authority of the ecclesiastical hierarchy (Ben Nabi 1986 p. 192). When Simon de Montfort, who massacred the inhabitants of Beziers during this unholy crusade, was asked how the soldiers could tell a 'heretic' from a Christian, his reply was: 'Slay them all, God knows his own' (Knight and Lomas 1998 p. 159).

In 1252 Pope Innocent IV established an approved pattern of repression. He officially sanctioned the use of torture to extract 'confessions' from suspected 'heretics'. In 1555, alarmed by the spread of Protestantism, Pope Paul IV urged a vigorous pursuit of dissenting suspects, not sparing bishops and cardinals. An index of forbidden books was published banning books that offended 'correct' beliefs.

In October 1536, William Tyndale who ventured to make the first English translation of the Bible met bitter resistance from the Church and was finally arrested, and, publicly executed by burning at the stake. Martin Luther, who in 1520 translated the Bible into German, earned his excommunication by the Pope. In 1633, the Inquisition arm of the Roman Catholic Church tried the famous Italian physicist and astronomer Galileo, for 'grave suspicion of heresy'. His belief in a revolving earth was considered 'heretical', and he was therefore condemned to life imprisonment. It took another 360 years for this injustice to be redressed. Only on October 1992 was a Papal decree issued acknowledging the Vatican's error.

The Spanish Inquisition, an instrument of brutal suppression, was established by Papal decree in 1478. It tried Jews suspect of not being 'sincere' in professing Christianity. After 1502 it turned its attention to Muslims, and in the 1520s to Protestant suspects. In turn Protestantism had, in its lands, proved as repressive as the Spanish Inquisition.

John the Seer and his Revelation

Nevertheless, Church propaganda made a point in later times of singling out Nero as the one dreaded persecutor of Christianity. Emperor Nero and Emperor Caligula, one of his predecessors, were both identified as the Antichrist, that is the ultimate enemy of Christ, the beast of Revelation (Fuller 1995 p. 3; McGinn 2000 pp. 49–50). In the Church's unwillingness to accept that the 'End of Time' was not after all as imminent as Paul and John had both predicted, it never despaired of its quest for the 'Beast of Revelation', the dreaded Antichrist. And indeed there has been an abundance of candidates for this title, proliferating from time to time. Such candidates ranged on a very wide and indeed contradictory spectrum, extending from the Pope himself as believed by some Protestants, to Saddam of Iraq (Fuller 1995 pp. 13, 144, 159–60). Not because of Saddam's tyranny, but because Iraq in the Christian fundamentalist's mind is a symbol of the former Babylon the Great, 'The Mother of Harlots and Abominations of the Earth' (Revelation 17: 5). Interest in identifying Saddam with the Antichrist, the beast of Revelation, peaked before and during the second Gulf war in 1991.

John, the author of Revelation, was one of the Christian residents in Rome who escaped Nero's atrocities. The catastrophe that befell his fellow Christians was for him a sign that that the long-awaited end of time, predicted by Paul, was finally forthcoming. Echoing Paul's prophecy before him he wrote in his Revelation, 'for the time is at hand' (Revelation 1: 3). A few years earlier, Paul had prophesied the end of history in his own lifetime (I Corinthians 7: 29, 31). The long overdue return of 'Christ', after thirty years of absence from the scene, combined with the catastrophe that befell Christians in Rome, fuelled renewed expectations in the Second Coming. Refusing to reconcile himself to reality, John fancied and elaborated the Second Coming in his own Revelation: 'Behold, he comes with clouds, and every eye shall see him, and they also which pierced him' (Revelation 1: 7), meaning in the lifetime of those who took part in 'killing' him! His Hellenistic Chrestos was required to return as a powerful warrior-king who would annihilate his enemies. Rome was historically the first to be stigmatized as the 'Beast' of John's Revelation, the persecutor of Christianity, symbolized as 'the dreaded Whore of Babylon'. For John, there was no other alternative but for Christ to return as an avenger to annihilate not only the Romans, but also all humanity except a chosen 144,000 sealed on their foreheads (Revelation 7: 1–8). Thus he wrote his visions, excerpts of which are quoted above. Ironically, this pattern of expectations was to repeat itself on various occasions throughout Christian history up to the present time.

John's stigmatization of Rome as the 'Great Whore', symbolized as Babylon the Great, 'The Mother of Harlots and Abominations of the Earth' (Revelation

17: 5) was descriptive. He presented Rome as a woman fornicating with a beast that had seven heads, alluding to seven successive emperors of Rome, starting with Augustus and ending with the short lived reign of Otho in 69 CE. This puts the date of authorship of Revelation squarely in the year 69 CE right after the fall of the seventh emperor Otho between January and April 69 CE (Revelation 17: 1–11), and definitely before the destruction of Jerusalem by the Romans in 70 CE, since its author anticipated that a mere one tenth of the city would be destroyed (Revelation 11: 13). He also predicted that the temple would remain unharmed (Revelation 11: 1–2), The sheer inaccuracy of John's prophecies was proven much sooner than he had expected. A mere one year after his writing of Revelation, Jerusalem and the temple were in ruin.

John's Revelation proved him to be ultra-fanatical, greatly biased and anti-Roman with an immense grudge. If John's feeling was representative of the sentiment of Pauline Christians of his time, at least in Rome, it may explain why Nero singled out Christians for punishment following the fire. We have noted that Tacitus, the Roman historian, mentioned that Christians, at the time of the fire, were arrested in Rome for their obvious extremism and hatred of non-Christians, something that made them natural candidates for the charge of arson (Tacitus 1996 p. 365). It was the kind of sentiment exhibited by John's Revelation, topped by his explicit prophecy and aspiration that not only Romans, but all humanity, excepting a chosen 144,000, should perish in a lake of brimstone and fire.

On the other extreme of Christian sentiments towards Rome, we read Paul's letters enjoining obedience to governing authorities as a sign of obedience to God. 'Let every soul be subject unto the higher powers, for there is no power but of God: the powers that be are ordained by God. Whosoever therefore resists the power resists the ordinance of God. And they that resist shall receive to themselves damnation' (Romans 13: 1–2). Notably, both Paul and John wrote their contrasting treatises during the reign of the same Roman Emperor, Nero. Some five decades later, Luke in his book of Acts adopted the same appeasing attitude towards the Roman governing authority when he addressed both his Gospel and his book of Acts to a Roman official, the 'most excellent Theophilus' (Acts 1: 1; Luke 1: 3).

The Rapture

The meagre number of 144,000 humans to be saved according to John's Revelation must have been a source of embarrassment to the Church, and a nightmare for the faithful. In response to this situation, fundamentalist Christian preachers during the last two hundred years devised a solution in the form of an end time escapism to soothe their credulous followers. The solution assured 'saved' Christians of their 'rapture' before the tribulations that will follow the Second Coming. Rapture means 'catching up'. This is in reference to Paul stating in his first Epistle to the Thessalonians: 'For the Lord himself shall descend from heaven with a shout, with the voice of the archangel, and with the trumpet of God, and the dead in Christ shall rise first; then we which are alive and remain shall be *caught up* together with them in the clouds, to meet the Lord in the air, and so shall we ever be with the Lord' (I Thessalonians 4: 16–17). In this manner those who are 'born again' Christians need not worry about the horrendous end that is to befall the rest of humanity (Halsell 1999 pp. 33–37; McGinn 2000 pp. 253–54). 'Therefore comfort one another with these words' (I Thessalonians 4: 18).

The Middle Eastern Legacy of John the Seer

It is perhaps true that John's Revelation, at the time of its writing, reflected the sentiment towards Rome of those Christians who must have been deprived and frustrated antagonists to Roman rule, perhaps willing to take part in insurgencies or subversive activities against the state. This was sharply contrasted by the view of other Christians of the time who accepted Paul's writings, which considered governing authorities – Nero at the time – to have been appointed by God. It may be that Paul wrote his views with the intention of both placating his followers and avoiding friction with the Roman authorities, while awaiting the return of Chrestos.

Although both Paul's and John's prophecies on the 'Second Coming' and the 'End of Time' were proven grossly in error, yet Pauline Christianity, which Paul never intended for future humanity, was able to proliferate not only in the Graeco-Roman world of his time, but also into future generations of Western civilization. More remarkable is that many Christians up to the present time have never despaired of the Second Coming. Even now in twentieth-century USA, no less than 53 per cent of the population, including former President Reagan, were reported to believe in the imminent 'Second Coming' and 'End of Time' (Fuller 1995 p. 4). Little wonder that Hal Lindsey was able to sell twenty million copies of his book *The Late Great Planet Earth* predicting the imminent End of History and claiming that humanity now lives an era of the Beast, the Antichrist (Halsell 1986 p. 9), to which Revelation designates the number 666 (Revelation 13: 18).

Conspicuously, such sentiment, together with the prophecies on the Second Coming and the End of Time, has been instrumental during Christian history in shaping the feelings and actions of the Christian West towards the Middle East and its people.

In 1095, Pope Urban II declared that the first Crusade to Jerusalem was designed by God to help Christianity 'flourish again in these "last times" so that when the Antichrist begins his reign there – as he shortly must – he will find enough Christians to fight [him]' (see Fuller 1995 p. 33).

Those Christians who share beliefs in the inevitability of the Second Coming and in the 'imminent End of Time' ideology are today called fundamentalists. The surge of the Christian fundamentalist mentality in the Western Hemisphere has been, not only a driving force behind Western policy in the Middle East, but also specifically punishing to the people of that region, first and foremost in Palestine, and second in Iraq, not to mention other Islamic countries opposed to Israel. The entanglement of the Jews into the picture of the Second Coming, having had a drastic effect on shaping Western policy in the Middle East, threatens catastrophe for the people of the region and for world peace at large.

John's Legacy on Palestine

On the strength of John's Revelation, Christian fundamentalists in the Western Hemisphere, some two millennia after John, are still able to convince themselves as well as their followers that the creation of Israel in Palestine was a most necessary prelude for the 'Second Coming' of Christ and the 'End of Time'. Many Americans who originally had been anti-Jewish on the grounds that the Jews rejected and 'killed' the Messiah later turned into ardent supporters of Israel because of the ostensible role that Israel is to play in the scheme of the 'Second Coming' and fulfilment of 'prophecies'.

Grace Halsell, a distinguished American journalist, writer, and speech writer for former President Johnson, documented in her book *Prophecy and Politics*, the most astonishing and compelling details in this regard. The fundamentalist mentality is neatly summarized in the words of one fundamentalist American: 'Jesus can't return unless there is an Israel for him to return to' (see Halsell 1986 p. 124). Put differently, now that the state of Israel has been established, the countdown to the End of Time has started.

Fundamentalist 'born-again' Christians in the USA strongly believe that Jews are God's Chosen People, and that God gave the Holy Land to the Jews. And that God blesses those who bless the Jews, and curses those who curse the Jews. In addition, and like their forefathers almost 2,000 years ago, they have not despaired of awaiting the 'imminent' End of Time, which will be signalled by the battle of Armageddon in Palestine. Armageddon is alleged to be the site of the final battle between the forces of good led by the returning Christ, and the forces of evil led by the Antichrist, a horrible battle from which the returning Christ will obviously emerge victorious though at a tremendous cost of devastation and human suffering. Christ's victory will be followed by the establishment of God's Kingdom on earth, literally not metaphorically, over which Christ will reign supreme for 1,000 years from his headquarters in Jerusalem. Acknowledging Christ as their awaited Jewish Messiah, Jews will then convert to Christianity and will participate with Christ in the administration of his millennial kingdom on earth! Satan will be chained during this period, giving rise to its description as the happy millennium. It is far from clear why Satan will be let loose again at the end of this period and allowed to deceive the nations in the 'four quarters of the world' (Revelation 20: 8).

The preaching of Armageddon theology has become the fashion within the American Christian Right, the fundamentalist Christians of America. Through a powerful network of hundreds of radio and television stations, tens of thousands of fundamentalist American preachers and TV evangelists of this belief are now able to penetrate the hearts and minds of tens of millions of Americans. The Armageddon theology is simplistic and based on the premise that the end of the world is at hand (Halsell 1986 p. 10). Its prerequisite, which is the establishment of Israel in Palestine, has been fulfilled. This in turn has ushered the Second Coming of Christ who will soon return as a militant warrior-king to crush his enemies in the horrible battle of Armageddon. The faithful have a role to expedite the Second Coming. Many believe that a nuclear holocaust at this time would be most desirable as the only means that ensures a quick Second Coming. Former President Reagan was not too far from this belief. Influential fundamentalist preachers such as Jerry Falwell, Jimmy Swaggart, Pat Robertson, Hal Lindsey, and their like, find delight in describing and preaching the horrors of Armageddon to their credulous audience (Halsell 1986 p. 28).

Fundamentalist preachers are not a marginal splinter group in the American scene but have made substantial inroads into American politics. One TV evangelist, Pat Robertson, who once personally participated in Israel's invasion of Lebanon 1982, became a US presidential contender in 1988 (Halsell 1999 p. 92). The fundamentalist common wisdom is that one need not worry about nuclear proliferation, nor about escalation of the Arab–Israeli conflict that may ignite a third world war, since such developments are parts of an inevitable divine scheme that will result in the Second Coming of Christ. Fundamentalist wisdom on predestination has it that one need not work for peace but accept war as the inevitable will of God. James Watt, once US Secretary of the Interior, indicated to a US House of Representatives committee that, in view of Christ's imminent return, he would not worry much about the destruction of natural resources (Halsell 1986 p. 10).

Falwell specifically predicted: 'I do not think we have 50 years left, I do not think my children will live their lives out' (Halsell 1986 p. 35). In turn, Falwell reported that Reagan had told him, 'Jerry, I sometimes believe we are heading very fast for Armageddon right now'. Hal Lindsey in *The Late Great Planet Earth* predicted that, with the creation of Israel in Palestine, the countdown towards the end of time has started. In a spirit identical to that of John the Seer, Lindsey claims that the returning Christ will 'lay waste' to the earth and scorch its inhabitants and that only 144,000 thousand 'Born Again' will survive (Halsell 1986 p. 30).

Since 1970 Billy Graham has been warning, 'the world is now moving rapidly towards Armageddon', and 'the present generation of young people may be the last generation in history'. In June 1971, the then Governor Reagan asked Billy Graham to deliver a spiritual 'State of the State' address to both Houses of the California legislature. After the talk Reagan asked Graham, 'Do you believe that Jesus Christ is coming soon?', to which Graham replied, 'The indication is that Jesus Christ is at the very door, he could come any time'. Reagan was reported to have been very much impressed, and went along with it. Reagan later said, 'All prophecies that had to be fulfilled before Armageddon have come to pass ... everything is falling into place. It can't be too long now.'

In 1980, presidential candidate Reagan addressed a group of Jewish leaders saying, 'Israel is the only stable democracy we can rely on as a spot where Armageddon could come'. As president, Reagan arranged for Jerry Falwell to attend National Security Council briefings and discuss with top officials, plans for a nuclear war with Russia. Reagan also approved Hal Lindsey for a talk to Pentagon strategists on the prospect of a nuclear war with Russia. Jerry Falwell, Hal Lindsey, Pat Robertson, and similar evangelists of the Christian right are of the belief that the Second Coming of Christ is assured after a period of global natural disasters, economic collapse, social chaos, and a nuclear war igniting Armageddon.

In 1983 President Reagan used the phrase 'evil empire' as a description of the then Soviet Union, in the sense that it was part of the evil powers of darkness backing the Antichrist in the forthcoming horrible battle of Armageddon. In 2002 US President George Bush Jr almost echoed Mr Reagan's description of the Soviet Union as an 'evil empire', by declaring Iraq, Iran and North Korea an 'axis of evil'. In the battle of Armageddon Israel and its allies, i.e. the powers of good, will fight alongside Christ in his Second Coming! In a conversation in 1983 with Tom Dine of the American Israel Public Affairs Committee President Reagan stated: 'You know, I turn back to your ancient prophets in the Old Testament and the signs foretelling Armageddon, and I find myself wandering if we are the generation that is going to see that come about ... Believe me [these prophecies] certainly describe the times we are going through' (Halsell 1999 p. 17).

With the 'End' in mind, Reagan felt a religious conviction to increase the military might of the USA in preparation for the final battle. There is little doubt that this apocalyptic belief considerably influenced Reagan's policy decisions on matters of economic policy, domestic spending, armament, and military spending. During Reagan's two terms of presidency the US budget deficit spiralled to a scale never before reached in US history. Reagan's economic policy of inflationary spending, 'Reaganomics' as it was called, stemmed from the premise that there was no need to worry about US spiralling national debt since it was God's plan to bring about the end of time soon. His view was that money should be optimally and primarily spent on arms. Domestic programmes requiring public finance could be cut down on the grounds that the End was near. Reagan was reported to have said, 'Armageddon can not take place in a world that has been disarmed' (Halsell 1986 pp. 40–50).

It is a chilling thought in retrospect, that the president of the most powerful nation on earth, having allied himself with Israel, firmly believed in the Armageddon theology, and was emphatically and energetically looking forward to a horrible apocalyptic outcome. It was perhaps no less than miraculous that Reagan's terms of office elapsed without an outbreak of a third world war propelled by self-fulfilling prophecies.

American fundamentalist Christian 'pilgrims' who visit Israel typically wear a pin proclaiming, 'Israel, we love you, because God loves you' (Halsell 1986 p. 51). Fundamentalist Evangelical preachers such as Jerry Falwell have succeeded in transforming John's Revelation into an Israel cult, a mythology that clearly and flatly perverted the message of Jesus the Messiah. The fundamentalists have elevated the cult of Israel above all Christian belief. The mythology of John's Revelation has been conveniently and deliberately misrepresented and employed as a powerful political tool for aiding Israel (Halsell 1986 p. 66). In a totally pro-Israeli fashion, it has shaped American policy towards the Middle East in general, and Palestine in particular. Falwell flatly proclaimed, 'If we fail to protect Israel, we will cease to be important to God'. Israel is a most necessary pillar of the fundamentalists belief system, without it, their belief crumbles.

On August 1985, the fundamentalist TV evangelist, Pat Robertson, summarized the general stand of the American Christian Right towards Israel and the Middle East, saying, 'There is regard and concern among Christian fundamentalists for the Arabs, but it pales into insignificance compared to our feelings toward Jews' (Halsell 1986 p. 67).

Sadly, Robertson's statement, typically and almost exactly, reflected official American policy on Palestine. On April 1998, the US Assistant Foreign Secretary, Martin Indick, declared that the term 'even-handed mediator between Israel and the Arabs, does not exist in the American [political] dictionary, because the relationship between the US and Israel is very special' (*Al-Riyadh*, 24 April 1998). In consequence of this 'very special' relationship, the USA, with its vast economic resources and tremendous military apparatus, continues to support, condone, and directly or indirectly encourage Israel's aggressions against its Arab neighbours and the Palestinian people. It may suffice to learn that Martin Indick was an officer in the Israeli army actively participating in the 1973 Arab–Israeli war. He then emigrated to the USA in 1993, only to become the US ambassador to Israel in 1995 (*Al-Sharq Al-Awsat* 9 April 2001 p. 8).

Curiously, one might ask the question: why Armageddon? What is so significant about this site in Palestine that a final cosmic battle of annihilation has to take place there? Armageddon is 'Tel Megiddo' in Canaanite, meaning the hill of Megiddo. In the tenth century BCE, Megiddo in Palestine was a typical Canaanite hill fortress strategically located some 30 km to the south-east of the present-day coastal city of Haifa. The prefix *har* means 'hill' in Hebrew; hence *har-megiddo* or *armageddon* meaning 'Hill of Megiddo' (Halsell 1986 p. 22). It seems that the Hebrew take over of Megiddo from the Canaanite, and subsequent battles to defend the city against the Egyptians, resulted in bitter memories. In 609 BCE a Jewish king Josiah was killed in battle while trying to defend the strategic Megiddo fortress against the Egyptians (Rhymer 1996 p. 53). Centuries later, John, author of Revelation and a Jew of the Pauline faith, decided to immortalize Armageddon memories in his own way!

In modern times, the British general Allenby commanded British troops in Palestine during the latter part of the First World War. He was able in September 1918, to cut off the lines of retreat of the defeated Ottoman army in Northern Palestine. Either in admiration of or in anticipation of the awaited cosmic battle, Allenby could not fail to give the name Megiddo to his successful skirmishes with the Ottomans (Halsell 1986 p. 22). Ironically, the two British regiments that Allenby was commanding consisted in their entirety of Jewish volunteers (Schonfield 1997 p. 129).

John's Legacy on Iraq, the Former Babylon

No less mysterious is John's stigmatization of Babylon the Great as the Mother of Harlots and Abominations of the Earth! With such stigmatization, Babylon became for the West a symbol of vice and every abomination of the earth.

Undoubtedly John was imbued with the Old Testament spirit that yearned to crush little Babylonian children against the stones. 'O daughter of Babylon, who are to be destroyed; happy shall he be, that rewards thee as thou has served us. Happy shall he be, that takes and dashes thy little ones against the stones' (Psalms 137: 8–9).

In 598 BCE, more than six centuries before John's time, the Chaldean king Nebuchadnezzar took Jerusalem after a three-month siege. He was remarkabley lenient to the Jews. The Jewish king Jehoiachin and his entourage were taken to a comfortable captivity in Babylon while Jerusalem and the temple were left intact. Zedekiah, a newly installed Jewish king in Jerusalem rebelled once more against Babylon with the result that the Babylonians in 587 BCE retook and destroyed Jerusalem and the temple. Zedekiah and many of his subjects were taken in chains to Babylon with only the poorest inhabitants left behind. The deportees remained in Babylon for 48 years (Rhymer 1996 pp. 54–55). Their return was made possible through the generosity of the Persian king Cyrus who overran Babylon and its territories including Palestine in 539 BCE and decreed that Jewish exiles could return. This in turn explains why the Jewish Bible later called Cyrus a 'Messiah' although he was a pagan. Needless to say, the Babylonian captivity hardly justified an everlasting grudge and hatred towards Babylon and its future generations; something which the Jewish clergy decided to immortalize in the Old Testament.

It is a sad irony of history that since John wrote his Revelation, one net result has been that Babylon became instantly recognizable in the Bible, by both Jews and Christians, as typical of any tyranny, and a symbol of oppression, vice, and corruption. When St Augustine wrote his confessions about his youth, he used the same metaphor: 'See with what companions I ran about the streets of Babylon, and how I wallowed in its mire as though in cinnamon and precious ointments. That I might cling to its navel ... for I was easy to seduce'. He symbolized his pious mother as 'the mother of my flesh, who had fled from the centre of Babylon' (Ryan 1960 p. 69).

It is hardly comprehensible that the Christian Church, in the fourth century, decided to include Revelation as part of Holy Scripture: the Christian Bible! It is also one of the great ironies of history that Revelation incorporated into Holy Scripture left such an indelible effect, not only on the Western public mind, but also on Western policy on the Middle East for many generations.

Since the end of the second Gulf war in 1991, the USA and Britain professed their intention to help Iraqis topple their dictator Saddam. But the net result of the US/British embargo policy has been to perpetuate the suffering of the people of Iraq while Saddam remains firmly in power. This may not have been accidental, nor an inadvertent by-product of Western policy. One need only remember that, in the immediate aftermath of the liberation of Kuwait, the people of Basra in southern Iraq led an insurgency against Saddam, only to face ruthless suppression by the Iraqi presidential guard coming from Baghdad. The US forces on site provided – intentionally or inadvertently – safe passage to Basra, for the Iraqi presidential guard to quell the rebellion.

There has been no shortage of books relating present-day Iraq to 'Babylon the Great Whore, mother of Harlots', for example, Charles Taylor's *Saddam's Babylon the Great*, and the book *The Rise of Babylon* by Charles Dyer of the Dallas Theological seminary, which shows Saddam's picture on the cover. Even after the defeat of Saddam, Dyer suggested, Iraq may still emerge as 'Babylon the Great Whore' and Saddam may still emerge as the Beast of Revelation, the Antichrist (see Fuller 1995 pp. 160, 222). It is small wonder that, more than a decade after the defeat of Saddam, economic sanctions are still exacted on Iraq in a fashion that can only hurt the Iraqi population without in any way affecting their dictator.

TEN

The Protestant Reformation and Christian Fundamentalism

And, had Thy Sustainer so willed, He could have made all people one single community – with one belief, but He willed otherwise – and so people continue to hold divergent views. Except those on whom Thy Sustainer bestowed His mercy, and to this end did He create them. (Qur'an 11: 118–19)

Christian Fundamentalism

The phenomenon of Christian fundamentalism seems to have first surfaced in Europe towards the beginning of the sixteenth century, with the eruption of the Protestant revolution onto the scene. The European Renaissance together with the Protestant revolution – better known as the Reformation – had set the stage for the modern history of the West. Since then the Jewish people, who were traditionally considered enemies of the Christian Catholic Church, began to figure prominently in a new Protestant perspective. A perspective which was to become both sympathetic and supportive of the concept that the Jews should 'reassemble' in Palestine in accordance with a 'Providential Scheme' for the 'Second Coming' of Christ. With the entanglement of the Jews in the picture, Christian fundamentalism took shape and eventually formed various beliefs and concepts (Canaan 1995 pp. 31–39), such as:

- a firm belief in the Jewish Bible as part of Christian Holy Scripture.
- a literal, rather than allegorical, interpretation of the Bible.
- renewed belief in the imminent 'Second Coming' of Christ, as Paul had prophesied during his missionary years.
- the necessity of creating a Jewish 'home' in Palestine, in which the Jews should 'reassemble', as a biblical pre-condition for the 'Second Coming' of Christ.

- looking forward eagerly to the 'millennium' whereby the returning triumphant Christ will reign supreme.
- the religious obligation of the faithful to exert human effort to expedite, and lay the ground, for the fulfilment of the 'Second Coming'.

The Reformation, started in Germany by Martin Luther (1483–1546), basing itself on the principle of returning to the 'original Scriptures'. According to Luther, Scriptures were inerrable, while the Pope was not infallible as had been believed until then. Therefore, Scriptures – not the Pope or the clergy – were the only basis for authority. To this end, the Bible was eventually translated into vernacular languages so as to be within the direct reach of every Christian and not remain a closed book – in the form of the Latin Vulgate, or the Aramaic Peshitta – which none but a limited elite could hope to approach. Roman Catholic practice theretofore had effectively restricted personal use of the Bible solely to the clergy.

While Martin Luther led a bitter struggle against the Church in Germany, King Henry VIII in England used his royal authority to sever relations with the Pope and bring Papal and Catholic Church domination to an end. In 1534 the king issued a series of Acts that were to free the Church of England from Papal authority. The king himself became head of the Anglican Church.

In addition to considering the authority of the Bible to be over and above that of the Pope, the Protestants went as far as identifying the Pope with the Antichrist. Luther openly referred to the Pope as 'the right Antichrist' and said 'the conviction that the Pope is Antichrist is a matter of life and death for the church'. Luther was not singling out an individual Pope for condemnation, but rather the Papal office in its entirety. He explicitly stated that 'the Papacy is indeed nothing but the Kingdom of Babylon and of the true Antichrist' (McGinn 2000 pp. 203, 206; Fuller 1995 p. 37). Thus, Protestants viewed Catholicism as a hopeless combination of heresies and superstitions. They considered the Roman Catholic Church to be a rival to true gospel faith; a rival conspiring with Satan to delude the faithful. At a later stage, American Protestants after their migration to the New World, identified the Roman Catholic Church with the 'false prophet' of Revelation (19: 20), assisting the Antichrist – the Pope – in his endeavour to be worshipped by the entire world (Fuller 1995 pp. 5, 145–48). But Protestants were not alone in their feelings towards the Pope. In modern times, when Pope John Paul VI visited Greece on 4 May 2001, Greek Orthodox multitudes demonstrating in Athens carried banners depicting the Pope as the arch-enemy of Christianity and portraying him as Satan with two horns.

Having translated the Bible into local languages, Christians started in the sixteenth and seventeenth centuries, for the first time in history, to buy, own,

The Protestant Reformation and Christian Fundamentalism

and interpret the Bible for themselves without the intervention of church authorities. Reading and understanding the Scriptures were no longer solely the privilege of the clergy.

Biblical scripture began to be read by children attending Sunday schools and church services, thus giving a sense of familiarity to names of places and characters in the Holy Land. Recurrent repetitions in church sermons, in Sunday schools and public meetings, made stories and personalities of the Old Testament quite familiar to the common European. With Jewish sermons becoming part of Christian prayers and texts of the Old Testament read regularly in Church, stories of the Old Testament became a main theme in European culture. This new attitude resulted in a new cultural approach greatly affecting Western outlook towards Palestine and the Middle East.

As part of this process, knowledge of Hebrew gradually became part of the culture, since it was the 'sacred' language supposedly spoken by Adam, Noah, and Abraham. It was also the language in which God spoke to Moses! As such, Hebrew was to become an important element, not only in pure religious studies but also taking its place side by side with European languages. Clergy and other sections of society spent a great amount of time and effort to study the Old Testament in its 'original language'. Many Protestants thought of Palestine as a Jewish land, and reduced its history before Christianity to such biblical stories narrating the Jewish presence in the land, notwithstanding its short duration. For the actual duration of Jewish history in Palestine see the Appendix.

The newly found zeal and interest in the Old Testament, the proliferation of Hebrew language and Hebrew studies in European Universities and cultural centres, culminated in charging the European mind with many new concepts and beliefs. A new Christianity had emerged, described as 'Judaized Christianity', 'Christian Zionism', or simply 'Christian fundamentalism'. Today, evangelical Protestants who share beliefs on Bible inerrancy, literal interpretation of the scriptures, and the requirement of a geographical Israel in Palestine as a necessary prelude to the Second Coming, are called Christian fundamentalists.

The new fundamentalist perspective went as far as considering Western civilization not merely as the collective Graeco-Roman heritage, but as Graeco-Roman-Hebrew as well (Shaban 1999 p. 10). It is in this context that the Protestant Reformation was described as a Jewish, or Hebraic, renaissance.

The Catholic Viewpoint

Classical Catholic ideology used to be of the belief that Jews had earned the wrath of God in consequence of the repeated crimes and sins they had committed throughout their history. Jews had thus deserved their Babylonian captivity (586–539 BCE) among many other divine punishments culminating in their final expulsion from Palestine in 70 CE. Prophesies of their return to the Holy Land already materialized, according to Catholic belief, when Cyrus the Persian king freed them from Babylon and allowed their return to Palestine (537–515 BCE).

Their expulsion from Palestine at the hands of the Romans, in 70 CE, was a direct result of their failure to acknowledge Jesus as their Messiah, thus bringing their existence as a nation to an end. This was something that they deserved not only for rejecting and 'killing' Christ, but for allying themselves with the Antichrist at every opportunity (Fuller 1995 pp. 139–44). In consequence they became traditional enemies of Orthodox Christianity.

Scriptural Jewish prophesies on the rise of the 'new Israel' meant, according to Catholic interpretation, the rise of the Christian Church as the only legitimate heir to Israel. According to Catholic belief, the Christian Church is the manifestation of the Kingdom of God on earth, exactly as St Augustine wrote and preached in the fifth century.

It is interesting that, prior to the Protestant Reformation, there was not the slightest notion among Christians of the 'requirement' of 'reassembling' the Jews in Palestine, or even in their presence as a Jewish nation. Palestine, according to Catholic belief, was simply the land from which Christ's light emanated to the whole world, and Jerusalem was the City of the New Testament that had replaced the Old Testament. Passages of the book of Revelation and other biblical passages on this matter were interpreted allegorically rather than literally.

Within this Orthodox Christian context, it is not quite understood why Protestant Christians came to believe, almost suddenly, that a 'new Israel' should literally be established in Palestine to which all Jews should return. For fifteen centuries orthodox Catholic Christianity did not hold this idea until the Protestant Reformation overturned the tables by rejecting allegorical interpretations of the Catholic Church. The net effect was that literal and narrow fundamentalist interpretations of the book of Revelation became catastrophic for Palestinians and Middle Eastern people in particular, and for world peace and international peaceful co-existence in general. This particular Protestant belief has been a major factor in shaping US and Western policies towards Palestine and the Middle East.

The Providential Plan According to Western Fundamentalism

The Protestants insisted that the 'New Israel' did not mean the Christian Church as St Augustine had metaphorically preached (Halsell 1986 p. 134; Halsell 1999 p. 60). To them, the New Israel was to comprise the children of Israel, the descendants of Jacob, i.e. the Jewish nation, which is to return to the 'Promised Land' and establish a geographical Kingdom of God. This was a necessary prelude to the Second Coming, and the fulfilment of the Utopian millennium, (Revelation Ch. 20). According to Protestant belief, Israel was to become the Kingdom of God on earth, while the Christian Church represented the Kingdom of God in Heaven. As a consequence, Protestants became staunch advocates of Zionism.

As the Providential Plan called for the Second Coming of Christ, it was necessary for the Jews, as the 'Chosen People', to return to the 'Promised Land' in order to pave the way for the Second Coming. The Jews should be back in Palestine irrespective of merit, but rather in fulfilment of scriptural prophesies, and because of an active role they must play in a Providential Plan for the 'salvation' of humanity. The Protestants have it that Christ will return to Palestine only after the Jews have 'reassembled'. The Pauline 'End of Time' ideology, reinterpreted, hinged on restoring a Jewish nation in Palestine to which Christ can return (Fuller 1995 pp. 144–45). In this respect there arose a slight difference between Jewish and Protestant aspirations. While Protestants are awaiting the Second Coming of Christ, Jews are awaiting his First coming, not as a Hellenistic Christ but as their own Messiah. To this end, the Jews are at the centre of a Salvation Plan that the Protestants are looking forward to. German Protestant, Paul Felgenhauer proclaimed in 1655, that Jews on the Second Coming of Christ would recognize Jesus as their Messiah (Halsell 1986 p. 135). According to Protestant belief, Jews and Christians will unite in faith after the Second Coming, a belief obviously rejected by the Jews.

Such a substantial change in ideology resulted in tremendous implications on the ground. On the practical level, Europeans, and subsequently Americans, felt a strong religious obligation to play an active role in making scriptural prophesies come true, which in turn should expedite the Second Coming and the beginning of the millennium prophesied in Revelation. This newly found enthusiasm was not confined to the popular level, nor to church missionaries, but proliferated among many prominent leaders, politicians, colonizers, and scholars.

Early American settlers, so-called pilgrims, often referred to themselves as the tribes of Israel in their flight from Europe across the Ocean to the New World. The extended metaphor described the Atlantic as the Sinai Desert or the

Red Sea, and the New World as the Land of Canaan, the Promised Land (Shaban 1999 p. 8).

An editor of *The Boston Medical and Surgical Journal*, J.V.C. Smith, wrote in 1853: 'As frequently expressed in the course of my observations on the future destiny of the Land of Promise, I fully believe in the final restoration of the Jews, and the re-establishment of their nation.' He also wrote in his 'Pilgrimage to Palestine': 'It is certain that until the present inhabitants are rooted out of the land, and a new race of men introduced in their stead, the Gospel will only be precious with a few, who can have little influence in changing the manners and customs of the whole' (Shaban 1999 pp. 3–4, 16).

In the field, some American missionaries and travellers had ambitious plans and were certain of their success. Many of them, having then despaired of converting Muslims, were of this opinion: 'you might as well convert bricks into brick-cakes. It is not the will of God that the East be Christianized'. The solution, many suggested, was that the local population be 'rooted out, and a better race of men be brought into the Orient' (Shaban 1999 p. 17).

The local population of Turks, Arabs, and Muslims, which they advocated rooting out, were presented in a variety of shades ranging from innocence to savagery, with many shades in between. One of them wrote 'This wild people continually remind us of our Indians' (Shaban 1999 p. 20).

Henry Jessup in *Fifty Three Years in Syria 1857–1910* and *The Mohammadan Missionary Problem* (1879), and Dr John Barkley in *The City of the Great King* (1858), offered the most detailed programmes for the future of the Orient. Their programmes prophetically included dividing the Orient among the major Western Powers, including Russia, and gathering the Jews of the world in the Holy Land in preparation for the establishment of the Kingdom of God. Some drew the borders of Greater Israel from the Euphrates to the Nile and from Mount Ararat to the Arabian Sea, and planned railroads to connect Israel with the West (Shaban 1999 p. 17).

> The destiny of the Orient was perceived as firmly locked to that of America, and the part to be played by the US was drawn by 'the hand of God'. The Orient, like the American West, seems 'to have been reserved by Providence to be the meeting place of the Anglo-Saxon on his eastern and western path of Empire.' The American duty is to fulfil the 'vision of Zion'. The missionary concern is to save the 'lost' Muslim souls. (Shaban 1991 p. 199)

Conspicuously, in 1968 Martin Luther King Jr expressed his passion for the new Israel in his famous 'I see the Promised Land' speech.

Such concepts and beliefs, having gradually taken root in the Western mind over the past four centuries, became the basis for missionary activities. It gained tremendous momentum towards the nineteenth century, and in the twentieth century such beliefs were translated into concrete political processes culminating in the creation of Israel, with the unconditional support of the USA, in particular, and the West in general.

In summary, 'American Orientalism has developed through the present century into a full-grown independent idiom. Its activities now take many directions: intellectual, academic, political, and religious. The "Middle East Studies Association of America" is an umbrella organization of many academic institutions that have made great strides in various fields of Oriental studies' (Shaban 1991 p. 197).

Pushing Forward the Providential Plan

John Adams, President of the USA 1797–1801, and Thomas Jefferson, President of the USA 1801–09, both members of a committee formed in 1776 to choose an official symbol for the new nation, recommended a representation showing Moses leading his people out of Egypt. John Adams repeatedly expressed his sincere desire towards the 'return' of the Jews, as an independent nation, to the 'land of Judah'. Benjamin Franklin, the well-known diplomat of the American Revolution suggested a symbol showing Moses splitting the Red Sea with his staff (Canaan 1995 p. 60).

In 1848 Warder Cresson, the US Consul in Jerusalem, helped establish a Jewish settlement in Palestine financed by a joint Christian–Jewish society based in the UK. In 1898 another US Consul in Palestine, Edwin Sherman Wallace wrote: 'The Land is waiting. The People are ready to come.' (Halsell 1986 p.139).

In England, in 1650, Oliver Cromwell, who became Lord Protector of the newly established Puritan Commonwealth of England, Scotland, and Ireland (1653–58), declared that the Jewish presence in Palestine would be the prelude to the Second Coming of Christ. One Fifth Monarchist John Spittlehouse urged Cromwell to carry the fight against Antichrist into the land of the Canaanites (McGinn 2000 p. 224).

In 1839, Lord Anthony Ashley Cooper, seventh Earl of Shaftesbury, known in Britain as the 'Great Reformer' urged all Jews to immigrate to Palestine. He saw them as the Christian's hope for salvation, playing a pivotal role in the 'divine plan' for the Second Coming of Christ. On Palestine he stated that it was a country without a nation for a nation without a country. He was instrumental in establishing a British consulate in Jerusalem with the devout evangelical William Young as first British Vice Consul. One of his official duties was to 'protect' all Jews residing in Palestine, at that time counting no more than 9690 in number (Halsell 1986 pp. 135–36).

In 1845, Edward Mitford of the London Colonial Office proposed 'the establishment of a Jewish nation in Palestine as a protected state under the guardianship of Great Britain.' He advocated that 'this state would place us in a commanding position in the Levant from whence to check the process of encroachment, to overawe our enemies and if necessary repel their advance' (Halsell 1986 p. 137).

T.E. Lawrence, the so-called 'Lawrence of Arabia', a British intelligence officer in Arabia during the First World War wrote: 'I was tired to death of these Arabs ... those petty incarnate Semites ... The Arab mind is strange and dark, full of depression and exaltations, lacking in rule.' About his role as leader of the Arab insurgents against the Ottomans he wrote: 'not being a perfect fool, I could see that, if we [the British] won the war, our promises to the Arabs were dead paper. Had I been an honourable adviser [to the Arabs] I would have sent my men home, and not let them risk their lives for such stuff' (Kabbani 1993 p. 110).

The British Prime Minister Lloyd George (1916–19), sponsor of the Balfour Declaration, was raised in a school that taught the history of the Jews more than it taught the history of England. Zionist leader Chaim Wiezman noted, after first meeting him, that he had met a man whose value to the Jewish cause was incalculable.

Arthur James Balfour, the British Secretary of Foreign Affairs (1916–19), to whom is attributed the infamous Balfour Declaration, was raised as a strict Protestant. Thanks to his Protestant upbringing he had been quite familiar with the Old Testament since his childhood. His mother whom he was accustomed to see reading the Old Testament over and over, had a tremendous effect on him. He described her as a woman of deep religious commitment. Balfour was deeply convinced of the inevitability of the 'return' of the Jews to Palestine as a necessary prelude to the Second Coming of Christ. His niece who wrote his biography said that he was strongly attached to the belief that Christianity owed the Jewish faith an incalculable debt. It was, in his opinion, a shame that Christianity did not adequately reward the Jews (Canaan 1995 p. 24).

Woodrow Wilson, President of the USA 1913–21, a strict Protestant and clearly a Jewish sympathizer, was quick to endorse the Balfour declaration on 31 August 1918.

Harry Truman, President of the USA 1945–49, carefully studied the Old Testament, and as a 'born-again' Baptist believed in every letter of it. He was strongly convinced of the 'religious justifications' for the establishment of Israel and made his Jewish sympathies very clear long before he became President. As such his hasty recognition of Israel in 1948 was not merely in

The Protestant Reformation and Christian Fundamentalism

pursuit of Jewish votes, nor due to mere pressure from the Jewish lobby as one may be inclined to believe, but a result of sincere personal religious convictions.

Jimmy Carter, President of the USA 1976–80, was a 'born-again' Evangelical with obvious fundamentalist convictions. During a speech at the Israeli Knesset in March 1979, he declared to the Israeli members of Parliament that: 'We share together the heritage of the Old Testament'. He firmly believed that the creation of Israel was a fulfilment of Old Testament prophecies. To him, peace in the Middle East meant nothing more than 'the secured and continued presence of the Jewish State in Palestine'. During a reception he arranged at the White House for the Israeli Prime Minister, Menahem Begin, he promised that the USA would, forever, support Israel. In a speech he declared that, since the destruction of Jerusalem (70 CE) the Jews had been praying that their coming year be in Jerusalem, and that now the Jews had returned to the land of the Torah after 2,000 years of exile, anguish, and discrimination (Canaan 1995 pp. 66–67; Halsell 1999 p. 61). Adding to his biased record, during his visit to Bosnia-Herzegovina in 1992 as a 'mediator' between Muslims and Serbs, Mr Carter proclaimed to the Serbs, famous for their heinous war crimes against humanity, that: 'The US people have misunderstood you'!

Ronald Reagan, President of the USA 1980–88, was an Adventist 'born-again' Christian, a strong believer in the Adventist ideology of Armageddon (Revelation 16: 16). He referred to quotations from the Old Testament on many occasions. Like John the Seer 2,000 years before him, he literally believed that the Second Coming of Christ was forthcoming in his own days. Under his presidency the USA accumulated spiralling budget deficits unprecedented in US history, mostly for armament presumably in preparation for the battle of Armageddon. To President Reagan, budget deficits did not matter because the End of Time was imminent. In his words there was 'no reason to get wrought up about the national debt if God is soon going to foreclose on the whole world'. As for domestic issues, since 'Christ is at the door' spending on domestic issues should not be taken too seriously (Halsell 1999 p. 102).

On 6 February 1983, Evangelical preacher Jerry Falwell declared that he favoured Israelis taking portions of Iraq, Syria, Turkey, Saudi Arabia, Egypt, Sudan, and all of Lebanon, Jordan and Kuwait. He stated that 'God has blessed America because we have cooperated with God in protecting that which is precious to him', meaning Israel (Halsell 1986 p. 141).

In Jerusalem, on 29 April 1998, while commemorating the fiftieth anniversary of the establishment of Israel, Netanyahu, then Prime Minister of Israel, declared to his audience, who included the US Vice-President Al Gore: 'The Americans were looking for the New Promised Land. This is the Real Promised Land. The Americans were looking for the City on the Hill. Jerusalem is the Real City on the Hill'. Not surprisingly, his statement was received with heated applause by Mr and Mrs Gore and the audience. Similarly President Clinton, during a speech to the Israeli Knesset on 27 October 1994, proved himself an obvious Zionist stating that 'sustaining Israel is important not only for American interests, but for all precious American values'. President Bush alluded to his 'born-again' experience and was indebted to the New Christian Right for his election. Afniri, the well-known Israeli peace activist, added that President Bush Jr is a typical representative of the fundamentalist Christian Right (*Al-Sharq Al-Awsat* 27 June 2001; Halsell 1999 pp. 11, 39, 102).

In short, the Protestant Reformation provided the Jews with a unique opportunity in history. They came to enjoy the support and respect of a massive portion of Western Christendom due to the very important role they were 'destined' to play in a 'Providential Plan'. Palestine is promised to them as the land of Israel and home for all the Jews. Simultaneously, for Christian fundamentalists, the Second Coming of Christ is thus guaranteed through the creation of Israel (Schonfield 1997 pp. 124, 129).

Awaiting the Messiah

John the Seer, a Jew who converted to the religion of Paul, and author of Revelation, which was destined to be the last book of the New Testament, portrayed a returning Christ similar to that awaited by the Jews. He had him stand on Mount Zion with 144,000 of his chosen, that is 12,000 from each of the twelve tribes of the children of Israel. His Christ would lead the final battle at Armageddon against the 'beast' and the kings of the earth and their armies of 'evil' gathered together. He would be the Lion from the Tribe of Judah, the root of David (Revelation 5: 5). He would see the Holy City, the New Jerusalem coming down from Heaven with its twelve gates, on which are written the names of the twelve tribes of Israel.

In parallel to the returning Christ of Revelation, the Jews have been awaiting their own military Messiah – not the same as Christ. Awaiting the military Messiah is one of the most important Jewish beliefs. The Messiah, the anointed warrior-king from the line of David is to appear and restore the Kingdom of David. He will save the Jews from 'exile' and bring them back to the Holy Land, whereby their enemies will be crushed, the temple of Solomon will be rebuilt, and Jerusalem will become their capital. They did not acknowledge Jesus as their Messiah because he denied any military associations with his mission, and made it clear that he was not destined to lead them against Rome. This is why they called him a pretender and imposter. Since then for 2,000 years they have been waiting for the advent of their military Messiah, the warrier prophet-king who will restore the kingdom of David.

Having waited that long, and having been greatly assisted in recent times by the eruption of Christian fundamentalism in the Western Hemisphere, they decided to take the initiative and come back to Palestine by sheer force. In retrospect, we can see that the Jewish Zionist movement was not born in a vacuum, but became possible only within the context of fundamentalist Christianity that recently permeated the West and which Zionist Jews have decided to exploit to the utmost. The Christian fundamentalist belief in the necessity to 'revive' a Jewish state in Palestine, and the return to Palestine of the 'exiled' Children of Israel, as a precondition for the Second Coming and the advent of the millennium, was a unique historical opportunity for Jewish Zionism.

This fundamentalist spiritual–political environment and driving force bore fruit with the convention of the first Jewish Zionist Congress in Basel, Switzerland in 1897, under an Austrian Jewish Journalist called Theodore Herzl. Herzl became the father of political Jewish Zionism. He appealed to Jews to live exclusively among Jews because, in his belief, they were hated worldwide, and this was the only way to guarantee their safety.

The first Jewish Zionist Congress notwithstanding, it is remarkable that Christian fundamentalists, in their effort to expedite the Second Coming of Christ, were far ahead of Jewish Zionists in their schemes for the 'return' of the 'Chosen People' to Palestine. The Protestant faithful consider it their religious obligation to act, in order to make/help biblical 'prophecies' come true.

Such religious zeal and belief was eloquently expressed by Van der Hoeven, at the first Christian–Zionist conference of the International Christian Embassy (ICE) (see below). In response to a view expressed by an Israeli participant that one third of the Israeli population was willing to trade land for peace with the Palestinians, Van der Hoevens' reply was that of a typical and fervent fundamentalist: 'We do not care what Israelis vote' he declared: 'We care what God says, and God gave that land [Palestine] to the Jews' (Halsell 1986 pp. 11, 133; McGinn 2000 p. 256).

Not many researchers have taken up the subject of the rise of Christian fundamentalism in the Western Hemisphere, which was simultaneously and ironically coupled, in the twentieth century, with a substantial defection rate from the Christian Church by disillusioned, disgruntled Christian intellectuals. One example of such defection is the more than two hundred theologians, professors, and doctors of divinity who participated in the 'Jesus' seminar' and produced their most valuable work 'The Five Gospels' (see Chapter 2). A substantial amount of Western critical literature has been forthcoming in the last century analysing and criticizing the untenable position of the Christian Church and Pauline Christian theology (Funk 1996 pp. 6, 13).

The International Christian Embassy

Having been instrumental in establishing the State of Israel in Palestine, the Christian fundamentalists further culminated their efforts, in the year 1980, by establishing a so-called 'International Christian Embassy'(ICE) in Jerusalem, as an umbrella group for Christian fundamentalists in the West in particular, and worldwide in general. Many believe that its funding comes from South Africa (Halsell 1986 pp. 98, 120).

On 27 August 1985 the ICE convened the first Zionist–Christian conference in Basel – to parallel the first Zionist conference convened by Herzl in 1897, and in the same auditorium as Herzl. The conference was attended by the director of the International Christian Embassy Johann Luckhoff of South Africa, by its fervent spokesman Van der Hoeven of Holland, its representative in Washington D.C. Richard Hellman, and Dr George Giacumakis, former director of the Institute of Holy Land Studies in Jerusalem (Halsell 1986 pp. 11, 132).

Conference resolutions urged all Jews throughout the world to leave their countries and proceed to assemble and live in Israel. The conference decided that Jerusalem the 'City of David' should be the unified capital of Israel forever, and that Judah and Samaria, misnamed the West Bank (sic), are part of Israel by virtue of Old Testament prophecies! The conference also urged the USA and all other nations having diplomatic missions in Israel, to move their embassies from Tel Aviv to Jerusalem. In addition, it 'demanded' that the USA and European countries desist from arming 'Israel's enemies'.

In 1988 the ICE convened its second Zionist–Christian conference in Jerusalem, celebrating the fortieth anniversary of the establishment of Israel. It decided that:

> the Jews have a sacred right to live freely on the land of Israel. That the evil spirits of Islam [sic] are responsible for spiritual slavery in the Arab world, for anti-Semitism, for oil blackmail, and for 'mocking God', due to the presence of a mosque in the most sacred Jewish site. Let everybody then pray against the spirit of Islam. (Canaan 1995 pp. 164–65)

Today tens of thousands of preachers in the USA are preaching similar concepts to more than half the American population, on hundreds of television and radio stations (Halsell 1986 pp. 13–17; Halsell 1999 p. 50).

The Islamic Perspective

Muslim beliefs on the mission of Jesus the Messiah, the Second Coming, the Promised Land, and the Kingdom of God, can be briefly summarized as follows:

The Awaited Messiah

Muslims are of the belief that Jesus was indeed the Messiah who had come to restore the Jewish religion to its pristine form, to rid it of pagan influence, and reform its moral and social standards. Jewish history abounds with a series of scandalous relapses into idolatry and moral decay, well-documented in the Old Testament. On this point the Qur'an has the following to say:

> The Messiah said: 'O children of Israel! Worship God – alone –, who is my sustainer as well as your sustainer' Behold whoever ascribes divinity to any being besides God, unto him will God deny paradise, and his goal shall be the fire; and such evildoers will have none to succour them. (Qur'an 5: 72)

> When Jesus came – to his people – with all evidence of the truth, he said, 'I have now come unto you with wisdom, and to make clear unto you some of that which you are at variance, hence be conscious of God, and pay heed unto me. Verily God is my sustainer, as well as your sustainer, so worship – none but – Him, this – alone – is a straight way'. (Qur'an 43: 63–64)

> And We caused Jesus, the son of Mary, to follow in the footsteps of those – earlier prophets – confirming the truth of whatever still remained of the Torah; and We vouchsafed unto him the Gospel – the Enjil –, wherein there was guidance and light, confirming the truth of whatever still remained of the Torah, and a guidance and admonition unto the God-conscious. (Qur'an 5: 46)

The Kingdom of God

The kingdom of God that Jesus meant and preached was not a triumphant Catholic Church, nor was it a visionary Utopian millennium that will materialize after his 'Second Coming', nor a geographical kingdom of one aggressor privileged nation, nor a kingdom composed of celestial beings of the spirits of prophets and saints. But it was the practical religion of Islam for all people, irrespective of race or ethnic origin, who believe in one God; a religion not confined merely to the spiritual concerns of men and women but which also regulates life and society; a religion that does not separate the spiritual from the mundane, and is to become worldwide, not bound by geography (Dawud 1990 p. 92; Izetbegovic 1989 pp. 194–200; Dawes 1999 p. 69). On this point the Qur'an states:

> O humankind! Behold We have created you all out of a male and female, and have made you into nations and tribes, so that you might come to know one another – not that you may despise each other –. Verily the noblest of you in the sight of God is the one who is most deeply conscious of Him. Behold, God is all-knowing, all-aware. (Qur'an 49: 13)

The Second Coming

The concept of the Second Coming may have penetrated Muslim thought at a late stage through what is known as 'Israelite thought intrusions', i.e. in Islamic Jurisprudence, whereas in fact there is no basis for such a concept in the Qur'an, nor in the authentic traditions of the Prophet. Contrary to Pauline theology, the Messiah did fulfil his mission during his lifetime on earth, and so there is no need for a Second Coming.

The Promised Land

The Muslims, who are the seed of Abraham through Ishmael, contend that prophecies in Genesis 15: 18 and 17: 20, promising the land between the Nile and the Euphrates to Abraham's seed, had already materialized with the advent of Islam. The Muslims were the only people from the seed of Abraham to have actually conquered the land from the River Nile in Egypt to the Euphrates in Iraq, fourteen centuries ago (Dawud 1990 pp. 27–28).

Islam and the Reforms of Luther

One of the most conspicuous – yet widely unnoticed – features of the Protestant Reformation is that many of the principles preached by Luther have their direct counterpart in what Islam preached 900 years ahead of Luther. Consider for example the following Lutheran principles that illustrate the point:

1. Human beings are not infallible. In particular, popes are not sacrosanct and should be made to face justice.

The Protestant Reformation and Christian Fundamentalism

In Islam, no human being, of whatever religious standing, is infallible. In comparison, the Pope's infallibility can be contrasted in Islam to the infallibility of consensus called *ijma'*. The Prophet is reported to have said: 'my people cannot agree on an error, and in case of disagreement the majority is to be followed' (Izetbegovic 1989 p. 197).

2. No human being – popes included – have power over purgatory. The Church indulgence system was no more than an aspect of papal corruption.

   Compare the Pope's supposed power with the basic Islamic tenet, *la ilaha illa allah*, meaning there is no deity except God. One corollary of this tenet is that all power rests with God alone in this world as well as in the hereafter. Put differently it means that power should be taken away from the clergy, the rulers, the wealthy, and returned to God alone (Izetbegovic 1989 p. 195).

3. Any Christian commoner should have access to Holy Scriptures without the mediation of clergy.

   Islam requires every Muslim to read and understand the Qur'an on his or her own. (Qur'an 47: 24).

4. Scripture is the only basis for authority. Considered as the 'word of God' Scripture is authoritative in its own right. The Bible alone should determine the practices and doctrines of the church.

   Islam agrees that Holy Scriptures are indeed the infallible word of God but only in their original pristine form as inspired to the Prophets.

5. Not only do all Christians have the right to read the Scriptures for themselves, but that papal claim to exclusive interpretive authority of the Bible is invalid.

   Since the dawn of Islam and to this day, hundreds of books on Qur'an exegesis have been produced by various individuals.

6. No church is needed to act as God's agent on earth. Divine grace is available without mediation.

   Every Muslim prays to God without mediation.

7. Priesthood is for all believers. Any layman is spiritually a priest. A ruler is himself a priest who can and should act to reform the church.

   Islam does not recognize any authority for clergy. In fact it does not recognize a separate clergy class. Every Muslim thinker is a theologian.

8. The doctrine of merits for saints has no foundation in the Gospels.
   Islam does not recognize an elite class of saints and monks.

9. Confession is voluntary, and can be made to any fellow Christian.
   Confession for a Muslim is unnecessary and is between man and God.

But Luther's decent intentions appealing to the intellect and to reason stopped short of radical reformation. Luther remained captive to Pauline theology, as he could not see beyond the mythical Christ of Paul. Or perhaps for him, as for most Christians, both the mythical Christ of Paul and the historical Jesus were one and the same. His reformation was unable to deal with the kernel.

For all his knowledge, or perhaps because of it, his doctorate of theology, his professorship, his search for evangelical perfection, his inner conflict, his struggle against uncertainties and doubts, Luther was unable to make a breakthrough and remained captive to dogma deeply ingrained in Pauline theology, which many before him found unintelligible and confusing. It was inconceivable for Luther to attempt to tackle what Bible scholars of the last two centuries had been working on. This was a point that stood at the heart of the reformation that Christianity needed, but which Luther was incapable of. Indeed Luther remained a deeply medieval figure, obsessed with the devil, the Antichrist, and the imminent End of Time. In the words of one theologian: 'Luther was proclaiming the Last Days, not the modern age' (McGinn 2000 pp. 201, 213). On the question of 'Bible inerrancy', Biblical criticism had to wait many centuries more, until modern scholars embarked on the quest for the historical Jesus, and on the study of the authorship of the Bible and its origins.

A notable figure in Luther's time was Franck Sebastian (1499–1542), one of the most modern thinkers of the sixteenth century, who was able to arrive at a radical cognition. Sebastian was fiercely anti-dogmatic and therefore strongly disillusioned with the concept of an institutional church. He had converted first from Roman Catholic to Lutheranism only to be disappointed in a 'Reformation' that dealt only with the surface. He looked at the Bible as a book full of contradictions veiling its true message, and believed that the 'Antichrist' entered the Church immediately on the death of the apostles so that there had never been a true church. It was only the heretics who have been members of the church. Sebastian's concept amazingly portrayed the original situation of the Christians in contrast to the Nazarenes during the first years of Christianity. The conclusion that Sebastian reached: 'All that we have learned since childhood, we must all of a sudden unlearn again. For one will sooner make a *good Christian* out of a Turk than out of a bad Christian or a learned divine' (McGinn 2000 pp. 216, 217). What Sebastian did not know is that a good Christian, i.e. a Nazarene, is in fact a Muslim.

As a matter of fact, the radical reformation that Christianity needed had come to it nine centuries ahead of Luther, but was largely ignored by the church institution. Islam came with a far-reaching reformation clearly drawing the line between the religion of Paul and that of Jesus. Islam's witness to the unity of God, and its attestation to the humanity of Jesus and his mother, were reformations which the church badly needed but sadly continues to ignore. The Church has always felt that the historical Jesus would pose a threat to its existence (Funk 1996 pp. 21–23

Fundamentalism

During the last decades of the twentieth century until the present time it has become common in the Western media to use the expression 'Muslim Fundamentalists' or 'Fundamentalist Islam' to imply the meaning of extremism, fanaticism, and even terrorism among Muslims. To the extent that many people in the West, became under the impression that the adjective: 'fundamentalist' has an ideological connotation in Islam. This is in spite of the fact that the word does not exist in Islamic terminology. As such there is no fundamentalist Islam or non-fundamentalist Islam, but simply Islam. Nevertheless, the recurrence of the term 'Fundamentalist Muslims' in the media has the effect of ascertaining that there exists a branch or category of Islam with this description. Whereas in fact there is none.

In contrast, we have already seen, that the connotation 'fundamentalism' is rather a Christian term that applies to those Christians who believe in the literal interpretation of the Bible, in the 'necessity' of 're-assembling' the Jews in Palestine as a 'prerequisite' for the Second Coming and the fulfilment of the Millennium, according to the prophesy by John the Seer in his Revelation.

Indeed, it is now estimated that fundamentalist Christians in the USA number about 62 million. That is more than one third of the entire American adult population believing that the End of Time at the battle of Armageddon is imminent. One poll showed that one half of American college graduates are awaiting the Second Coming of Jesus. A full 90 per cent of Protestant American missionaries around the world are fundamentalists having a powerful propaganda apparatus at their disposal in the form of an awesome network of radio and satellite TV stations. Evangelical preacher Jerry Falwell boasted that there are some 200,000 evangelical pastors in America willing to use their influence in support of Israel. The US Christian Right represents, at the present, more than a third of the Republican Party's total membership, and within the Party the Religious Right has tremendous institutional power, planning literally to hand-pick the next US president. If so, the USA is moving fast from a democratic into a theocratic government (Halsell 1999 pp. 8, 9, 19, 40, 44, 94, 102, 111).

This kind of present fervent religious mood seems to be in tune with past American history of religious revivals among Protestants. Since the early eighteenth century, intense religious interest marked by evangelical preaching and prayer meetings, frequently accompanied by intense emotionalism, were characteristic of American history.

Parallel instances of religious enthusiasm are also noted in Europe's Middle Ages where revivals took place in connection with the Crusades under the auspices of the papacy and monastic orders, sometimes with strange local adjuncts, as in the case of the Flagellants and the dancing mania. The Lutheran Reformation was also accompanied by religious revivals.

But it is more accurate to limit the application of the term 'revival' to the history of modern Protestantism, especially in Britain and the USA where religious revivals flourished with unusual vigour. The eighteenth century in particular was marked by two massive waves of religious revivalism in America. The first revival wave designated as the 'Great Awakening' took place in New England and other parts of North America. It started about 1720, culminated around 1740–42 and was characterized by renewed interest in millenniarism, the belief that the Second Coming of Christ was imminent. This in turn created the urgency to convert as many people as possible before the forthcoming end. Both Princeton University and Dartmouth College had their origin in this Great Awakening. Later generations would call this movement Evangelical Protestantism.

Toward the end of the eighteenth century a fresh series of revivals began in the USA lasting intermittently from 1790 to 1860. This second wave was called the 'Evangelical re-awakening', or simply the 'Second Great Awakening' culminating in 1859–61, rapidly expanding into western frontiers but also extending to New York and other eastern states. It is believed that in a single year half a million converts were received into the churches.

Churches soon came to depend upon revivals for their growth and even for their existence, and as time went on, missionary work was also taken up by itinerant preachers. The early years of the nineteenth century were marked by great missionary zeal extending to foreign lands (Wilson, B. 1999 pp. 70–74, 82–98).

APPENDIX

Palestine and Jerusalem, Chronology of Conflict

BCE

1630–1521	The domicile of Joseph in Egypt coincides with the Hyksos reign
c.1292–25	Reign of Ramses II Pharoah of persecution
1213	Exodus of the Israelites from Egypt with Moses – reign of Meneptah
970	Building of Solomon's Temple in Jerusalem
935	Death of King Solomon, the division of the Kingdom into Israel the North Kingdom (Samaria), and Judah the South Kingdom. Egypt's Pharoah, Shoshenq, occupies Jerusalem
721	Fall of Israel, capital Nablis (Schikkim), to the Assyrian King Sargon II, who deported the greatest part of the Jewish nation, never to return (the ten lost tribes). Since then various people have claimed to be the 'lost tribe of Israel', including British and American groups.
586	Fall of Judah, capital Jerusalem, to the Chaldean King Nebuchadnezzar, destruction of the Temple. Deportation of the Jewish population of Judah to Babylon, as a result, the city of Babylon becomes a symbol of oppression and corruption instantly recognizable in the Bible by both Jews and Christians as typical of any tyranny.
539	Persian King Cyrus II 'the Great' occupies Babylon.
537–515	Cyrus allows the return of the Jews to Palestine under their leader Zerobabbel. Reconstruction of the Temple in Jerusalem.
332	Alexander III 'the Great' occupies Palestine, spread of Hellenistic culture
320–198	Palestine under the Ptolemies of Egypt
198–63	Syria under the Seleucids

Appendix

167	Antiochus Epiphanes IV, the Seleucid King of Syria occupies Jerusalem
164	The Maccabees revolt, the Jews achieve self-rule in Jerusalem
62	The Romans under Pompey occupy Palestine

CE

30–37	Probable interval of the Mission of Jesus the Messiah
66	Jewish revolt in Palestine is crushed by the Roman general – later emperor – Vespasian during the reign of Emperor Nero.
70	Roman general Titus (later emperor) – son of Vespasian – occupies Jerusalem, destroys the temple, the Jewish Diaspora begins
135	Roman Emperor Hadrian completely destroys Jerusalem and the Temple and expels the remaining Jews. Jerusalem is renamed Aelia Capitolina, after Hadrian's forename Aelius.
135	Hadrian builds a pagan temple and calls it Jupiter to replace Solomon's Temple, later to be destroyed by Emperor Constantine I 'the Great', 325 CE
325	The first Ecumenical Council of Nicaea under Emperor Constantine convenes to settle the Arian dispute. The council decides that Jesus Christ was the Son co-substantial with the Father.
335	Construction of the Church of the Holy Sepulchre
431	The Third Ecumenical Council in Ephesus calls Mary Mother of God
570	Birth of Muhammad (20 August)
620	*Al-Isra'* (The Night Journey) and *Mira'j* (The Ascension) of The Prophet.
622	Migration of The Prophet to Madinah
638	Muslims under Omar conquer Jerusalem
691	Construction of Dome of the Rock Mosque
715	Construction of Al-Aqsa Mosque
1095	The First Crusade
1099	The Crusaders occupy Jerusalem
1187	The Muslims under Salah ad-Din retake Jerusalem from the Crusaders
1361–1452	Ottomans occupy large parts of Eastern Europe

Appendix

1452	Muhammad the Conqueror takes Constantinople
1492	Fall of Granada, Andalusia.
1516	Ottomans occupy Syria, Egypt and Hijaz (Sultan Salim the First)
1520	The Protestant Reformation underway
1534	King Henry VIII separates the English Church from the Pope with the Act of Supremacy
1538	Suleiman the Magnificent rebuilds the walls of Jerusalem
1653	Oliver Cromwell dissolves the English Parliament and replaces it with the Parliament of Saints, a council of Puritans imitating the Sanhedrin, the old Supreme Jewish Council
1656	Cromwell allows the return of the Jews (having been expelled in 1290) to England
1798	Napoleon I of France issues a statement during his occupation of Egypt urging the Jews to re-establish the old Jewish Kingdom in Jerusalem.
1860	Ernest Laharan, personal secretary of Napoleon III, publishes his book *The Eastern Problem, re-building the Jewish Nation*.
1865	Establishment of Palestine Discovery Fund under the auspices of Queen Victoria and the leadership of the Archbishop of Canterbury.
1878	Rev. William Blackstone publishes his book *Christ is coming*, translated into 48 languages, millions of copies are sold. When Herzl contemplates establishing Israel in Uganda, Blackstone presents him with a copy of his book saying that the will of God requires that Israel be in Palestine as a pre-condition for the coming of the Messiah.
1897	Herzl convenes the first Zionist conference in Basel
Nov. 1917	James Balfour, British Foreign Secretary issues his declaration for the establishment of a Jewish State in Palestine.
Dec. 1917	The British occupy Palestine and facilitate Jewish immigration
1948	The British withdraw from Palestine and the Jews proclaim their state.
1967	Israel occupies all of Jerusalem, Sinai, the West Bank, and Gaza
1977	Egypt's President Anwar Sadat visits Jerusalem, offers peace to Israel
1979	Sadat signs peace treaty with Israel
1980	Establishment of the International Christian Embassy in Jerusalem

Appendix

1982	Israel invades Lebanon and expels the Palestinians from it
1985	The International Christian Embassy convenes the first Zionist–Christian conferen on 27 August 1985 in Basel to mirror Herzl's first Zionist conference in 1897 and in the same hall.
1988	The International Christian Embassy convenes its second Zionist–Christian conference in Jerusalem, celebrating the 40th anniversary of the establishment of Israel.
1993	Palestinian Authority signs a peace treaty with Israel.
1994	Jordan signs a peace treaty with Israel.
2000	Israel evicted from South Lebanon.

Select Bibliography

Ali, Abdullah Yusuf, 1992, *The Meaning of the Holy Qur'an*, Amana Corporation, Maryland.
Allegro, John M., 1992, *The Dead Sea Scrolls and the Christian Myth*, Prometheus Books.
Asad, Muhammad, 1984, *The Message of the Qur'an*, Dar Al-Andalus, Beirut.
Baigent, Michel and Leigh, Richard, 1993, *The Dead Sea Scrolls Deception*, Touchstone Books, New York.
Ben Nabi, Malek, 1986, *The Qur'anic Phenomena*, Dar Al-Fikr, Damascus.
Canaan, Georgie, 1999, *Muhammad and Judaism*, Bisan Press, Beirut.
Canaan, Georgie, 1995, *Christian Fundamentalism in the Western Hemisphere*, Biesan Press, Beirut.
Crossan, John Dominic, 1992, *The Historical Jesus*, Harper Collins.
Dawes, Gregory W., 1999, *The Historical Jesus Quest*, Deo Publishing.
Dawud, Abdul Ahad, (Reverend Professor David Benjamin Keldani), 1990, *Muhammad in the Bible*, Islamic Propagation Center International, Durban.
Deedat, Ahmed, 1994, *The Choice: Islam and Christianity*, Abul Qasim Publications, Jeddah.
Eisenman, Robert, 1997, *James the Brother of Jesus*, Penguin.
Eusebius, 1989, *The History of the Church*, Penguin.
Ferguson, Everett, 1993, *Backgrounds of Early Christianity*, 2nd ed., Erdmans Publishing Company, Michigan .
Freke, Timothy and Gandy, Peter, 1999, *The Jesus Mysteries*, Harmony Books, NewYork.
Friedman, Richard Elliott, 1987, *Who Wrote The Bible*, Harper Collins, San Francisco.
Fuller, Robert, 1995, *Naming The Antichrist, The History of An American Obsession*, Oxford University Press.
Funk, Robert W., 1996, *Honest to Jesus*, Harper Collins, San Francisco.
Funk, Robert W., 1993, *The Five Gospels – The Jesus Seminar*, Macmillan, New York; Harper Collins, San Francisco.
Grant, Michael, 1999, *Jesus*, Phoenix Giant.

Select Bibliography

Grant, Michael, 1996, *The Twelve Caesars*, Phoenix Giant.
Halsell, Grace, 1999, *Forcing God's Hand*, CrossRoads.
Halsell, Grace, 1986, *Prophesy and Politics: The Secret Alliance Between Israel and the U.S. Christian Right*, Lawrence Hill Books.
Hart, Michael, 1992, *The 100: a ranking of the most influential persons in history*, rev. ed., Citadel.
The Holy Bible, King James Version.
Hoffman, Murad, 1993, *Islam The Alternative*, Garnet Publishing, Reading.
Izetbegovic, Alija Ali, 1989, *Islam between East and West*, American Trust Publications.
Kabbani, Rana, 1993, *Imperial Fictions, Europe's Myths of Orient*, Pandora/Harper Collins, San Fransisco.
Kelber, Werner H., 1997, *The Oral and the Written Gospel*, Indiana University Press.
Kirsch, Jonathan, 1997, *The Harlot by the Side of the Road*, Ballantine Publishing Group.
Knight, Christopher and Lomas, Robert, 1998, *The Second Messiah*, Arrow, London.
Lang, Jeffrey, 1995, *Struggling to Surrender*, Amana Publications, Maryland.
Lang, Jeffrey, 1997, *Even Angels Ask*, Amana Publications, Maryland.
Laidler, Keith, 2000, *The Divine Deception*, HeadLine Publisher, London.
Larson, Martin A., 1977, *The Story of Christian Origins*, Village Press, Oklahoma.
Le Glay, Marcel, Voisin, Jean-Louis and Le Bohec, Yann, 1997, *A History of Rome*, Blackwell.
Livingstone, E.A., 2000, *Oxford Dictionary of the Christian Church*, Oxford University Press.
Maalouf, Amin, 1984, *The Crusades through Arab Eyes*, Saqi Books, London.
Maccoby, Hyam, 1998, *The Mythmaker, Paul and the Invention of Christianity*, Barnes and Noble.
McGinn, Bernard, 2000, *AntiChrist*, Columbia University Press, NewYork.
Mack, Burton L., 1995, *Who Wrote The New Testament?* Harper Collins, San Francisco.
Miller, Robert J., ed., 1994, *The Complete Gospels*, Harper Collins, San Fransisco.
Mitchell, Stephen, 1991, *The Gospel According To Jesus*, Harper Collins, San Fransisco.
Pagels, Elaine, 1989, *The Gnostic Gospels*, (TGG), Vintage Books, New York.
Parrinder, Geoffrey, 1992, *Son of Joseph*, T. & T. Clark, Edinburgh.
Parrinder, Geoffrey, 1979, *Jesus in the Qur'an*, Sheldon Press, London.
Razi, 1990, *Tafsir al-Kabir*, Dar Al-Kutub al-Ilmiyya, Beirut.
Rhymer, Joseph, 1996, *Atlas of the Bible*, Chartwell Books, New Jersey.
Robinson, James, 1990, *The Nag Hammadi Library*, Harper Collins, San Francisco.
Robinson, Neal, 1996, *Discovering The Qur'an*, SCM Press.
Rubenstein, Richard E., 1999, *When Jesus Became God*, Harcourt.
Ryan, John K., 1960, *The Confessions of St Augustine*, Image Books Doubleday.
Said Edward, 1979, *Orientalism*, Vintage Books, New York.
Sanders, E.P., 1996, *Paul*, Oxford University Press.

Select Bibliography

Sanders, E.P., 1993, *The Historical Figure of Jesus*, Penguin.
Sanders, E.P., 1977, *Paul and Palestinian Judaism*, SCM Press, London.
Schonfield, Hugh, 1997, *The Mystery of the Messiah*, Open Gate Press, London.
Schonfield, Hugh, 1994, *The Passover Plot*, Element Publishers.
Schonfield, Hugh, 1993, *The Essene Odyssey*, Element Publishers.
Shaban, Fuad, 1999, 'Tapestry of Colors: The Orient in the Mind of America', *Journal of the University of Jordan*, Special Issue, Amman.
Shaban, Fuad, 1991, *Islam and Arabs in Early American Thought:The Roots of Orientalism in America*, Acorn Press, Durham, N. Carolina.
Spong, John Shelby, 1998, *Why Christianity Must Change or Die*, Harper Collins, San Francisco.
Spong, John Shelby, 1996, *Liberating the Gospels*, Harper Collins, San Francisco.
Spong, John Shelby, 1992, *Rescuing The Bible From Fundamentalism*, Harper Collins, San Francisco.
Tacitus, 1996, *The Annals of Imperial Rome*, Penguin.
Vermes, Geza, 2000, *The Changing Faces of Jesus*, Penguin.
Vermes, Geza, 1998, *Jesus The Jew*, SCM Press, London.
Wells, G.A., 1999, *The Jesus Myth*, Open Court Publishers.
Wilson, A.N., 1997, *Paul, The Mind of the Apostle*, Norton.
Wilson, A.N., 1992, *Jesus, a Life*, Fawcett Columbine.
Wilson, Brian, 1999, *Christianity*, Routledge, London.

Qur'an quotations are in most cases translations from Asad (1984) and to a lesser extent from Ali (1992).
Bible quotations are from the Holy Bible King James Version.

Index

Abraham 18, 23, 107, 116, 142, 187, 198
abrogation, theory of 24
Acts of the Apostles 34, 37, 45, 73–5, 78–80, 94, 102, 153, 158, 175
Adam 106, 116, 127, 187
Adams, John 191
Admetus, husband of Alcestis 96
Adonis 58
Agrippa, King Herod 59, 63
Albert of Aix 173
Albigensian 'heretics' 173
Alcestis, wife of Admetus 96
Alexander the Great 46, 58, 62, 101, 114
Alexandria 33, 172
Allenby, General E.H.H. 181
Ammianus 89
Ananias 73–4, 154
Antichrist, the 'Beast of Revelation' 174, 176–9, 183, 186, 200
Antioch 62, 73, 97, 114, 125
Antium 170
Apocalypse of James 119
Apocalypse of Peter 147
Arab-Israeli War 181
Arabia 24, 27, 28, 162–3, 192
Aramaic 36, 42, 114, 122
Aretas IV, King of the Nabateans 61
Arianism 67, 84, 85, 122, 172
Arius, Bishop of Alexandria 84
Armageddon 168, 169–70, 178–81, 193
Artemis 65
Asia Minor 172
AUA (American Unitarian Association) 86
Augustus Caesar 62–3, 114, 159
Aurelian 103

Babylon 32, 168, 169, 182, 188
The Bacchae (Euripides) 59
Balfour, Arthur James 192
Balfour Declaration 192
Barabbas 153
Barkley, Dr John 190
Barnabas 63
Basra 183
Begin, Menahem 193
Bethlehem 116
Beziers 173
Bible
  Arabic translation 42
  Authorized Version 43
  authors and editors 44–5
  definitions 31
  Disciples and authorship 45–8
  English versions 42–3
  eyewitnesses, authors as 46
  'foreign' in Arabia 163
  German translation 43
  historical development 42–4
  King James Version (KJV) 43
  Paul's letters, attribution of 44–5, 47–8
  'Peshitta' version 42, 51, 163, 167, 186
  Protestant Bible 41–2
  Qur'an and 48–9, 70–1
  rejection of 'Last Prophet' 144
  Revelation of St John 47
  Revised Standard Version (RSV) 43
  Roman Catholic Version (RCV) 41, 43
  'Scholar's' version 44
  'Son of Man,' references to 127–9, 137–40
  Trinitarian formula 43
  versions 41–2

Index

Vulgate Bible 42, 43, 51, 163, 186
  see also Old Testament (OT); New Testament (NT)
Bosnia-Herzegovina 193
The Boston Medical and Surgical Journal 190
Bultman, Rudolf 128–9
Bush Jr, George 179, 194
Byblus 58
Byzantium 26, 27–8, 28

Caesar Augustus 175
Caesarea 61, 153–4
Caiaphas 151
Caligula 63, 174
Calvinism 85–6
Canaanite religion (Baal) 74
Canaanites 181
canonical gospels 36–7
Capernaum 132
Carter, Jimmy 193
Cerinthians 167
Chaldeans 182
Channing, William Ellery 86
Chediac, Father R.P. 42
China 25
Chrestos (Hellenic 'Christ') 55–7, 64, 75–6, 94, 97–8, 115, 130, 174174
Christian Bible *see* Bible
Christian Fundamentalism
  awaiting the Messiah 194–6, 197
  beliefs and concepts in 185–6
  Biblical scripture and 187
  'born-again' Christians 177–8
  Catholic viewpoint 188
  International Christian Embassy (ICE) 196–8
  phenomenon of 185–7, 201–2
  providential plan of 189–94
  Western fundamentalism 189–91
  see also Orientalism; Revelation of John
Christianity
cannibalistic rites and 100
Christian-Nazarene dilemma 76–8
Christian persecutions 171–3
  Dark Ages and 166
  'Deliverer' and 'Messiah,' perspective on 129–30

enigma of 55–7
Eucharist 41, 98–103
fundamentalism in 201–2
gulf between Jesus and 77
Hellenism and 39–40, 55–71
heretics, persecution of 172–3
introduction of term 62, 73
Mithraism and 102
Nazarenes and 64–6, 73–92
Orientalism in 165–7
Orthodox Church 41, 186, 188
paradox of 67–8
Pauline claim on 77–8, 93–109
'Prophet' and 'Messiah,' distinction between 130–1
Revelation of John and 167
salvation and 23
term absent from writings of Paul 103–4
  see also Christian Fundamentalism; Pauline Christianity; New Testament (NT)
Cleopatra 172
Cleophas 118, 155
Clinton, Bill 194
Cologne 42
Constantine, Emperor 34, 36, 64, 66, 83, 84, 167
Contra Celsus (Origen) 119
Cooper, Lord Anthony Ashley 191
Coptic Gospel of Thomas 38–9, 146
Cresson, Warder 191
Cromwell, Oliver 191
Crucifixion
  evidence for 145–7
  eyewitnesses 149–50
  Passion narratives 147–9
  Roman Justice 150–1
  scriptural 'evidence' 149–50
Crusades, Christian 29, 172–3, 177
Cyrenius 159
Cyrus, King of Persia 114, 182, 188

Damascus 60–1, 94
Daniel, Book of 104, 127, 128, 129, 131, 138, 152
Dark Ages 166
David, Prophet-King 128, 132, 134, 139, 142

Index

'Day of the Lord' 103–5
de Montfort, Simon 173
Dead Sea 33, 88
Demeter 65, 155
Deuteronomist 33
Diana 65
Dine, Tom 179
Diocletian 101
Dionysius, Bishop of Alexandria 167
Dionysus 58–9, 62, 97, 100, 103, 115, 129, 130, 136
Douai 43
Dyer, Charles 183

Ebionites 82, 85
   see also Nazarenes
Ecumenical Council of Constantinople 41
Edessa 42
Egypt 28, 123
Eleazar, high priest of Jerusalem 33
Eleusis 155
Elias 130
Elijah 113, 136
Elohist 32–3
Emmaus 114, 157
enjil, Gospel of Jesus 37–8, 39, 90
Ephesus, Council of 65
Epiphanius 81
Epiphany 103
Epistles of Paul 34, 35
Essenes 74, 82, *88*
Eucharist 41, 98–103, 148–9
Euphrates River 168, 190
Euripides 59
Eusebius, Bishop of Caesarea 66–7, 106, 167
Eve (and Adam) 106

Falwell, Jerry 178, 179, 180, 193
Felgenhauer, Paul 189
Ferenc, David 85–6
Fifty Three Years in Syria, 1857-1910 (Jessup, H.) 190
fight, permission to 27
France 25
Franklin, Benjamin 191
Funk, Professor Robert 145, 150

Galilee 87, 113, 118, 132, 150, 159
Galileo 173
Gethsemane 79, 148
Giacumakis, Dr George 196
Gnostics 146–7
God
   'Creator of all things' 21
   Divine Revelation of 143–4
   Jesus's ascent to 161
   'Kingdom of God' 104, 131, 133–7, 140, 197–8
   omniscience of 19–20
   'Oneness' of 142
   salvation and belief in 23
Gog and Magog 170
Gore, Al 193–4
Gospels 34
   as biography 36–8
   canonical 36–7
   canonization of 34
   chronology 34
   Crucifixion 145–6
   evolution 39–41
   eyewitnesses to Crucifixion 149–50
   gospels 35, 37, 159–60
   historical Jesus 113–19
   innovativeness 128
   Jerusalem, Jesus's triumphant entry 151–3
   of Jesus, Islamic perspective 87–92
   ministry of Jesus 132–6, 159–60
   narrative content 34–9, 130
   Passion narratives 147–9
   reappearances (resurrection?) of Jesus 155–8
   of Secret James 158–9
   titles of Jesus 111–12
Graham, Billy 179
Grant, Professor Michael 154
Gulf War 182

Hadith 39
Haifa 181
Halsell, Grace 177
Hebrew Bible *see* Old Testament (OT)
Hecate 155
Helios 66, 101, 103, 121
Hellenistic

Index

Age 58–9
'Chrestos' 55–7, 64, 75–6, 94, 97–8, 115, 130, 174
Christianity 39–40
culture 55, 98
Hellman, Richard 196
Henry VIII, King of England 186
Heraclius, Emperor 26, 27–8
Hercules 62, 63, 96–7, 115, 130
Herod Antipas 113, 150, 153, 159
Herod the Great 159
Herzl, Theodore 195, 196
Hijaz 28
Hippolytus 104
Holy Bible *see* Bible
Holy War 29
Homer 97
Horus 65, 99–100
Hugo, Victor 166
Hussein, Saddam 174, 182–3

Iconium 63
ideological compromise, preclusion of 30
Indick, Martin 181
Innocent III 173
Innocent IV 173
International Christian Embassy (ICE) 195, 196–8
Iraq 28, 174
Isaac 142
Ishmael 142, 198
Isis 65
Islam
  'abodes of peace and war' 28
  authority within 15
  'Awaited Messiah,' perspective on 197
  biblical research and 141
  Crucifixion, perspective on 160–3
  'Deliverer' and 'Messiah,' perspective on 129–30
  dogma, insufficiency in 30, 52–4
  establishment of 'Kingdom of God' 140
  etymology of *jihad* 29
  fundamentalism in 201–2
  Gospel of Jesus, Islamic perspective on 87–92
  Gospel of Jesus *(enjil)* in 37–8, 39, 90

  intellect, appeal to 106–9
  Jesus, Islamic perspective on 68–71
  'Kingdom of God,' perspective on 197–8
  Lutheran principles and 198–201
  mission of Jesus, perspective on 91–2, 125–6
  policy towards those outside Arabia 24
  'Promised Land,' perspective on 198
  protection of non-believers 30
  religious tolerance of 108
  'Second Coming,' perspective on 198
  'Son of Man,' perspective on 140–4
  spread of 24–5
  study of traditions of the Prophet 44
  war in 23–8
  Western attitude to 166
Al-Isra 140
Israel, tribes of 168
Israeli Knesset 193, 194
Iznik *see* Nicaea

Jabal, Mua'z Ben 27
al-Jabbar, Abd 90
Jacob 142
James *see* Nazarenes
Jefferson, Thomas 135–6, 191
Jehoiachin 182
Jeremiah the Prophet 150
Jerusalem 29, 32–3, 38, 61, 81–2, 94, 97, 113, 128, 130, 133–4, 136, 151–3, 170
Jerusalem Church 74, 75–6
Jessup, Henry 190
Jesus Christ
  acceptance of 64
  appearances, post-Crucifixion 158–9
  ascent to God 161
  blood brothers and sisters, lack of 118–19
  Davidic ancestry 116–18
  deified Jesus 122
  denial of role of 'Deliverer' 131, 138–9
  as Divine Saviour 94–8
  genealogy of 116–18
  gospels as biography 36–8
  and Hellenistic 'Chrestos' 55–7, 64, 75–6, 94, 97–8, 115, 130, 174
  historical Jesus 35–8, 112–19

Index

Islamic perspective on 68–71
Islamic view of mission of 91–2, 125–6
'Last Supper' of 98
lifetime of 159–60
Messiah Jesus 114–15, 129–30
ministry of 132–3, 159–60
mission of 91–2, 125–6, 133–7
mythical Jesus, titles of 119–24
as 'Paschal Lamb of God' 123–4
Paul and the 'Heavenly' 78
Prophet Jesus 112–14
reappearance (resurrection?) of 157–9
sepulchre of, women at 155–7
as 'Son of Man' 123, 128
on 'Son of Man' 127–9, 137–40
titles according to the Gospels 111–12
transformation of 55–6, 57–8
trial of, contrast with Paul's 153–4
triumphant entry to Jerusalem 151–3
virgin birth of 115–18
see also Crucifixion
Jesus in the Qur'an (Parrinder, G.) 54
Jesus Seminar 44, 47, 48, 52–3, 70, 145
Jewish Bible *see* Old Testament (OT)
Jewish exodus from Egypt 123
Jewish Zionist Congress 195
Jihad
　fighting, preclusion of 29
　inaccuracy of use by media 29
jizya (Islamic tribute) 28
John Paul II 109, 119
John Paul VI 186
John the Baptist 23, 37, 81, 99, 113–14,
　123–4, 130–1, 140, 159, 160
John the Seer 133, 167, 170, 174–83
Johnson, Lyndon B. 177
Joseph of Arimathea 155
Josephus, Flavius 87, 160
Judaism 23, 32, 74–5, 77, 102, 122, 129–30,
　142–3
　see also Old Testament (OT)
Judas Iscariot 147
Julius Caesar 62–3, 114, 121, 150–1
Justin Martyr 101, 104

Keldani, Rev David Benjamin 87
Kerygma, Jesus of the 57–9
King Jr, Martin Luther 190

Kuwait 183
Kyrios ('Lord') 122

The Late Great Planet Earth (Lindsey, H.)
　176, 179
Lawrence, T.E. 192
Lebanon 178
Levites 114, 130
Lindsey, Hal 176, 178, 179
Lloyd-George, David 192
Luckhoff, Johann 196
Luke *see* Acts of the Apostles; Gospels
Luther, Martin 42–3, 173, 186, 198–201
Lystra 63

Ma'arrah 172–3
Mack, Professor Burton L. 145–6, 147
Madinah 26
Magians 23
Magis of Persia 103
Marcion 41
Mark Antony 63
Mark *see* Gospels
Mary, deification of 65
Mary Magdalene 118, 149, 155, 156, 157
Matthew *see* Gospels 81
Mazdeans 102
Mecca 140
Megiddo 181
Messiah
　awaiting the 194–6, 197
　'Deliverer' and, perspective on 129–30
　'Prophet' and, distinction between
　　130–1
Middle East Studies Association of
　America 191
Mitford, Edward 192
Mithraism 40, 100, 101, 130, 147
The Mohammadan Missionary Problem
　(Barkley, J.) 190
Mosaic Law 32, 118, 139
Moses 13, 28, 32–3, 74, 95, 130, 135, 142, 187,
　191
Mount Ararat 190
Mount Zion 168
Muhammad *see* Prophet Muhammad

Nabateans 61

214

Index

Nag Hammadi Library 38–9, 119, 146–7, 158–9
nasara 88
Nazarenes 23, 37, 39, 45, 47, 120, 125
   acknowledgment of Jesus as Messiah 74–5
   Christian-Nazarene dilemma 76–8
   to Christians, transformation 64–6
   'Jerusalem Church' of the 74–6
   legacy of the 81–3
   opposition to Pauline doctrine 79–80
   unitarianism and the 85–7
   who were they? 73–5
Nazareth 87, 113, 116
Nebuchadnezzar 32, 182
Nero, Emperor 47, 63, 170–1, 174–5
Netanyahu, Binyamin 193
New Testament (NT)
   Acts of the Apostles 34, 37, 45, 73–4, 75, 78–80, 94, 102, 153, 158, 175
   anonymity of authorship 36
   canonical gospels 36–7
   choice of scriptures in 34–5
   Coptic Gospel of Thomas 38–9, 146
   Epistles of Paul 34, 35
   evolution of the Gospels 39–41
   fixing of 31–2
   Gospels 34, 35–41
   Greek language of 36
   narrative Gospels 38–9
   as 'New Covenant' 32
   Q (Quelle) Gospel 38–9, 40
   sayings Gospel 38
   synoptic gospels 35, 37, 159–60
   'Word of God' 36, 41, 47
Nicaea, Council of 34–6, 39, 41, 55, 57, 64, 66–7, 106, 120–1, 125, 166–7, 172
Nicene Creed 34, 83–4, 121–2, 141, 172
Nile River 190, 198
Noah 17–18, 187
Nonadorantes 86

Odyssey (Homer) 97
Old Testament (OT)
   Deuteronomist as source 33
   Elohist as source 32–3
   Greek translation 33
   as 'Old Covenant' 32
   pagan Greece and the 46–7
   the Pentateuch 32
   preserving message of Jewry 31–2
   Prophets-Psalms-Proverbs as source 33
   Septuagint 33, 45, 100, 163
   sources 32–3
   the Torah 32, 38, 50, 70, 107
   Yahwist as source 32
Omar (successor to Muhammad) 28
Orientalism 165–7
Origen 41, 87, 119, 149–50
Orthodox Church 41
Osiris 58, 99–100

Pagans 23–4
Palestine 36, 42, 46, 61, 64–6, 103, 122, 132, 181, 190–4
Palm Sunday 151–3
Parrider, Geoffrey 54
'Passion,' narratives of the 147–9
Passover 98, 102, 123–4, 145, 147, 148–9, 153, 172
Paul
   the 'Apostle' 60–4
   conversion of 59
   Epistles of 34, 35
   faith in Jesus 94–8
   'Heavenly Jesus' and 78
   Hellenistic influences on 96–8
   Hellenistic mentality of 62
   letters, attribution of 44–5, 47–8
   ministry of 76–8
   originator of Christianity 93
   as originator of Christianity 93
   Peter and 80
   trial of, contrast with Jesus's 153–4
Paul, the Mind of the Apostle (Wilson, A.N.) 170
Paul IV 173
Pauline Christianity 34, 37, 39, 68, 78
   Christian enigma 55–7
   Christianity or Paulinism? 93–109
   continuity aspect 32
   foundations 60–4
   letters of Paul, only valid Gospel 105
   Nazarene-Christian dilemma 76–8
   Nazarene ideology, 'heretical' nature of 45

Index

schismatic movements within 40–1
slavery, attitude to 106
social values 105–6
'Son of Man,' Second Coming 105, 128
submission to Governing Almighty 105–6
women's status within 106
the Pentateuch 32
Pentheus of Thebes 59
Perea 81
Persephone 103, 155
Persia 28
Peshitta Bible 42, 51, 163, 167, 186
Peter, Paul and 80
Philo 46, 47
Phoenicians 74
Pilgrimage to Palestine (Smith, J.V.C.) 190
Plato (and Platonism) 85, 86, 97
Polish Diet 85
Polycarp, Bishop of Smyrna 49
Pontius Pilate 115, 150–4, 155, 160
Poppaea 63
predestination 19, 54
Priestley, Joseph 86
Prophesy and Politics (Halsell, G.) 177
Prophet Muhammad
    Arabian emphasis 24, 27
    chronologically last (in a series) 141
    as 'Deliverer' 129, 131
    divine writ vouchsafed unto 22–3
    historical records, access to 162
    self-defensive against enemies 26–8
    as 'Son of Man' 129, 140–4
    Tabuk expedition 26
Prophets-Psalms-Proverbs 33
Protestant Reformation 42–3, 85, 108–9, 185–96, 198–201
Ptolemy II Philadelphus 33
Pyramid Texts 99

Q (Quelle) Gospel 38–9, 40
Qumran scrolls 33, 74, 96
Qur'an
    on aggression 25–6
    appeal to reason 52–4, 108
    Arabian emphasis 24
    Bible and 48–9, 70–1
    on Bible and message of Jewry 32
    on blasphemous talk 15
    challenge of the 51–2
    on coercion in matters of faith 18, 24
    credibility 49–51
    on definitive knowledge, striving for 29
    on dignity of mankind 19, 22
    enjil, Gospel of Jesus 37–8, 39, 90
    final divine message, presentation as 14
    final revelation 50–1
    on forbearance 21–2
    on freedom of choice 16–22
    on freedom of religious belief 18–19, 24
    on frivolous talk 15
    ideological compromise, preclusion of 30
    Jesus's Disciples, noble support for 148
    last days of Jesus's mission in 161–2
    on lawful war 25–6
    on lying 15
    message, argument concerning the 16–17
    message, manner of delivery of the 17–18, 22
    on mission of God's apostles 14–15
    on moral responsibility 19–21
    nasara, use of term 88
    Nicene Creed and the 83–4
    on non-believers 16–17, 22
    on oppression 26
    on Pagans, dealing with 23–4
    permission to fight 27
    on personal responsibility 15
    on predestination 19
    on re-creation 107
    reason, appeal to 106–9
    recognition of God's apostles 13–14
    rejection of the Crucifixion 146
    on scepticism 20–1
    on self-sufficiency 22
    'sword verses' 23–4
    uniformity, denial of 23
    war, statement of object of 25
Qur'anic Law 25

Ra' 58

Index

Radulph of Caen 172–3
Reagan, Ronald 176, 178–80, 193
'Reaganomics' 180
Reimarus 120
Republic (Plato) 97
Revelation of John 104
    Antichrist, the 'Beast of Revelation' 174, 176–7
    Armageddon 168, 169–70
    on Babylon 169
    Christian conviction 167
    excerpts 168–70
    fanaticism of John the Seer 174–5
    Iraq, legacy in 181–3
    Middle Eastern legacy 176–7
    on the 'New Jerusalem' 170
    Palestinian legacy 177–81
    rapture in salvation 175–6
    on salvation 168
    vials of wrath 168
    on women, defilement of 168
Rheims 43
The Rise of Babylon (Dyer, C.) 182–3183
Robertson, Pat 178, 179, 180–1
Roman Empire 104, 128, 133–4, 166, 172
Roman Justice 150–1, 154
Rome 170–1, 174–5

Sabbath 139–40, 150
Sabians 23
Saddam's Babylon the Great (Taylor, C.) 183
Sadducees 136
Said, Edward 165–6
St Augustine 182, 188
St Petersburg 42
salvation, conditions for 23
Sanhedrin 135, 153
Satan 13–14, 15, 170
Sayings Gospel 38
Sebastian, Franck 200–1
'Second Coming' 105, 128, 174, 176–7, 178–80, 185, 189–94, 192, 198
Sepphoris 87
Septuagint 33, 45, 100, 163
Serapis, Temple of 172
Servetus, Michael 85
Seth, Second Treatise of 146
Sibylline Revelation 141

Simon Peter 79, 156, 159
Smith, J.V.C. 190
Socinus, Faustus 85–6
Sol Invictus 66, 101
Solomon 32, 117
'Son of Man' 104, 123, 127–9, 137–44
Soviet Union 179
Spain 24–5, 103
Spanish Inquisition 173
Spittlehouse, John 191
Spong, John Shelby 83–4, 100, 109
Stephen the Martyr 135
Swaggart, Jimmy 178
'sword verses' 23–4
synoptic gospels 35, 37, 159–60
Syria 28
Syriac dialect 42

Tacitus 171, 175
the Talmud 33
Tammuz 58
Tarsus 101–2
the Taurah 32
Taylor, Charles 183
Tertullian 101
Tetragrammaton 100–1, 122, 151
Theodosius, Emperor 172
Theophilus, Bishop of Alexandria 46, 84, 175
Theotokos (Mother of God) 65
Thirty Years War 89
Thomas, the doubter 158
Tiberius 160
the Torah 32, 38, 50, 70, 107
Transcendentalism 86
Transylvania 85–6
Truman, Harry S. 192–3
Tynedale, William 42–3, 173

uniformity, denial of 23
Unitarianism 85–7
United States of America 44, 86, 167, 177–81, 189–90, 191–4, 201–2
Urban II 29, 172, 177
UUA (Unitarian Universalist Association) 87

Vermes, Professor Geza 146

Index

Victor, Bishop of Rome 172
Visigoths 166
Vitellius 154
Vulgate Bible 42, 43, 51, 163, 186

Wallace, Edwin Sherman 191
war
    holy 29
    in Islam 23–8
    statement of object of 25
Watt, James 178
Wilson, Woodrow 192
'Word of God' 36, 41, 47

Yahwist 32
Yemen 27
Young, William 191–2

zakat (purification of alms) 28
Zechariah 151–2
Zedekiah 182
Zeus 63, 96, 121, 136
Zionism 194–6
zummi (protected by Islam) 28